Lewis M. Haupt

A Move for Better Roads

Essays on Roadmaking and Maintenance and Road Laws

Lewis M. Haupt

A Move for Better Roads
Essays on Roadmaking and Maintenance and Road Laws

ISBN/EAN: 9783743400696

Manufactured in Europe, USA, Canada, Australia, Japa

Cover: Foto ©Suzi / pixelio.de

Manufactured and distributed by brebook publishing software (www.brebook.com)

Lewis M. Haupt

A Move for Better Roads

A MOVE FOR BETTER ROADS.

ESSAYS

ON

ROADMAKING AND MAINTENANCE

AND

ROAD LAWS,

FOR WHICH PRIZES OR HONORABLE MENTION WERE AWARDED THROUGH THE
UNIVERSITY OF PENNSYLVANIA BY A COMMITTEE OF
CITIZENS OF PHILADELPHIA,

WITH A

SYNOPSIS OF OTHER CONTRIBUTIONS AND A REVIEW

BY THE SECRETARY,

LEWIS M. HAUPT, A.M., C.E.,
PROFESSOR OF CIVIL ENGINEERING, UNIVERSITY OF PENNSYLVANIA,

ALSO AN

INTRODUCTION

BY

WILLIAM H. RHAWN,
CHAIRMAN OF THE COMMITTEE.

PHILADELPHIA:
UNIVERSITY OF PENNSYLVANIA PRESS,
1891.

INTRODUCTION.

SINCE Peter Cooper built the first American locomotive, sixty years ago, there has been a prodigious growth and improvement in the railroads of the country, until a system of transportation has been developed that infinitely transcends that of any previous age known. This marvelous development was only possible through the employment of the highest scientific, engineering and financial talent and skill.

During the same period our common roads, while necessarily increasing with the settlement of · new territory, have exhibited no marked improvement in character, and since the death of Macadam, in 1836, his mantle appears to have fallen on no other great prophet or apostle of better roads.

A belief that the same character of scientific and engineering talent and skill that achieved such stupendous results in the development of the railroad system of the country should be, as far as possible, employed in the improvement of its common roads, induced the writer, in November, 1889, to offer to contribute, through the University of Pennsylvania, a prize for the best paper upon the construction and maintenance of common roads. The encouragement the project received from Doctor William Pepper, the Provost, and Professor Lewis M. Haupt, the head of the Civil Engineering Department of the University, led to an enlargement of the plan through the organization of the Committee on Better Roads and the opening of a subscription to a fund for its contemplated work. The responses to the solicitations of the committee for subscriptions to the fund were extremely gratifying, as showing the general interest felt in the matter.

Prizes of $400, $200 and $100 were offered by the Committee for the best papers upon Road Making and Maintenance, the competition to be open to all.

The Committee is indebted to the authors of a large number of papers received by Doctor Pepper and referred to a Board of Adjudicators appointed by him. The Board was composed of Alexander J. Cassatt, C.E., Chairman; William Sellers, M.E,; Joseph M. Wilson, C.E.; William H. Wahl, Ph.D.; Thomas M. Cleeman, C. E.; Hon. Wayne MacVeagh, and Professor Lewis M. Haupt, C.E., Secretary.

During the examination of the papers and until the awards were made, their authors remained entirely unknown to the Board, which, after long and careful consideration of all the papers received in competition, awarded the first prize, of $400, to Henry Irwin, B.A., C.E., Assistant Engineer, Canadian Pacific Railway, Montreal, Canada; the second prize, of $200, to David H. Bergey, B.Sc., M.D., North Wales, Pa.; and the third prize, of $100, to James Bradford Olcott, South Manchester, Conn.; and honorable mention without reference to order, to Edwin Satterthwait, Jenkintown, Pa.; Charles Punchard, Philadelphia; George B. Fleece, C.E., Memphis, Tenn.; Frank Cawley, B.S., Swarthmore College. Pa.; and Francis Fuller McKenzie, C.E., Germantown, Pa.

The papers for which prizes and honorable mention were awarded, together with notes and a carefully prepared digest of all other papers, by Profesor Haupt, are here presented, as a contribution to the cause of better roads.

It is intended to present a draft or drafts of a model legislative bill for a road law in an appendix or an additional volume.

The Committee here makes most grateful acknowledgment to the contributors of papers, the Board of Adjudicators, to Doctor Pepper, and to Professor Haupt, for their zealous coöperation.

WILLIAM H. RHAWN,
Chairman.

CONTENTS.

SECOND PRIZE PAPER. No. 35.
By D. H. Bergey, B.S., M.D.
1.—General Consideration of the Subject.

2.—Advantages of Good Roads.

3.—Construction of Public Roads.

THIRD PRIZE PAPER. NO. 25.
By James Bradford Olcott.

CONTENTS.

Value of sand as a permanent cushion for stone; a case in actual street
practice, ... 111
Variation in relative value of stone, sand and clay in different districts;
refuse stone, brickbats, etc., ... 112
Necessity of keeping a clay foundation dry; drains and ditches, . . . 113
Provision against water; drainage to be done separately from road
work; R. R. Bramley's caution against stones with clay in them, . . 114
Danger from clay and how to avoid it, ... 115
Sample of the "greedy" stone road work, ... 116
Objections to hastily built "better roads," 117
Roads of broken stone in Southern England, ... 118
Effect of corrupt examples of metropolitan engineering on rural road
making; macadamizing as defined by some encyclopædias, ... 119
Cubic measurement for broken stone a fraud, ... 120
Size of stone; MacAdam's statement to the Parliamentary committee, . 121
Examples of "bogus" engineering, ... 122
Radical repairs on an old stone road; where the fault generally lies
in old broken stone roads, ... 123
Value of sand in stone road making, ... 124
Objections to porous road work, ... 125
Fallacy of our philosophy of stone road work, ... 126
Principles of common road business; criticism of private road making, 127
Iron pipes for surface draining, ... 128
Cement and vitrified pipe for draining; advantages of trees on a road, . 129
Best grasses for roads; definition of the word turf as given by a London
schoolgirl, ... 131
Example of wrong stone road making; objections to the arrangement
by which road stones are assorted at the crusher, ... 132
Proportions of coarse and fine stone to make solid work; manner of
disposing the stone on the bottom; variety in the shape of the raw
road metal; objections to the application of chips and rock dust to
the top of a new stone road, ... 133
To make stone roads in difficult regions solid and permanent; the cost
of smooth roads no more than that of rough ones; failure of macadamizing streets in Toronto, ... 134
Red gravel and the graveling craze; the proportion of finer filling must
be determined by experiment, ... 135
Neglect of fit packing in common stone road work, ... 136
Highway robbers of the Nineteenth Century; blunders of schools of
engineering, ... 137

DIGEST OF THE CONTENTS OF THE REMAINING CONTRIBUTIONS TO THE ROAD PRIZES.

By Prof. Lewis M. Haupt.

A MOVE FOR BETTER ROADS.

PHILADELPHIA, January, 1890.

Many facts have recently brought sharply to notice how little attention has been paid to the scientific and economical building and care of our streets and common roads, as compared with our railroads, and have led to the conclusion that much of the lack of appreciation of good common roads and of the necessity for skilled civil engineers in their construction and maintenance is due to the want of practical knowledge on the part of most people as to what constitutes a really good road and its economic advantages over a poor one, and likewise to insufficient laws upon the subject.

In the historical sketch of its road published by the Pennsylvania Railroad, it is stated that at one time the supervisors and track foremen were satisfied with an excellence far below the ideas of perfection entertained by the managers, and to remedy this the latter adopted the plan of having each supervisor prepare on his division one mile of sample track, not limiting him as to cost, but requiring that it be made as perfect as possible. The officers, supervisors and foremen, then passed over these sample miles, carefully examining each, and at the conclusion of this inspection the most experienced supervisors acknowledged that they had never before known what a perfect track was. May not much the same be said of the majority of people in regard to our common roads—that they have little realizing conception of a perfect road and its economic advantages over an indifferent one? Manifestly, such is the case, and the remedy lies in the direction of the education of the people up to a better knowledge of good roads, which will be followed by a greater appreciation of and a determination to have them.

Like all such education, this must begin at the top, and it is therefore encouraging to notice that there has been an awakening upon the subject of better roads and an evident desire for more knowledge as to their scientific and economic construction and maintenance. This has been shown in a marked degree during the past year in the numerous articles that have appeared in pamphlet form and in the journals and periodicals of the day, among which may be mentioned, "Notes on the Making of Common Roads," by James B. Alcott, and "The Road Question in Pennsylvania," by Samuel R. Downing, in *The American;* "Road Legislation for the American State," by Professor Jenks, of Knox College, published by the American

Economic Association; "Roads and Road-Making," by Captain Francis V. Greene, and "What I Know About European Roads," by Joseph Pennell, in *Harper's Weekly*, of which a second edition was required to meet the demand for the illustrated article by Captain Greene; "Highway Improvement," an address by Colonel Albert A. Pope before the Carriage Builders' National Association; "The Common Roads," by Professor Shaler, of Harvard University, in *Scribner's Magazine;* "Resurfacing," a letter by A. J. Cassatt, in "A Plea for Better Roads," by William H. Rhawn; "Municipal Engineering," by Professor Haupt, of the University of Pennsylvania, read before the Franklin Institute and published in its *Journal;* "Improvement of Highways," a series of articles on the making and care of good roads, with the draft of a proposed bill for legislative enactment to secure them, published by the League of American Wheelmen—an organization that is now endeavoring to educate the people up to a higher appreciation of better roads and streets, and to secure the enactment of laws providing for them in the several States—and the articles that appear almost continuously in the *Manufacturer*, and in the *American Athlete* and other journals devoted to "wheelmen."

The Governor of Pennsylvania in his last annual message called attention to the subject, and the Legislature, in April last, enacted a law which he approved, providing for the appointment of "a commission to revise and consolidate the laws relating to the construction and improvement of the roads and public highways in this Commonwealth, and also to consider the advisability and practicability of the State assisting in the construction and improvement of the same."

It would appear that there are few subjects of greater importance to the country at the present time than the establishment of the best and most direct means of communication between its people, over its highways. That these highways may be greatly improved by a better and more scientific treatment than they have generally received is now undoubtedly engaging the attention of the intelligent and thoughtful. As aids to a solution of the question, it is deemed desirable that exhaustive papers upon the subject shall be prepared by competent writers, upon the making and care of common roads in accordance with the latest and most approved methods of engineering, in which the economic and legislative questions involved shall be treated.

It is proposed to make these papers the basis of an effort to secure an efficient organization for the creation and maintenance of better highways, not only in our immediate vicinity but also throughout the State, and it is believed that the general benefits to be derived from so important a work will prove to be a strong incentive to all public-spirited citizens to co-operate in securing so laudable a purpose.

The Committee named below have arranged to offer, with the approval of the Board of Trustees of the University of Pennsylvania, a number of University prizes for the best papers upon the subject, in accordance with the conditions hereto annexed. Upon the receipt and publication of these papers, it is proposed to offer prizes for the best drafts of a bill for legislative enactment, embodying all the most essential features of a good road-law, the passage of which, it is hoped, may be secured.

The Committee will be pleased to have your co-operation in this most important work, and request you to aid them by enclosing to the Chairman your check for TEN DOLLARS to the order of William Hacker, Treasurer. Copies of the successful papers will be sent to the contributors.

COMMITTEE ON BETTER ROADS.

Charles Richardson,	George W. Childs,	Charles C. Harrison,
Joel J. Baily,	George de B. Keim,	Edward C. Knight,
Edward Longstreth,	Henry W. Sharpless,	Alexander J. Cassatt,
Joseph Wharton,	Henry H. Houston,	Charles Hartshorne,
George B. Roberts,	Justus C. Strawbridge,	John H. Converse,
Jay Cooke,	Benton K. Jamison,	John Sellers Jr.,
John R. Fell,	N. Parker Shortridge,	Craige Lippincott,
T. Broom Belfield,	Beauveau Borie,	Joseph E. Gillingham,
Charles F. Berwind,	Eben C. Jayne,	John Lowber Welsh,

Lewis M. Haupt,	William Hacker,	William H. Rhawn,
Secretary.	*Treasurer.*	*Chairman.*

CONDITIONS OF COMPETITION

FOR THE

UNIVERSITY OF PENNSYLVANIA ROAD PRIZES

OF

$400, $200, and $100,

Offered by the Committee for the best three papers on Road Making and Maintenance, to be submitted subject to the following conditions:

1. The competition shall be open to all, and will be under the auspices of the University, with the advice of the Committee.

2. The subject should include the *engineering*, *economic* and *legislative* features of construction, reconstruction and maintenance, and the advantages of thoroughly *scientific* treatment, but omit *history*, excepting where necessary to illustrate or impress an argument.

3. The papers should be terse, logical and original [not compilations], written on one side of a sheet only. It is preferred that they should be in type-writing. A paper may be the joint production of two or more persons.

4. The author's name should not appear upon his paper, nor be otherwise prematurely disclosed, but his name and address should be enclosed in a sealed envelope attached to his paper in such manner that it may be readily removed without injury. The papers and envelopes will be correspondingly numbered as received, and the envelopes will remain unopened until after awards of prizes or honorable mention are determined upon, when only those will be opened which correspond to the successful numbers; the rest will be destroyed and the identity of the writers remain unknown.

5. All communications should be addressed to Dr. William Pepper, Provost, University of Pennsylvania, Philadelphia, Pa., and be presented on or before April 5th, 1890.

6. The papers received will be submitted to a Board of five or seven Adjudicators, to be appointed by Doctor Pepper with the advice and consent of the Committee, which Board shall be the sole judges of all papers and will not consider any paper that fails to comply with these conditions. They shall report, if possible, within one month from the date of receiving the

(4)

papers   The vote of a majority of the Board upon the merits of any paper shall be final.

7. For the paper adjudged to be entitled to the first prize there shall be paid four hundred dollars.

For the paper adjudged to be entitled to the second prize there shall be paid two hundred dollars.

For the paper adjudged to be entitled to the third prize there shall be paid one hundred dollars.

Honorable mention may be made of other contributions, at the discretion of the Board of Adjudicators.

8. When the adjudication shall be made and reported to the Provost he shall call a meeting of the Committee, at which meeting he shall open the envelopes corresponding with the successful papers, and award the prizes in accordance with the adjudication to the authors then disclosed and entitled to receive them.

The papers for which prizes have thus been paid shall become the property of the University for early publication, after which it is proposed by the Committee to invite a second competition for the best drafts of legislative bills designed to carry out the features developed by the first competition.

LEWIS M. HAUPT,
Secretary,
University of Pennsylvania.

WILLIAM H. RHAWN,
Chairman,
  313 Chestnut Street.

REPORT OF THE BOARD OF ADJUDICATORS
TO THE COMMITTEE ON BETTER ROADS.

PHILADELPHIA, October 18th, 1890.

MR. WILLIAM H. RHAWN,

Chairman Committee on Better Roads.

SIR:—The Board of Adjudicators, appointed by Dr. William Pepper, Provost of the University of Pennsylvania, to examine the prize papers submitted for competition on the subject of Road Making and Maintenance, have the honor to submit to your Committee the following resolutions as embodying the substance of their recommendations in relation to this subject.

RESOLUTIONS.

Irrespective of the relative merits of the several papers which have been selected for publication, the Board of Adjudicators would respectfully recommend to the Committee on Better Roads:

1. That in the improvement of roads, the Macadam system, consisting of small angular fragments, in sizes not exceeding from two (2) to two and a half (2½) inches in their longest dimension, according to quality, should be used, wherever a stone surface is both practicable and justifiable.

2. That the minimum width of the metaled surface for a single track should be a demirod (eight and one-quarter feet), of such depth as the amount of traffic and character of the subsoil may require; to be determined by the engineer in charge.

3. That the bed to receive the stone must be so prepared that it cannot be saturated with water, and to accomplish this

great attention should be paid to the character and drainage of the subsoil.

4. That there should be legislative enactment regulating the width of the tires of wheels, and that the minimum width of all cart, dray, wagon or other heavy draught vehicles should be four (4) inches, to be increased when the capactity of the vehicle exceeds half a net ton per wheel, at the rate of one inch for each four hundred (400) pounds in excess.

Respectfully submitted,

A. J. CASSATT, *Chairman*,
WILLIAM SELLERS,
JOSEPH M. WILSON,
WAYNE MACVEAGH,
THOMAS M. CLEEMAN,
WILLIAM H. WAHL,
LEWIS M. HAUPT, *Secretary*.

ANNOUNCEMENT OF THE AWARD

OF THE

UNIVERSITY OF PENNSYLVANIA ROAD PRIZES.

The Board of Adjudication having completed the examination of the papers submitted for competition on the subject of Road Making and Maintenance, and having reported their findings to the Provost, Dr. William Pepper, he takes pleasure in announcing to the public that the authors of the selected papers entitled to premiums, or to commendations, are as follows :

For the First Prize—
    HENRY IRWIN, B.A., C.E., Canadian Pacific Railway, Montreal, Can.
For the Second Prize—
    DAVID H. BERGEY, B. Sc., M.D., North Wales, Pa.
For the Third Prize—
    JAMES BRADFORD OLCOTT, South Manchester, Conn.
And for honorable mention, without reference to order—
    EDWIN SATTERTHWAIT, Jenkintown, Pa.
    CHARLES PUNCHARD, 1223 Hollywood Ave., Philadelphia.
    GEORGE B. FLEECE, C.E., Memphis, Tenn.
    FRANK CAWLEY, B.S., Swarthmore College, Pa.
    FRANCIS FULLER MCKENZIE, C. E., 5774 Germantown Avenue, Philadelphia.

These papers, with a digest of others submitted in competition, will be printed for the information of the public by the Committee on Better Roads. Application for copies may be made to the Secretary, Prof. Lewis M. Haupt, University of Pennsylvania, Philadelphia.

WILLIAM PEPPER, M.D., Provost,
University of Pennsylvania.

PHILADELPHIA, October, 1890.

(8)

ROAD MAKING AND MAINTENANCE.

FIRST PRIZE PAPER. NO. 37.

BY

HENRY IRWIN, B. A., C. E.,

Canadian Pacific Railway, Montreal, Can.

BASIS OF REMARKS.

The following remarks, so far as they refer to the locating, grading, draining and forming of roads in general, and also to the macadamizing of them in particular, are based on the writer's experience while in charge of a district adjoining a large town where some of the finest macadamized roads are to be found, and while driving for many years over some of the worst highways in the adjacent county. The remarks on asphalt, block stone and wood are based on observations extending over fifteen years.

DIVISIONS OF SUBJECT.

The subject is arranged according to Article No. 3 of the Conditions, under the following divisions, viz. :

First.—The engineering.

Second.—The economic, and

Third.—The legislative features of road making and maintenance.

DIVISION NO. I.

This part is subdivided into three sections, viz. !

SUBDIVISIONS.

Section 1st.—Construction.

Section 2d.—Reconstruction, and

Section 3d.—Maintenance.

(9)

Road Construction from an Engineering Point of View.
LOCATION.

Section 1.—In the older States of the Union, where few new roads are required, except more direct roads between large towns, and in the newer States, where the highways are made along section and township lines, this question would generally become one of alteration of alignment where hills are met with, rather than of complete new location. While it is very proper that the side lines of townships, sections and farms should be straight and should run due North and South or East and West, it would be much better, in many cases, to locate the roads so as to give as easy grades as possible without incurring too much expense on excavations or embankments, and so as to avoid marshy ground or expensive stream crossings.

The second division would seem to be the proper heading under which to discuss the actual advantages of easy grades; but with reference to location, the question as to whether it is better to have a straight, short, hilly road or one that is winding, longer and with easier grades, resolves itself into one of determining how much a road may be lengthened by going round a hill in order to avoid a bad grade in going straight over the hill.

For an example, let it be assumed that a practically level road round a hill can be obtained by increasing its length by one mile; let the average cost of the road be $10,000 per mile for construction and $300 per mile for repairs and maintenance.

The $300 per annum represents a capital of $6,000 at five (5) per cent., therefore the total cost of the extra length of one mile would be really $16,000; in addition to this, the cost of hauling would be increased by the extra length. This item, however, is difficult to calculate on a practical basis. It is the farmers who are principally to be considered in such a case, and unless the extra mile prevents the farmer from making a second trip to town per diem, the extra mile in length really costs him very little extra except in a slight increase of wear and tear of harness, etc.

The above item of $16,000 has to be compared with the cost of hauling up the steep grade which is to be avoided by the detour ; suppose this grade to be one in fifteen (1 in 15) and of too great a length for a horse to draw the same load on it that he can on the level, even by making a spurt ; let the tractive force on the level road be one-fortieth (1-40th) of the total, or fifty (50) pounds per ton ; the extra force required on the grade of one in fifteen (1 in 15) would be about one-fifteenth (1-15th) or one hundred and thirty-three (133) pounds per ton, making a total tractive force required on the grade of (50 + 133) = one hundred and eighty-three pounds per ton, against fifty (50) pounds per ton on the level. Now, supposing that the hill is not too long for a horse to exert double his usual pull on it, the proportion of the load he could draw on the level to that which he could draw up the hill would be fifty (50) to the half of one hundred and eighty-three (183-2) or of one (1) to one and eighty-two hundredths (1.82).

If one hundred farmers, using the hilly road, required an average of one hundred and fifty days' work of one horse each to market their produce, with the new road, by taking heavier loads, they would only need an average of about eighty-two and one-half (82½) days each, or a total of eight thousand two hundred and fifty (8250) days, against fifteen thousand (15,000) days on the hilly road, showing a saving of six thousand seven hundred and fifty (6750) days' work of a horse ; there would also be added to this, if two-horse teams be used, half that time for a man, or three thousand three hundred and seventy-five (3375) days. Estimating labor at one dollar ($1.00) and the cost of a horse at fifty cents (50 cents) per day, the level road would thus effect an annual saving of six thousand seven hundred and fifty dollars ($6750), representing a capital of one hundred and thirty-five thousand dollars ($135,000), and an annual saving to each farmer of sixty-seven dollars and fifty cents ($67.50). Now, even if the saving were only one-fourth of the above item, or thirty-three thousand seven hundred and fifty dollars ($33,750), it would be still more than double the estimated cost of the improvement.

The advisability of improving the grades on a road without altering its alignment may be arrived at in a similar manner.

In altering the alignment of a road, provision has often to be made for providing properties with access to the new road across adjacent properties.

In locating highways in hilly country, it will generally be found advantageous to follow along water-courses—a practice which is very often adoped in the case of railways.

In going from a valley over a hill care should be taken to avoid running down hill, if possible. The advantage of having a road run close to quarries from which good road metal can be obtained should also be kept in view.

GRADES.

Before the profile of the located road can be completed the exact grades have to be decided on.

It may here be mentioned that tables are often to be found in works on location giving the amount which can be drawn up various grades as compared with what can be drawn on the level. Such tables are of little use unless they also give the tractive force required on the level, because the effect of gravity in the case of a hill varies in proportion to the sine of the angle of inclination, and practically, for any reasonable slope, it varies as the tangent of that angle, and is independent of the road surface, whereas the tractive force required, due to the inequalities, adhesiveness and yielding of the roadbed, is the same whether on a grade or on a level, and as these last-mentioned items vary very much on different roads, the proportion of the force required to overcome them, as compared with the force necessary to draw a load against both them and the force of gravity on a grade will also vary considerably according as the road be good or bad.

The steepest grade that should be allowed on a public road is one in twelve (1 in 12), and the length of such a steep hill should not be more than about one hundred (100) feet, in order that a horse may not be overworked before reaching the top with a heavy load ; such a grade, however, should not be permitted except on roads of little importance.

A grade of one in fifteen (1 in 15) may be permitted for about two hundred (200) feet in length, but even this slope should be avoided on important thoroughfares.

A good load can be taken up a grade of one in twenty (1 in 20) for a length of four hundred (400) feet. This is the steepest slope which should be allowed on a road where there is much traffic.

If it be necessary to have more than five hundred (500) feet of such a grade, it is best to divide it by having intervals of about one hundred (100) feet in length of level road spaced about three hundred (300) feet apart, or at places that will best suit the contour of the ground, as there is nothing more tiring on a horse than a long, steady uphill pull ; however, unless the cost of reducing the grade to one in thirty (1 in 30) be too great, it would be better to fix this latter grade as the maximum for first-class roads.

In fixing the steepest allowable grade it should be remembered that the better the road surface is, the better and flatter should be the grades, or else the benefit arising from the good road surface will not be fully realized.

If hills be not too long to tire out a horse and use up his reserved strength, it may be assumed that he can exert an extra pull on a hill at least double his regular pull on the level ; more than this should not be counted on except for very short slopes.

On a *very good* macadamized road, in first-class order, the required tractive force due to the road bed is about one-fiftieth ($\frac{1}{50}$) of the load ; the tractive force to overcome gravity on a grade of one in fifty (1 in 50) is equal to this, so that the last-mentioned grade should be the maximum on such a road.

On an ordinary good road, however, the tractive force due to the road surface is probably nearer one in thirty (1 in 30), and as a grade of one in thirty would require one in thirty (1 in 30) more, the latter grade would seem to be the proper maximum for long hills, if the cost of securing it be not too great.

A DEAD LEVEL TO BE AVOIDED.

A long stretch of a perfectly level road is, however, by no means an unmixed good, for the water tables or gutters at the sides of the roadway require to have a fall of at least one in one hundred and twenty (1 in 120), or one inch in ten feet (1″ in 10′), so that on a level road the water table would gradually increase in depth below the surface of the road, which is not desirable, as it tends to diminish the available width of roadway, or else the exits into the longitudinal drains or ditches must be more frequent, which always adds to the cost of construction. The surface water on the roadway also drains off better when there is a slight longitudinal slope.

Having determined on the grades of a road, the methods of construction have next to be considered.

DRAINAGE.

The first item to be attended to is the drainage, and it is as important as any other.

It is almost impossible to make a good road on a wet, yielding soil, except by going to great expense in providing a heavy concrete foundation.

Money spent in securing a good, firm, dry roadbed will save a vast amount of trouble in attempting to maintain a good surface and to keep it clean.

In Northern latitudes the remark is frequently made in the Spring that "the frost has heaved the road."

It is true that the roadway would probably not have heaved had there been no frost; but yet the frost does not spoil a *dry* roadway; and, in fact, it is the ice thawing that does the mischief, and not the frost. The proper remark to make in such a case would be " The road is badly drained."

All roads should have a ditch or drain about four (4) feet deep on each side ; these side drains are generally open except in villages and towns, or in some cuttings, as noted later on. These side drains should be outside the fences to prevent accidents. In wet places, low-lying lands, clayey soils and localities where springs are met with under the roadbed, it should be thoroughly sub-drained.

SUB-DRAINS.

French drains are the best for such cases. In Northern latitudes the bottom of the drain should be kept low enough to prevent the water in it from freezing.

From five feet to five feet six inches (5' to 5' 6") would be deep enough to meet all ordinary cases, but where there are no severe frosts, four (4) feet is deep enough.

TILE PIPES. STONE COVERING.

Ordinary unglazed circular tiles three (3) inches in diameter should be laid in the bottom of the trench, except in cases where extreme economy is necessary. The stones immediately over the tiles should be laid with their lower edges on the bottom of the trench, and their upper edges meeting so as to form an inverted covering over the tile pipes ; over these, cover stones, to a depth of eighteen (18) inches, are laid. Rounded or field stones from two (2) inches to six (6) inches in diameter are better for this purpose than those with angular edges, which fill up the spaces between the stones. In using coarse gravel of mixed size it is advisable to separate the larger from the smaller by screening, and to put in the larger first and the smaller on the top, as the mixed sizes fill up the interstices more than when each size is used separately. The smaller screenings can be used on the sidewalks, or as binding for macadam, if clean and sharp enough. Over the stones a layer of brushwood or coarse straw should be placed to prevent the soil from filling in between the stones before they become compacted.

The excavations for these French drains may be made about eight (8) inches wide at the bottom, and, if four (4) feet deep, twenty (20) inches wide at the top; when the drain is only three feet six inches (3' 6") deep, it may be eighteen (18) inches wide at the top.   Where flat-bedded stones, which break readily into pieces with parallel sides, can be cheaply procured, the tiles may be dispensed with, and the bottom of the drain formed by setting two stones vertically against the sides of the trench and covering them with a third flat-bedded stone.

DISTANCE APART OF SUB-DRAINS.

The distance apart of sub-drains, when required, must be governed by the nature of the soil.   When this is gravelly and pervious to water, the open ditches on each side of a road, even if sixty-six (66) feet wide, are sufficient for draining the roadbed, as they will act from twenty-five to thirty (25 to 30) feet on each side under such conditions; but if there be any springs under the road, especially if they rise through an impervious soil, a sub-drain leading directly to the side ditches is required.   Again, should the road be on a side hill, a deep open ditch on its upper side, and none on the lower side, may be sufficient to keep the roadbed dry.   In such a case the surface water from the water table on the lower side of the road would, unless there were ditches at proper distances on the lower side, have to be conducted across and under the road by ordinary dry stone culverts at suitable intervals, depending on the grade of the road.   In such a case the question would have to be considered as to whether it would be cheaper to make a French drain under the water table, on the lower side, and to leave openings for the water table to drain into, instead of making culverts at such intervals as might be required.

When a cutting is deep and takes up too much land, it may be advisable to make a French drain under the water table on each side instead of open ditches; a comparative estimate would have to be made to ascertain which is the more advantageous method.

CLAYEY SUB-SOIL.

When the road passes over clayey or impervious soil, sub-drains become necessary along the centre of the road, unless the roadway be extremely narrow. A drain in such soil will not be efficient for more than from ten to fifteen (10 to 15) feet on each side. It is obvious that in the case of a sixty-six (66) foot road having open ditches outside the fences, with their inner sides at least twenty-seven (27) feet from the centre of the road allowance, a French drain will be necessary in the centre of the roadbed where a clayey or impervious soil is passed over.

CATCH-WATER DRAINS.

In all cuttings over four or five (4 or 5) feet in depth small catch-water drains should be made along the top of the bank to prevent the surface water from washing away the slopes ; such drains are, of course, not necessary when the original surface of the ground slopes away from the cutting.

BERM AT FOOT OF SLOPE.

A berm of about (1) foot in width should be left between the foot of the slope and the sidewalk in a cutting ; and the sidewalk should be raised six (6) inches above the foot of the slope to keep it clear of the water from the slope.

UNIFORM INCLINATION FOR DRAINS.

In constructing all drains care should be taken to preserve a uniform grade in the bottom. For this purpose the workmen should use " boning rods," which seem to be seldom thought of in this country. Three are used at a time, made of pine about three (3) inches wide and one (1) inch thick ; two of them are about four (4) feet long and pointed at the end, and the third is about three (3) feet long and left square at the end ; all have a cross piece at the upper end about one foot long, set square to the upright part. The pointed rods are driven into the ground

2

where the grade pegs are given till the top of the cross piece is as high above the desired grade as the entire length of the unpointed rod ; then by sighting along the tops of the two rods driven into the ground, when the top of the third rod is brought level with the tops of the fixed rods its foot will be at the desired grade.   By this means the bottom of the drains can be perfectly graded from grade pegs set two hundred (200) feet apart.   These "boning rods" should also be used in grading the roadway.

GRADES OF DRAINS.

In determining the grades for drains it is well to make them so that they shall be a certain number of inches in ten (10) or twelve (12) feet.   A plank with one edge bevelled off to the given grade is generally used ; thus, for example, one (1) in one hundred and twenty (120) is one (1) inch in twelve (12) feet, one (1) in sixty (60) is two (2) inches in ten (10) feet, and so on.

CULVERTS.

Culverts to carry the drainage across a road should, if possible, be made of stone, as timber does not last long, and the caving-in of wooden culverts is a common cause of accidents. In all cases they should be made larger than sufficient to discharge the greatest known or estimated quantity of water which has to pass through them, and their slope should not be less than one (1) in one hundred and twenty (120).

Small culverts up to about two feet six inches (2' 6") square may be built of dry stone, but where they have to carry considerable streams they should be built in cement or good hydraulic mortar.   It would be better not to build any culverts with openings less than two feet by one foot six inches (2' x 1'6"), as a boy can then pass through them to examine them.   The cover stones should have a bearing of at least six (6) inches on each side wall, and should not be less than nine (9) inches thick for a two (2) foot opening and about twelve (12) inches thick for a three foot opening ; the side walls should be about two (2) feet thick, with their foundations separate from the pavement of the water-way, and they should be extended beyond the culvert itself at a slope of one and a half to one (1½ to 1) to retain the bank on each side. The bottom should be paved with stones, and each end protected from scour by extending the pavement to the ends of the side walls, and setting stones about one foot six inches (1' 6") long vertically across the ends of the pavement.

Where stone is scarce tile pipes may be used to advantage; these are now made specially for this purpose. Their ends should be well protected from scour by a wooden or stone sheeting.

CROSS SECTION OF ROAD.

The proper cross section of the road is the next point to be settled.

Across all level lands the crown of the road should be raised at least one foot above the surface of the ground. If the side ditches be made three (3) feet below the surface, one foot wide at the bottom and with their slides sloping one to one (1 to 1), they will be each seven (7) feet wide at the top, the two together forming twenty-four (24) square feet in section. The earth from these ditches will raise the sidewalk spaces one (1) foot high and six (6) feet wide, and will also fill in the margins of the road to the necessary height, while the paving and road metal will raise the central paved portion from thirteen (13) to fifteen (15) inches above the natural surface.

TRANSVERSE SLOPE.

In the case of a well-maintained macadam road a trans-verse slope of one (1) in thirty (30) from the centre to the sides is ample. But unless the road is to be very well kept, it would be advisable to give two (2) or three (3) inches more slope to the last four (4) or five (5) feet; one (1) inch per yard or one (1) in thirty-six (36) is sufficient for wooden blocks or stone pave-ment; while one in forty (1 in 40) is enough for asphalt.

EXPLANATION OF TERMS.

To avoid any misunderstanding as to the precise meaning of the terms " Road Allowance," " Roadway" and " Roadbed," it may be stated that the full width of land reserved for road purposes will always be referred to below as the " Road Allowance," the portion thereof used by vehicles as the " Roadway," while the term " Roadbed" will be applied to the surface of the roadway at sub-grade, on which the stone or other foundations for upper coating of the roadway is placed.

TRANSVERSE SECTION.

Some prefer a circular section of uniform radius, while others advocate a plane uniform slope from the centre to each side, with the apex at the centre rounded off.   The writer prefers the latter section, provided that the longitudinal drainage is very efficient ; but in places where there are heavy snowfalls, which thaw rapidly, or where there are very heavy rains lasting for some time, the writer would prefer to combine both sections in giving the paved portion of the roadway a plane uniform slope, with the apex rounded off, and then rounding off the last five (5) or six (6) feet of the margin with a quicker slope, leaving the last foot level for the water-table.   On a thirty (30) foot roadway the transverse slope should be four (4) inches for the first nine (9) feet, two (2) inches for the next three (3) feet and two (2) inches for the next (2) feet, leaving one foot horizontal for the water-table.

SIDEWALKS.

The sidewalk spaces may be made six (6) feet wide, with an allowance for a one to one (1 to 1) slope at each side, though when once the earth has become consolidated and some grass has grown at the sides, the edge next the road may be cut down almost vertically.   If the water tables be paved and curb stones be used, this edge will be vertical from the first.

In the case of a sixty-six (66) foot road allowance, where there is no cutting or filling, a thirty (30) foot roadway, the longitudinal ditches and a six (6) foot sidewalk on each side will take up the full width of the road allowance.

WIDTHS OF ROADWAY.

Country roads, however, do not require a thirty (30) foot roadway. If extreme economy be necessary, the central part of the roadway may be macadamized for a width of only eight (8) feet ; this is about the least width that a vehicle can be readily driven on. In such a case it would not be advisable to make the entire roadway less than twenty (20) feet wide, so that vehicles may pass on either side of the central portion, and that the macadamized part may be easily widened in the future.

To provide for a pretty constant traffic in both directions, the macadamized portion of the roadway should be sixteen (16) feet wide, as the axles of wagons or buggies are usually five feet eight inches (5' 8") in length, or five feet two inches (5' 2") from one wheel to the further end of an axle ; therefore, allowing a space of two (2) feet between the ends of the axles of two vehicles when passing, and two (2) feet from the further wheel to the outside of the paved part of the roadway, sixteen feet four inches (16' 4"), or, in round numbers, sixteen (16) feet, would appear to be the proper width to allow vehicles always to keep their own side of the road without going off the paved portion, while it will also give a play of nearly two (2) feet on each side, and of nearly four (4) feet altogether, in the width allowed to the vehicles to travel over, thus leaving space enough for vehicles to avoid always going in the same track and wearing the roadway into ruts.

If any further addition is to be made to the width of the macadamized part, it should be enough to allow three (3) vehicles to pass over it abreast, i. e., sixteen (16) feet and seven (7) feet four (4) inches, or twenty-three feet eight inches in all ; twenty-two (22) feet, however, is a common width for the paved part of a roadway of this description, as the difference of one foot eight inches (1' 8") can be gained by reducing the two (2) feet of spare width at the outsides by ten (10) inches on each side; however, the clear width between the sidewalks should not be less than twenty-four (24) feet, while a thirty (30) foot roadway will allow four vehicles to meet abreast, and thirty-five (35) feet is enough for a regular traffic of four vehicles.

WIDTH FOR DITCHES AND SIDEWALKS.

After deducting the width required for the roadway, allowance must be made for the side ditches; if these be one (1) foot wide at the bottom and three (3) feet deep below the original surface of the ground, they will be seven (7) feet wide at the top, provided that the slopes be made one to one (1 to 1), which is as steep as the sides will usually stand at. One (1) foot more should be allowed outside the ditch to the limit of the road allowance, and also a berm of at least two (2) feet between the side of the ditch next the road and the fence, which should always be placed between the ditch and the roadway to prevent accidents, and not outside the ditch, as is often the case. The two ditches, then, with the spaces on each side, will take up twenty (20) feet of the road allowance. Two feet would be required from the outside of the fence to the edge of the sidewalk, and six (6) inches more for the slope down from the sidewalk to the roadway; allowing six (6) feet for the sidewalk, a total width of eight feet six inches (8' 6") would be required for the fence and sidewalk on one side, and twenty-eight feet six inches (28' 6") for the two ditches and the fence and sidewalk on one side.

If the roadway be made twenty-four (24) feet wide and the road allowance be sixty-six (66) feet wide, there would still remain thirteen feet six inches (13' 6"), of which two feet would be required for the fence and the slope up to the road margin, next the inside, leaving eleven feet six inches (11' 6") to spare on one side where there is no cutting or embankment.

BEST SIDE FOR THE SIDEWALK.

This space should, as far as may be practicable, be left on the South and West sides of the road, so as to allow the sidewalk, if there be only one, to be made on the North and East sides, on which the sun shines the most, and, therefore, will dry the sidewalk the most quickly.

PLACES FOR STORING MACADAM.

The space on the opposite side from the sidewalk is, in the case of macadamized roads, utilized for storing the macadam, which is generally placed where there is most land to spare at level parts of the road.

SLOPES IN CUTTINGS.

In cuttings or embankments in ordinary loose earth or gravel, the side slopes should be made one and one-half horizontal to one vertical ($1\frac{1}{2}$ to 1); in rock one-quarter to one ($\frac{1}{4}$ to 1) is sufficient; for stiff clay two to one (2 to 1) should be allowed, and soft greasy clay requires a slope of three to one (3 to 1) to be allowed for. In the case of ordinary earth, when cuttings or embankments are not more than five (5) feet high, a slope of one to one (1 to 1) is sufficient, and one-half to one ($\frac{1}{2}$ to 1) for stiff clay.

SLOPING GROUND TO BE STEPPED.

In the case of embankments, the surface of the ground, when it has a transverse slope, such as would cause the bank to slide laterally, should be cut into steps before the embankment is commenced. The necessity for this for any particular slope can only be determined by the conditions of the case, it being remembered that water getting in between the original surface and the made ground will render the embankment very liable to slide.

All trees, stumps, brush and vegetable matter should be cleared off the surface before the embankment is commenced.

PLANKS ON CLAY ROAD.

Where a bank has to be made of soft clay, it is well to lay two (2) inch planks over the roadbed before placing the stone on it, as the clay can then consolidate before the wood could rot away sufficiently to let the stones get out of level. A clay filling, however, should be avoided as far as possible, as there are some clays which will stand in an almost perpendicular bank while being excavated, and yet when exposed to the weather on an embankment will spread away till they take a slope of four (4) or five (5) to one (1).

SOWING GRASS ON SLOPES.

The slopes of all cuttings or banks should be sown with grass seed, so as to prevent their being washed away by rain and damaged by frost. If the cost be not too great, the surface soil should be reserved and spread over the side slopes.

SAVING EXTRA WIDTH.

In cuttings or embankments over six (6) or eight (8) feet deep the roadway may be reduced to a width of twenty (20) feet to save taking extra land, and in cuttings French drains may be made under the water-tables instead of open ditches for the same object.

DRY STONE WALLS. TREES TO BE KEPT FROM DRAINS. TREES ON NORTH AND EAST SIDES.

In some cases it may be found economical to build dry walls about five (5) feet high at the foot of slopes to save width. Where French drains are made trees should not be allowed near enough to them for their roots to get into and block the drain. In this connection it must be remembered that the roots of a tree will spread out further from the stem than the branches, and that in dry ground they will always spread out toward water. In general, trees should only be allowed on the North and East sides of roads, so as to allow the sun and wind to dry them as much as possible ; this precaution is specially necessary in damp or level places.

ROADBED TO BE ROLLED.

The roadbed, having been brought to the required grade both transversely and longitudinally, should be rolled several times so as to make the surface firm and compact. While the rolling is in progress all inequalities caused by it should be levelled up and rolled, and it is well, in the first place, to make allowance for the settlement due to the rolling according as the portion to be rolled be in cutting or embankment.

WEIGHT OF ROLLER.

If it can be obtained, a roller of not less than ten tons in weight should be used. A steam roller is best both for the road-bed and for the subsequent paving, as it does not disturb the surface, and if it could be frequently or continuously used would be as economical as a horse roller. If horses are used, a suffi-cient number should be employed to draw it easily, and so as not to cut up the surface by straining too much to pull the load.

SURFACE MATERIAL.

The next point to consider is the material of which the sur-face of the roadway is to be formed.

ROADWAYS IN CITIES.

For large cities either asphalt, stone blocks or wooden blocks, or brick are largely used, and their use will increase as people begin to realize that the first cost of a roadway is not the only item of expense, and that the annual cost of keeping up badly-made roads often represents a capital sum far greater than that which would be required to make a first-class road.

FOUNDATION.

For the four classes of pavement just mentioned concrete forms the best, and in the long run the most economical foun-dation. The concrete need not be so rich in cement as it is sometimes made. The annual report of the City Surveyor of Montreal, for 1888, shows that a concrete foundation six (6) inches deep, and composed of one (1) part of Portland cement to three (3) parts of sand and four and one-half (4½) parts of two and one-half (2½) inch broken stone is amply strong enough to support a heavy traffic and also to withstand the effects of the severe frosts in that city. This foundation costs from ninety-five (95) cents to one dollar ($1.00) per square yard. Before definitely fixing the proportions of the cement, sand and broken stone for the concrete, it is well to try how much cement is required to fill the voids in the sand and allow about ten (10) per cent. extra, and also to try how much sand will fill the voids in the broken stone that is to be used, and add about ten (10) per cent. to this. If less cement or sand than the quantities thus found be used, the concrete will not be strong or compact. When a good concrete foundation is once laid, it will last for an almost indefinite period; all the materials, however, should be first-class, the sand clean, coarse and gritty, and the broken stone quite free from mud or earth. The concrete should be rammed till the water shows on the surface, and in hot or dry weather it should be protected from the sun and wind with old boards or tarpaulins until it is covered with the pavement. Traffic should be kept off the road until the concrete has had time to set properly.

FOUNDATION OF CONCRETE.

On such a foundation any class of pavement can afterward be laid; for instance, if brick or wood be laid at first, when it is worn out and the traffic has become so heavy that block stone must be laid, then all that is required besides the stone is the sand, or if asphalt is to be laid, all that is necessary is to add enough concrete to make up for the thinner layers of asphalt.

STONE BLOCKS.

Where block-stone pavement is used it is very poor economy to set it on anything but a concrete foundation, as the first cost of the stone is more than that of any other pavement, and it lasts much longer. On the concrete the stones are set. Experienced men should be employed to do the paving. The joints between the stones are filled in with sand, or, better still, with grout of Portland cement or with hot pitch. A layer of sand is spread over the finished pavement and is packed between the joint of the stones by the wheels of the vehicles. The writer has always seen streets paved with the stones at right angles to the direction of the street lines, but is of opinion that the pavement would remain in good condition longer, and that the noise and jar to vehicles would be greatly diminished, if the stones were laid in rows diagonally across the street. If laid at an angle of forty-five (45) degrees with the street lines the effect on the traffic would be the same in both directions.

TRANSVERSE SLOPE.

A transverse slope of from one in thirty-six (1 in 36) to one in forty-eight (1 in 48), according to evenness of surface, is sufficient to drain the surface of a block-stone roadway.

Though block stone lasts so long that its annual cost, including interest, cleaning and repairs is usually less than that of either asphalt, wood or brick, yet the noise that it causes, as well as the jar to passengers driving over it, and the shaking loose of bolts and springs of vehicles, make it a very undesirable kind of roadway except where the traffic is very heavy, and where there are factories the noise from which is so great that the extra noise from the pavement is of no consequence.

ASPHALT.

Where the traffic is not too heavy, and the expense can be incurred, asphalt makes much the finest roadway, the only objection to it, besides its cost, being that it is slippery in damp weather ; it is, however, so smooth that horses falling on it do not often get badly hurt, and in London they seem to have got used to it, and seem to know how to slide down without hurting themselves or damaging vehicles.

Asphalt, when well laid, will last from ten (10) to fifteen (15) years, according to the traffic. The writer has seen Trinidad asphalt, as laid by the Warren Scharf Company, stand very well under a range of temperature from twenty degrees below zero to one hundred degrees in the shade, showing that it is not liable to get too brittle when cold, or too soft when hot.

FOUNDATION.

Asphalt should be put down on a concrete foundation.   It is made up of two layers, of which the upper or wearing surface alone requires renewing, so that repairs can be easily made and are not very expensive.   Great care should be taken to connect the asphalt with the curb stones in a perfectly water-tight man-ner.   Existing block-stone pavements can be used as a founda-tion for asphalt by coating the stone with the materials of the lower layer sufficient to bring it up to the proper grade, and then laying on the upper coating.

LIMESTONE AND ASPHALT.

As limestone is found in a natural state impregnated with asphalt so as to form a good material for roads, the writer thinks that an artificial mixture might be used with advantage.   As an asphalt roadway has such a smooth surface, the dust and rubbish must be constantly removed and put into dust bins at the sides of the street, or else it will blow up under the slightest wind. By keeping the surface thoroughly clean, it is not so liable to be slippery in damp weather.

WOOD BLOCKS.

Though granite blocks make a very durable, and asphalt a very smooth and pleasant roadway, yet for smaller towns wooden blocks or bricks are more desirable, on account of their being cheaper at first.

Wooden block roads, of either tamarac, yellow pine or cedar, seem to have been in longer and more general use than brick.

Wood makes a noiseless pavement, which, when it is in good order, is smooth and pleasant to drive over. The great objections to it are that it does not last long in good condition, and that it absorbs a great part of the liquid refuse on it, which ferments or decomposes and gives rise to very unhealthy and disagreeable exhalations, during hot weather especially.

The transverse section of a wooden road should not be too

flat, so as to enable it to shed the water from it quickly and effectually. In London, England, the wooden pavements put down some years ago had a transverse slope of one (1) inch per yard; one (1) inch in four (4) feet is probably sufficient in almost any place.

FOUNDATION.

The best foundation is concrete as above described, but a cheaper foundation can be made of gravel well watered and rolled; a layer of sand well rolled and covered with two (2) inch planks, and another layer of sand, on which the blocks are placed, also makes a good foundation if the roadbed be well drained.

KINDS OF WOOD USED.

Of the various kinds of wood used, pitch pine wears the best. In London, after four and a half (4½) years' use, the wear on its surface was almost imperceptible; its cost, however, is too great to admit of its use in a general way. Elm and oak will not stand the exposure to the weather, and creosoting the blocks does not seem to be economical, as the advantages obtained from its use are more than counterbalanced by its cost.

WOODEN BLOCKS.

Tamarac, yellow pine and cedar seem to last the best. The first two are used in the shape of rectangular blocks about three (3) inches wide, by nine (9) inches long, and six (6) inches deep, though probably five (5) inches is depth enough, since when the blocks get worn down to a depth of about three (3) inches the roadway must be renewed.

The blocks should be laid with the fibres upright and with joint spaces about three-eighths (⅜) of an inch wide; these spaces are filled in with sand, cement grout or pitch, the last of which would seem to be the best, as it keeps the joints water tight. The surface should be covered with fine gritty gravel or coarse sand. Yellow pine or tamarac will last from six (6) to ten (10) years in fair condition if defective blocks are promptly removed; seven (7) years, however, is the most that should be counted on.

CEDAR BLOCKS.

When cedar blocks are used they should be stripped of their bark and sapwood, which causes the blocks to wear round on the top like cobble stones. Cedar is always used in the shape of full sections of the tree, and is never squared, as it would then split too readily. The blocks should not be less than four (4) inches in diameter, nor more than nine (9) inches, when stripped of the bark and sapwood. The smaller blocks should be laid alternately with the larger, so as to fill the spaces better. The interstices between the blocks are filled in the same manner as the spaces between square blocks; gravel or sand is rammed in with iron rods, and may be covered with pitch, and the whole surface covered with fine gravel or coarse sand. Blocks, when laid on sand, should be well rammed with a maul at least seventy (70) pounds in weight.

REPAIRS.

Blocks which show signs of decay or uneven wear should be immediately removed, and the whole surface should be kept free from dirt. Coarse sand should be occasionally spread on it, and it should also be well watered in dry weather.

BRICK PAVEMENTS.

The writer has had no experience of brick roadways, but thinks it well to give a brief account of them, as they seem to be coming more into use lately. Brick can be laid on the same kinds of foundation as wood; besides these, two layers of brick are sometimes used, the first laid on its side on a layer of sand and rolled or rammed into place. On this a layer of sand about one (1) inch thick is spread, and on this the upper layer of brick is set on edge; the spaces between the bricks may be filled with sand, cement grout or pitch, and a layer of sand should be spread over the surface. This gets well worked into the joints by the traffic.

The pavement would probably last longer and cause less

noise and jar in driving over it, if the bricks were laid in rows diagonally to the street.

The surface of either stone, wood or brick pavements, when laid on sand, would be improved by rolling.

Paving bricks should be of uniform quality, tough and burnt almost to vitrification ; in fact, some authorities claim that they should be completely vitrified. This would prevent them from absorbing moisture, but would tend to make them brittle and slippery.

In Vienna the clay is mixed with a little lime, which seems to make a very durable brick. Paving bricks should be burnt in special kilns, as the ordinary kilns cannot be relied on to give a uniform quality.

Good bricks will last from fifteen (15) to twenty (20) years, according to the traffic, and its first cost does not seem to be as great as that of wood, while it is much more healthy. It will not stand heavy traffic like granite blocks, but for moderate traffic it makes a clean roadway, with much less noise and jarring than are caused by block stone.

STONE TRACKWAYS.

In towns where there is heavy traffic on hills, stone trackways may be laid to diminish traction, as the force required to draw a load on a smooth stone trackway on the level is only about one one hundred and eightieth (1-180th) of the weight.

The stones may be about sixteen (16) inches wide, ten (10) inches deep, and five (5) feet long. The space between the trackways should be paved ; for this some authorities say block stone should be used, but the writer's experience in driving for many years, with his instruments, in front of street cars, leads to the conclusion that horses are very liable to slip and strain themselves in going up hill on stone blocks when drawing a heavy load, and that wooden blocks would be much better for the horses, though they would not last so long as stone.

For country roads, however, macadam is the most suitable.

Plank roads may be used in places where lumber is very cheap, from want of transportation facilities; such places, however, are quickly disappearing on this continent, and a plank road may be regarded as a thing of the past.

EARTH ROADS.

With regard to earth roads, the remarks already made as to draining, grading and forming the surface applies to them also. As earth roads do not shed the surface water readily, the water-tables should be kept about a foot lower than the crown of the roadway. The roadway itself should not be more than twenty (20) feet wide, in order that the water-tables may be able to keep the surface as dry as possible.

No stones larger than three (3) inches in diameter should be left on the road. The writer has often seen the ruts filled in with large round stones, with the result of making an extremely rough and bad road. In all cases the materials of the roadway should be uniform. No sods or vegetable refuse should be used in grading up the crown of the road or in filling in ruts, but the earth chosen for that purpose should be as gravelly as possible. The transverse slope of the roadway should not be less than one in twenty-four (1 in 24) or one inch in two feet (1″ in 2′). In the case of clay roads, sand, old broken bricks, or even charcoal, may be spread on the roadway to prevent the clay from sticking to the wheels; it is, however, almost impossible to keep a clay road in good order in wet weather, and the time and money spent in trying to do so would be much better invested in macadamizing the road. A very sandy road, which is at its worst during dry weather, might be improved by putting a little clay on it.

GRAVEL ROADS.

If gravel is to be put on the surface of the roads, the road-bed would be formed as already described. The gravel should be first screened, so as to remove all stones of more than two and one-half (2½) inches in diameter. The larger stones may be broken and used on the road, or may be reserved for drains;

the remainder should be screened again to remove all earthy matter and the small gravel which may be less than about three-quarters (¾) of an inch in diameter. The small screenings, if clean enough, may be used for the sidewalks, or for blinding the last coat of gravel.

ROLLING.

The gravel should be put on in layers. The bottom layer may be four or five (4 or 5) inches thick, and should be well rolled; the next layer may be three or four (3 or 4) inches thick, and should also be well rolled.

As the use of gravel implies want of money, a roller may not be obtainable; in that case the first layer should be allowed to remain till packed together by the traffic before the second layer is spread.

REPAIRS.

When ruts appear they should be immediately filled in, and the traffic should be directed over all parts of the road by putting logs or large stones on the parts most travelled over till the whole surface becomes consolidated. The same treatment should be applied to newly-constructed macadam roads.

Where the traffic has to pass over the first layer of the gravel, for want of a roller, it should be blinded as well as the second coat.

In the case of both earth and gravel roads special attention should be paid to the drainage, for if the roadbed be not very dry and firm, it is useless to expect to make a passable road.

MACADAM ROADS.

With regard to roads coated with broken stone, the comparative advantages of the ordinary macadam road as compared with those of the Telford-macadam combination, do not seem to be quite settled yet among many engineers.

The writer's experience has convinced him that the Telford-macadam system is by far the best, except where the road is to be made over rock, hardpan or very compact gravel; in these

3

cases the roadbed should be levelled off to at least six (6) inches below the finished surface, and the macadam laid direct on the roadbed.

The writer remembers well a piece of road, not in his own district, over which he drove twice a day for over six years, and at intervals for some twelve years more. On this road large quantities of macadam were spread, only to sink into the yielding roadbed, and become mixed up into a shifting mass of mud and stone, which must have been at least two (2) and possibly three (3) feet deep, and which was no better the last day the writer saw it than at the first. Had the roadbed been well drained and paved to begin with, at least half of the macadam would have been saved.

The Telford-macadam system is not, after all, so much more expensive than simple macadam, if a sufficient quantity of the latter be used. The grading, draining, and the forming of the roadbed cost the same in both cases, and the total amount of stone costs nearly as much in one case as in the other, there being three (3) or four (4) inches less in depth under the macadam system, while in the Telford-macadam plan the material of the bottom pavement is cheaper, having to be laid by hand instead of being broken. The total difference in the cost of the two systems is probably not more than the value of two (2) inches in depth of macadam laid on the road, and the cost of that will be saved in a few years' maintenance; for when the road has a good bottom to it, the macadam does not sink into the roadbed.

In this connection the writer would refer to an item in *Engineering News* of 22d of February, 1890, on page 189, referring to roads to be made in Franklin County, New Jersey. From this item it appears that it is proposed to make a macadam road with only four inches of stone, without any foundation whatever. It is stated that such a road will cost $4,700 per mile, whereas a Telford-macadam road would cost $12,000 to $15,000 per mile, thus making it appear that a Telford-macadam road would cost an average of $13,500 per mile, or $8,800 per mile more than an ordinary macadam road.

Now, while the various items of cost thus mentioned are doubtless correct, still the statement is liable to mislead those who read it with regard to the comparative cost of the two systems.

The roadway referred to is to be stoned for a width of fifteen (15) feet ; this would require about one-third (⅓) of a cubic yard of Telford bottom pavement per foot run, which, at say $2.00 per cubic yard, would amount to 66⅔ cents per foot run, of $3,520 per mile ; as for the macadam required, if four (4) inches in depth be enough on an unpaved roadbed, it would be ample on a Telford pavement. On the above basis then the Telford-macadam road would not cost more than $3,520 per mile over the cost of a simple macadam road.

But in point of fact, while four (4) inches of macadam laid on earth is better than nothing, it will only make a very poor road, and one (1) foot in depth, as laid before rolling, is necessary to make a good road when laid on earth, and as a depth of only eight (8) inches is required on a Telford-macadam road, the cost of the extra four (4) inches of macadam should be deducted from the cost of the Telford bottom pavement before arriving at the extra cost of the Telford road.

The four (4) inch macadam road above alluded to will probably not be in a satisfactory condition till eight (8) inches more macadam has been spread on it, and even then will not be as clean or as smooth as a Telford-macadam road.

TELFORD-MACADAM ROAD.

The roadbed having been formed and rolled, the Telford foundation is laid on it by hand. It should be eight (8) inches deep at the centre and six (6) inches deep at the sides, if the paved portion be sixteen (16) feet wide ; but if the paved portion be twenty (20) feet or more in width, and the traffic be not very heavy, and not increasing, the minimum depth at the sides of the road may be reduced to five (5) inches. The larger face of these stones should not be less than five (5) inches wide and ten (10) inches long, so as to give each stone a sufficient bearing on the roadbed; and no stone should be more than fifteen (15) inches long and nine (9) inches wide, so that they may not be liable to tilt up under a load.

These stones should be set with their larger face downward and the spaces between them well wedged up with spawls or quarry chippings. This wedging should not be carried along too close to the unfinished face of the pavement, but kept so far back that the chippings may be driven in tight without disturbing the stones or pushing them apart; generally, about fifteen (15) feet is far enough to keep back from the unfinished face.

The pavement thus formed should correspond in slope and cross section to the finished surface of the roadway, and should have an even, uniform surface without any projections or irregularities.

As this pavement has not to stand any grinding action from the traffic, it need not be of very hard or tough stone, such as the macadam should be made from, but any good, sound stone, if free from cracks, may be used.

MACADAM.

On this pavement the macadam is to be laid.

Before describing the manner of so doing, a few remarks should be made as to the macadam itself.

DESCRIPTION OF STONE.

The best stone from which it can be made is a good, compact, fine-grained syenite, or a basalt of a similar quality. Granite is not nearly so good for this purpose, as when broken up in small pieces the mica in it causes it to break up and grind away too easily when exposed to traffic and to the effects of the weather; but when the mica is in small grains it makes a very fair road. Gneiss makes worse macadam than granite; slaty rock generally breaks up too easily; mica-schist makes very poor road metal, as does also sandstone ; quartz rock or flint, though it is very hard, yet it is brittle, and it is difficult to break it into the proper cubical shape, and it is not so good as either syenite or basalt.

MACADAM VARIETIES OF STONE.

There are also other rocks, such as hornblend, actinolyte, dioryte, or greenstone, and some trap rocks, besides basalt, which make good macadam. Limestone from the older rocks makes a very poor macadam, as it is too soft ; however, it is easily broken into good cubical pieces, though it grinds away quickly, and the powder seems to burn to a certain extent under a hot sun, making a very disagreeable dust, which is very injurious to clothes.

SIZE OF STONES.

Stone for macadam should be broken into uniform, well-shaped cubical pieces ; for the first coating on the Telford pavement it may be of such a size as that the smallest stones should not be less than two (2) inches in diameter, and that the largest should pass, in any direction, through a three (3) inch ring, and the best quality of stone need not be used for this coating, if good, sound second quality of stone can be procured.

For the top coating, and for all future repairs, the smallest stones should not be less than one (1) inch in the least diameter ; seventy-five (75) per cent. of the total should pass in any direction through a two (2) inch ring, and the remaining twenty-five (25) per cent. should pass in any direction through a two and a half (2½) inch diameter ring.

Stones less than one (1) inch in diameter will not stand the pounding of the traffic. They will break up and hinder the other stones from binding properly ; while stones which will not pass through a two and a half (2½) inch ring make a rough road, and do not bind together well, being very liable to tilt up under the wheels.

HAND-BROKEN STONE.

Hand-broken stone is much superior to that crushed by a machine, which is generally of irregular shape and seldom cubical, so that it does not readily bind together, which is the essential qualification of macadam. Hand-broken stone, however, costs more than that broken by a machine, but it is a question whether the article which is more expensive at first cost is not the cheapest in the long run. The breaking of the stone to a uniform size and sufficiently small is of great importance. A few large stones projecting above the general surface considerably increase the resistance to traction, as the vehicle has to be hauled up over the stone, and in dropping down upon the other side, pounds a hole into the surface. This hole itself increases the evil which caused it, and an uneven road is the result.

CAUSES OF RESISTANCE.

It must be remembered that the two principal causes of resistance on a macadam road, besides the effects of grades, are this pulling of the vehicle over projecting stones and the friction of the wheels in their axles.

The friction of the wheels on the road surface does not, as some authors seem to state, offer resistance to traction, except when the wheels skid ; indeed, where there is no such friction the wheels would always skid, as the friction of the axle would keep them from turning.

Most people are well aware that sand has often to be put on rails to make enough friction for the locomotive to be able to pull its load. The extra power required to draw a load on account of the unevenness of the surface is well shown by the fact that a horse can draw twice as much on a common block-stone pavement, three times as much on the best block stone, and six and a half times as much on a stone trackway, as he can on a cobble-stone road, where the same sort of stone is used for each sort of the roads above mentioned, and therefore the friction between the wheel and the roadway is the same in all cases.

There are two other causes of resistance on a road which should not exist on one that is macadamized, except to a very trifling extent. One of these is the yielding of the surface under the wheel. This has the effect of opposing an inclined plane to the wheel, so that vehicles have then to be virtually pulled up a hill even when on a level road.

The other cause of resistance is the stickiness of the roadway, as in the case of a clay road in wet weather.

The above are the principal causes of resistance to traction when the vehicle is in motion, though the wind also offers considerable resistance sometimes. This is, however, independent of the nature of the road.

When a vehicle is at rest its inertia has of course to be overcome when starting.

The advantage of having a firm foundation and a smooth, hard and clean surface seems therefore apparent.

SPREADING THE MACADAM.

Having then procured good uniform-shaped macadam of the proper size, a first coating four (4) inches thick of the larger size as above mentioned should be laid on the Telford pavement and rolled until it is well consolidated. If possible, it should be well watered or advantage should be taken of wet weather to facilitate the binding of the materials. On this layer a top coating four (4) inches thick of the smaller broken stone as above described is to be laid. This should be coated with a layer of fine screenings from the broken stone or with fine gravel sufficient to fill the surface interstices between the stones and to cover them about half an inch. If screenings or fine gravel cannot be obtained, a thin coating of very coarse and perfectly clean river sand may be used instead, but on no account should any fine or dirty pit sand be put on the road ; coarse pit sand may be allowed after having been thoroughly washed so as to remove all earthy matter and the finer particles of sand, which would work down between the stones, prevent them from binding and convert the macadam in a short time into a loose mass of rounded stone little better than ordinary gravel. In this connection it must be remembered that the whole reason for using small uniform-shaped macadam is that it will of itself consolidate, under traffic, into a firm, compact and smooth roadway through the stones being wedged together among themselves, and that if any loose earthy or other fine material be mixed with the stones, they cannot become properly consolidated.

ROLLING.

The last coat, after being properly blinded, should be watered and well rolled with a heavy roller, preferably one driven by steam and not less than ten (10) tons in weight.

The sidewalks should also be given a coating of fine gravel or fine screenings; if these be considered too expensive, cinders may be substituted, and, in default of these, if wood be plentiful, a coating of charcoal will be of service in keeping the mud from rising too much to the surface.

The various works above described would complete an ordinary country road or the roadways in cities.

SIDEWALKS.

For the latter better sidewalks must be provided, either of asphalt, concrete set in panels, generally known as granolithic pavement, flagstones, planks, wooden blocks, or brick; of these flagstones are the dearest and last the longest; asphalt or concrete are very pleasant, but should be laid on a proper foundation; wooden blocks dipped in creosote last well, as they are not subject to much wear; well-laid brick also makes a good sidewalk; while three (3) inch planks, though pleasant enough to walk on when newly laid, are very unhealthy, as the under side soon begins to rot. To prevent this as far as possible, the planks should be set on sills, the upper faces of which should be at least three (3) inches above the ground, and spaces of not less than one (1) inch should be left between the planks to allow air to circulate under them.

STONE ON MARGINS OF THE ROADWAY.

On a country road where the Telford pavement does not cover the full width between the sidewalks, the margins on each side may receive a coat of macadam four (4) to six (6) inches deep, so that vehicles which have to leave the central portion may not sink into the earth too much and cut it up so as to prevent the water from draining off the central part. If no stones be put on, the margins should be at least well rolled, and the surface, therefore, before rolling should be left a few inches higher than the finished central part, the exact extra height depending on the nature of the material.

FRENCH DRAINS IN VILLAGES.

In villages and small towns French drains should be substituted for the side ditches for sanitary reasons, though they are often planked over, and the planking used for sidewalks, thus economizing space.

The water-tables also may be paved and curbstones put along the edges of the sidewalks. These should be deep enough in Northern latitudes to keep the frost from getting under them and heaving them up.

STEEP HILLS.

Where there are steep hills the macadamized part of the roadway should be made as wide as possible, so as to allow horses to cut the road from side to side in going up with heavy loads. On hills also, the centre of the road should be raised three (3) or four (4) inches more than on the level, to prevent the water from flowing longitudinally down the surface, and if the hill be several hundred feet long, it is well to make shallow water-courses across the road at intervals of about two hundred and fifty (250) or three hundred (300) feet ; these should slope from the centre toward both sides in a flat V shape, with the apex up hill, and may be about one (1) foot wide at the bottom ; the side slopes should not be steeper than one inch (1″) per foot : and the bottom and lower side should be paved for a width of

five (5) or six (6) feet. These watercourses will intercept any
flow of water down the hill and turn it off to the sides.

SOFT STONE ON HILLS.

The writer has found that on steep hills with a grade of
one in twenty (1 in 20) or steeper, a softer stone, such as limestone or the softer trap rocks, binds better and makes a safer
road, as there are fewer loose stones left on the surface, and
the softer stone wears well enough on a steep hill where the
vehicles go at a slower pace.

DEPOTS FOR STONE.

Macadam is usually stored in heaps along the roadside at
intervals of about six hundred (600) or eight hundred (800) feet,
the distance varying considerably, according to the amount of
macadam used and the frequency with which it is spread.
When hand broken, the stone is usually measured at the site
of these heaps, either before or after being broken. The writer
prefers the latter method, as unbroken stone can be loosely
piled up so as to leave a very large percentage of voids in the
centre of the pile. In making up heaps of stone ready for
measuring it is a very common trick to dig out all round the
sides and ends, so as to make the heap appear much larger
than it really is. To avoid this, and to keep the stones clean,
paved recesses are often made, with walls at the back and at
both ends. Another dodge is to put unbroken stones in the
centre of a pile of broken stone.

MARKING MEASURED STONE.

Immediately after stones are measured they should get a
good coat of whitewash, as the writer has known of old stones
being mixed up with new, and of measured stones being afterward carted to a neighboring town to be sold a second time.
These tricks are often disclosed by the presence of a few white-
washed stones.

On one occasion the writer knew of a contractor taking
macadam from a short road, which was measured up in the

forenoon, and piling it up on another road, which was measured up on returning in the afternoon, and the trick was not discovered for a few days.

Reconstruction from an Engineering Point of View.

Section 2.—If, in reconstruction, part of a road is to be relocated, or if the grade is to be changed, the various parts of Section 1 would equally apply to this part.

RECONSTRUCTION.

In reconstruction on the original road allowance, and without materially changing the grade, the first work would be to thoroughly clean out all ditches, drains and culverts, and to bring them to a uniform slope, so as to get the roadbed as dry as possible; then, if French drains are also found necessary, they should be put in next, but only one-half of the width of the roadway itself should be taken in hand at a time, unless the traffic is to be suspended altogether. However, if the surface is to be lowered, this would be done before making the drains. The next step is to remove all large stones from the roadway. These can be broken up and used again, and if the road has been previously coated with gravel or macadam, this should be taken up and screened for use on the surface of the roadbed, or if it be sufficiently uniform and angular, it may be used again as macadam.

The surface should then be brought to the proper grade and transverse slope, and well rolled. If there is to be no Telford pavement, the macadam will be spread on the roadbed of such thickness as may be decided on, and in layers of not more than four (4) inches in thickness, each layer being well rolled. One such layer is better than an earth surface, but will not last long, as the stones are sure to work into holes, for want of a proper foundation.

Two such coatings will last for some time, provided that the roadbed is dry and has been thoroughly rolled; but if a good hard roadway is required, three such coatings should be applied, which will be reduced to about nine (9) inches in thickness by rolling and a few months of traffic.

If the Telford-macadam roadway is to be made, it should be laid as described in Section 1, which also gives method of making gravel roads.

Roadways of asphalt, block stone, wooden blocks or bricks should not really require reconstruction, unless the foundation has been badly or too cheaply made at first. Should this be the case, a good concrete foundation, as described in Section 1, should be made, and on this the new pavement may be laid.

As already noted, a block-stone roadway may be used as a foundation for an asphalt road if the foundation be good; brick, under similar conditions, might also be converted into the foundation for an asphalt roadway.

MAINTENANCE.

SECTION 3.—This may be divided into three (3) subdivisions, as A, B and C, under the heads of "Cleaning the Roadway," "Repairing the Surface," and "Cleaning out the Drains or Water-courses at the edges of the Roadway."

SUBDIVISION A.—CLEANING.

Cleaning in the larger towns is generally done with brushes or scrapers drawn by horses, except in the case of asphalt roads, from which the refuse should be swept up by hand and deposited in boxes fixed at the sides of the road. On roadways paved with either stone, brick or wood or macadamized, the mud is best removed by machines when in a pretty liquid state; the other refuse can be easily swept up when dry. In towns all sweepings should be immediately removed, and not left along the sides of the roads to be spread out again by passing vehicles.

On country roads the scrapings are generally left on the roadside till dry and removed when convenient. It is well to encourage farmers to take the scrapings for top-dressing their fields.

On macadamized roads where horse machines are not used, and where the expense can be incurred of keeping two or more men at work on one section, hand machines are the most economical. The writer has not, however, seen any such machines in use in America; they work best when the mud is not so liquid as to spread too much when gathered into small heaps, nor too stiff to scrape up easily and efficiently.

These scrapers are used by two men and are about five (5) feet wide. Two men with a scraper can clean more road surface than four men with hoes, as the action of the machine is continuous, whereas a hoe requires to move backward and forward too much. It is not well to clean a macadam road too closely or to sweep it too clean either of mud or dust, or the stones may get loose on the surface.

This statement should not be considered contradictory of the opinion already expressed that no earthy or fine material should be used for blinding, since the blinding is put on loose stone, and would work down through the mass when rolled; whereas, a thin coat of mud or dust only covers the surface after the mass is made compact.

The irregularity of the surface of the stones will, however, generally retain enough binding material for the surface; if any more mud than this be allowed to remain, it not only makes travel more difficult and soils everything passing over the road, but also helps, when liquid enough, to grind away the stones.

SUBDIVISION B.—REPAIRING THE SURFACE.

In the case of roads paved with stone, brick or wood, or coated with asphalt, all defects should be made good as soon as possible and the surface kept even.

On macadamized roads, before spreading the stones, all mud should be cleaned off and the surface should be picked up a little to allow the new stone to bind well into the old. Where a heavy roller can be had, this picking may be done by teeth or spikes set into the wheels with screws; the teeth should only project about two inches (2″) from the surface and be spaced about five (5) or six (6) inches apart in alternating rows. The spikes should on no account be made too long, or they will break up and destroy the bond of the stones, which is an essential condition of a good macadam road.

The writer saw such a roller some five years ago, with spikes about six (6) inches long, which completely broke up the road surface and left it a yielding mass of stones and mud. Of course, macadam laid on this and well rolled would bind into the old soft surface and look smooth and good, but would not make nearly so firm a road as if the old surface had been only loosened on the top. Had the spikes been much shorter the roller would have been much more useful. The new, coating need not be more than three (3) inches thick, unless the surface has been worn away so much as to require raising more than the three (3) inches to bring it to the proper grade.

If less than the three (3) inches be put on, the stones will be unable to bind together, as there would then be a layer of new macadam only one stone thick. The writer has recently seen a specification for making new roads in one of the leading New England cities, in which it was required to lay a first coating of four (4) inch stone only four (4) inches thick, to be well rolled; on this a second coat was to be spread of two and a half (2½) inch stones only three (3) inches thick, which was also to be rolled, and the final coating was to be of one (1) inch stone only one (1) inch thick. The writer does not see how these successive coats would bind well together when only one (1) stone thick each; the two upper coatings would have bonded together better had the second rolling been omitted. In fulfilling the contract, however, it is probable that the several layers were about two (2) inches thicker than the specification called for, as it is not easy to spread a one-stone layer.

The stones when laid in large sections at a time, as is usual in towns, should be blinded with clean screenings, watered and well rolled.

On country roads, where the traffic is not very heavy, the stone should be put on in patches, laid in such a manner as that the traffic should come on them gradually from the side; these patches may vary from ten (10) to sixty (60) feet long and from three (3) to six (6) feet wide; on a narrow road the lesser width is sufficient. No road scrapings should on any account be put on the new stone, as it will prevent it from binding, and the result will be a yielding and uneven surface.

The writer has fully tried this question of blinding on one of the roads under his charge which was subject to a very heavy traffic from quarries. The road in question had a considerable grade down toward town, and carts with about three thousand (3000) pounds of stone used to come along down the grade in strings of twenty (20) at a time, all in the same track, and cut up the roadway badly. The writer found that the men in charge of the repairs used the road scrapings for blinding. He ordered them to stop this practice altogether, and by careful watching its use was altogether prevented. The result was that in a year the roadway became firm and even, with no more loose portions. Where a roadway has become cut up with ruts, all the loose stones and mud should be removed before the new stones are spread.

The best time to apply the stone is during wet weather in the Spring and Fall.

During dry weather in Summer all loose stones should be cleared off the road and used for patching the surface or else stored in heaps along the roadside for future use.

Newly-laid patches should be looked after, and any loose stones raked into place, and, if necessary, new patches laid to divert the traffic so as to gradually come on to the new stones.

SUBDIVISION C.—CLEANING OUT DRAINS AND WATER-TABLES.

This should be carefully attended to. The ditches and culverts should be well cleaned out in the Spring, and all mud and refuse which may have accumulated during the Winter removed. In Northern localities, where snow lies for some time, the outlets of all ditches and culverts should be opened out before the Spring thaw sets in. In the Fall all weeds and grass in the ditches should be cut, and the culverts and ditches left in good shape for the Winter.

At all seasons the water-tables should be kept free of mud and refuse of all sorts, in order that the surface water may be able to escape freely to the side ditches.

The road scrapings should not be allowed to remain on the sides of the roadway any longer than necessary, and care should be taken to prevent mud from accumulating along the sides near the water-tables, as it will prevent the surface water from draining from the centre of the roadway.

CLEANING DITCHES.

The time spent in attending to the drainage of the road should not be grudged, as a dry roadbed is more cheaply kept in good order than one that is always wet.

PRICES.

The following are approximate prices for various works and materials in connection with roads. It must be remembered, however, that prices vary considerably, both on account of the cost of labor and supplies varying in different localities, and from differences in the amount of competition among the contractors who may tender for works.

Excavation, per cubic yard.....................$0.15 to $0.30

Rock excavation, per cubic yard................ 1.00 to 2.50

French drains, three-inch tile and stone, without excavation, per lineal yard, .22 to   .30

Macadam, with Telford foundation, per square yard, .90 to 1.40

Concrete foundation—one of cement ; three of sand, and four and a half of two and a half inch stone, six inches thick, per square yard, .96 to 1.20

Granite blocks, supplied only, per square yard,	1.50 to	1.90
Granite blocks, supplied and laid (Scotch), per square yard,	2.94 to	3.25
Syenite blocks from locality, supplied and laid, per square yard,	2.75 to	3.10
Wooden blocks, supplied and laid, per square yard,	.95 to	1.25
Granite blocks on sand, including sand and laying, per square yard,	3.00 to	3.40
Granite blocks, including concrete foundation and laying, per square yard,	3.10 to	4.50
Asphalt, per square yard, including concrete foundation,	2.75 to	3.75
Red cedar on sand, including sand, per square yard,	2.00 to	2.40
Cedar and pine blocks, on concrete included, per square yard,	2.30 to	3.10
Wooden blocks, including concrete foundation and excavating old roadway, per square yard,	2.35 to	3.25
Brick on concrete, including concrete, per square yard,	2.05 to	2.50
Brick on sand, including sand, per square yard,	1.00 to	1.50
Brick, two layers on sand, including the sand, per square yard,	1.25 to	2.00
Repairs to wooden blocks per annum, per square yard,	.06 to	.10
Repairs to macadam and cleaning per annum, per square yard, for light traffic,	.06 to	.12
Ditto, for heavy traffic,	.20 to	.40

The writer has recently seen the results of investigations made by Mr. Rudolphe Hering, as to the cost per square yard of block stone, asphalt and wooden blocks laid on concrete, for a period of fifteen years, including the first cost and interest on same, and repairs, with cleaning, in London, Paris, Vienna and New York.

4

These results are given in a table, as follows :

MATERIAL.	CONSTRUCTION.	MAINTENANCE FOR 15 YEARS.	TOTAL.
Block stone,	$4.00	$1.05	$5.05
Asphalt,	3.65	2.25	5.90
Wood,	3.40	3.16	6.56

From this table, it appears that block stone is cheaper in the long run than either asphalt or wood, and that asphalt is also really cheaper than wood.

Division No. 2.—economic features.

There is nothing strikes a European more, on his arrival in North America, than the excellence of the railroads and the inferiority of the roads.

This inferiority may partly be due to the fact that the rich, both in the United States and Canada, almost invariably live in the cities, where the roads are better kept up, or else in the immediate neighborhood of towns which they can reach by rail.

The country roads seem to be principally used by farmers, to whom time seems to be no object, and who do not apparently realize that good roads can be profitable, since they do not actually place dollar bills in their hands, and who seem to think that the only way to increase their income is to sell more produce, no matter how much it may cost to draw it into market, and accordingly they spend a great part of their lives slowly plodding over bad roads without a thought of trying to improve them.

The writer has recently seen an account of investigations made by Captain D. Torrey as to the extra cost of bad roads in wear and tear of vehicles and harness, the result being that he estimates it at one (1) cent per mile per vehicle over what it would be on proper roads.

The principal advantages of good roads are that larger loads can be carried with greater speed, that farmers can market their produce at whatever time they can get the best prices, without being dependent on the weather, and that they can also use the roads in wet weather during the Winter and Spring, when they cannot plough, thus utilizing their horses when they would otherwise be idle.

In general, good roads practically shorten distances, encourage intercommunication between town and country, benefit trade, enhance the value of all adjacent properties, and effect a large saving in money uselessly expended in hauling materials over bad roads.

The following table gives the approximate percentages which can be drawn on the level over various descriptions of roads as compared with what can be drawn on an iron track, viz:

On an iron track	100	per cent.
On a good stone trackway	64	"
On asphalt	60	"
On best block stone	30	"
On common block stone	20	"
On good Telford-macadam	18	"
On common macadam	13	"
On cobble-stone	10	"
On gravel over earth	5½	"

From the above it appears that a horse can draw on a common macadamized road more than twice as much, and on a good solid Telford-macadam road more than three times as much as he could on a gravel road. Therefore, a farmer who might send produce into market for two hundred (200) days in the year, using a pair of horses to draw a load of about a ton on a poor gravel road, could, if the road were well macadamized, dispense with one of the horses. Supposing that the horse cost him forty (40) cents per day, including interest on first cost, he would save on this single item eighty dollars ($80) per annum.

The resistance due to grades, as alluded to already in Division No. 1, really varies as the sine of the angle of inclination, but for grades of one in twenty (1 in 20), or flatter, it practically varies as the tangent of the angle. Thus, for example, on a grade of one in twenty (1 in 20) the resistance due to gravity is practically one-twentieth ($\frac{1}{20}$) of the entire road.

On a good macadamized road where the resistance to traction on the level is, say, one-fortieth ($\frac{1}{40}$) of the load, a grade of one in twenty (1 in 20) will increase this resistance by one-twentieth ($\frac{1}{20}$) of the load, the total resistance then being three-fortieths ($\frac{3}{40}$) of the load ; therefore, a grade of one in twenty (1 in 20), if of considerable length, will considerably reduce the amount which a horse can draw over it, hence it is false economy to put a road into first-class condition, and yet leave on it a hill with a grade which practically destroys a great part of the advantages to be derived from the excellence of the roadway.

Since good roads virtually shorten distances and render travel over them much pleasanter, they make property through which they pass much more valuable, especially in the vicinity of towns, where many would live further out in the country were the roads kept in good order.

There are also many cases where farmers could bring two loads per day into town if the bad condition of the roads did not prevent them.

Besides this, the continued jolting of heavy vehicles over rough and badly-kept roads strains the horses in such a manner as to shorten their lives, and to develop in them such diseases as often render them unfit for heavy work.

Engineering News of 22d of February, 1890, publishes a statement made by Captain Brown, manager of Hollywood truck farm, in Virginia, to the effect that a pair of horses can draw fifty-five (55) barrels of produce over the roads on that farm, which are in excellent condition, whereas, on the ordinary country roads they can only draw twelve (12) barrels.

Such country roads must entail enormous unnecessary expense to the farmers who have to use them.

The mud and rough surface of bad roads also tend to destroy the wheels and framework of vehicles, and to break the springs and bolts.

Again, in dry weather the dust of badly-kept roads is very annoying, destroys clothes, and tends to prevent people from travelling.

The fact that people on this side of the Atlantic insist on having such first-class railway accommodation, and yet put up with such bad roads, has always been a mystery to the writer.

In towns, good roads increase the renting value of adjoining buildings very largely, as the traffic always follows the best roads, and it is in this connection that asphalt proves superior to all other pavements, as it is so free from noise and mud. Stone-block pavement should not be used on business streets, but kept for those where the noise from factories is such that the extra noise from the pavement is of no consequence.

The waste of gravel and broken stone on a bad foundation, or on no foundation at all, should also be alluded to in this section.

Frequently, large quantities of macadam or gravel, costing large sums of money, are spread in any sort of way on an eneven, dirty and uncompacted roadway, and then left to be scattered all over the road, part being mixed with the mud, and eventually carted off the road, part gradually worked over to the edges of the road, where it prevents the water from draining off the surface properly, and the remainder driven into the roadbed in a useless and uncompacted state.

The New York Times last year reported that the land owners in New Jersey are very well pleased with their new roads, even those who opposed them on account of their cost being well satisfied.

In concluding this division the writer will quote from a statement from Professor J. W. Jenks' "Road Legislation for the American State," as published in *Engineering News*. The Professor states that "In Illinois it is found that a full load can be carried on the State roads only three months during the year ; two-thirds of a load three months, and half a load six months. Good dirt roads there would reduce the cost of hauling one-half, and good permanent macadamized roads three-fourths. The defective highways the State now possesses cost it an extra $15,346,320 for hauling, and depreciate the value of its farms $160,000,000."

DIVISION NO. 3.—LEGISLATIVE FEATURES.

The district in which the writer had charge as assistant-engineer of the roads and bridges formed part of a county which occupied about eight hundred (800) square miles. A county engineer, eight assistants and a clerk formed the engineering staff.

The assistants drew up half-yearly estimates of the cost of making new and repairing existing roads and bridges ; these were inspected by the county engineer, and, after his approval, were submitted, with the tenders for their execution, to the rate payers of the various baronies, of which there were about twelve (12) in the county.

The tenders were called for by advertisement in certain newspapers.

The various contracts as then passed were brought before the grand jury (whose duties, in this respect, might, in America, be performed by the county council), and the various works and contracts passed by them were carried out.   In cases where no satisfactory tender was given in for a necessary work the county engineer was entrusted with it and had it carried out in his name.

The county engineer had power to grant such amounts on the various contracts as had actually been earned.   The contracts were usually let for a period of three (3) years, but when favorable prices could not be obtained they only ran for one (1) year.

These contracts, which were often taken by farmers, included, in the case of repairs and maintenance, stone delivered at the regular stone depots along the roads and there broken by hand, as well as the spreading of the stone and the necessary cleanings ; but in the case of roads on which there was much traffic it also included the pay of a certain number of men who were to be employed for a specific number of days in each week in cleaning and spreading stone.

Where machines for breaking the stone are used they are worked at the quarry.

The cost of the maintenance of the public. roads in and adjoining the largest towns was met half by the barony and half by the town ; the maintenance of all other roads in the barony was paid for by the barony.

The cost of new roads and bridges was borne half by the county at large and half by the barony in which the work was situated, and each barony paid its own proper rate of taxation.

Under this system, which worked very smoothly, the taxes were evenly distributed, and the whole of the county roads being under the control of an able and *trustworthy* engineer, there was a proper uniformity in the system of making and maintaining all roads and bridges and in the keeping of the accounts.

Legislation with a view of improving roads should give to a county council, or, if the county prove too small, to a council elected by two or three counties together, power to take all public roads and road bridges under its control ; to abolish all toll gates whether on roads or bridges ; to compensate the owners of such toll roads and bridges for taking possession of them, with the proviso that the amount of compensation may be fixed by three arbitrators and be subject to ratification by the courts; to appoint a county engineer, assistant engineers and clerks, whose tenure of office should be permanent, and should only be terminable by death, superannuation or their proving unfit for office, either through incapacity, negligence or misconduct; to fix the salary of such officers ; to decide what works shall be paid for, either in whole or in part, by the county at large, and to decide what proportion of the total cost shall be so paid for ; to determine what works shall be paid for entirely by the various sub-divisions of the county, whether they be townships or parishes; to arrange how many of such sub-divisions should be grouped together for_ taxation purposes ; to arrange with all towns which have roads under their control the amount to be paid by them toward keeping up the county roads ; to impose taxation for county roads and bridges, which should be limited to a rate to be fixed by the State ; to cause said taxes to be collected by the county treasurer and kept by him for payment of accounts ; to examine the tenders submitted by the county engineer for all works, and to ratify all contracts for county work on roads and bridges or for the supply of stationery and printing ; to decide on the making of new and the reconstruction or repair of existing county roads and bridges, and other minor works ; to attend to all petitions for or against the opening of new roads or for the execution of various works which may come under their control ; to acquire all lands necessary for the opening of new or the widening of existing roads ; to sell or otherwise dispose of any abandoned roads or portions of roads ; to compel property owners along county roads to keep their fences along the roads in proper repair, and also to keep their ditches in such repair and at such grades as shall permit of the proper drainage of the roads ; and to fix the time and place of their meeting, which should be at least held once a year, and of which due notice should be given.

DUTIES OF COUNTY ENGINEER.

The county engineer should have control of all his assistants and clerks, with power to dismiss them for misconduct: should have all necessary contracts and specifications drawn up ; should keep a road map of the county, showing its various subdivisions for taxation purposes, and all roads and bridges, each road being properly numbered; should have plans and profiles of all roads, also plans and sections of all bridges and large culverts. He should have a set of books showing the nature and amount of work to be done on each section of a road, according to its name, map, number or other designation, together with the contractor's name and the amount paid annually or half yearly for each description of work.

He should certify all amounts to be paid to contractors ; report annually to the council on all work done under his control during the year, showing the amounts paid for each work, and giving a statement of the condition of all roads and bridges, together with any information which may show the advantages of the works executed.

He should also prepare estimates of work to be done each year, showing the proportions to be paid by each subdivision of the county and by the county at large, and also the unexpended balances on any contracts which may remain over to the credit of the various subdivisions of the county or to the credit of the county at large. He should also see to the advertisement for tenders of all works under his charge.

DUTIES OF ASSISTANT ENGINEERS.

The assistant engineers should personally attend to the execution of all works within their districts, measure up all stone or other material supplied, estimate as closely as possible the amount of macadam on hand at the end of each year, report on how much shall be required on each section for the ensuing year, attend closely to the manner in which the various contractors execute their work, instruct the men under them in the performance of their duties, see that the roads are not encroached on or interfered with, except on permission from the county engineer in writing, assist the county engineer in making surveys, taking levels and preparing plans, profiles and estimates, and furnish the county engineer with the data necessary for drawing up his annual report.

POWER TO ENTER ON LAND.

The county engineer and his assistants should be empowered by law to enter on and traverse the property of any person whatever, when it may be necessary to do so for the purpose of surveying or taking levels on the route or proposed route of a new road or drain, provided that they do no damage to such lands or pay for any necessary damage,

CONVICTS ON ROADS.

It would be well if provision could be made for the employment of convicts in repairing and cleaning the county roads or in breaking stone at the county jails : their performing these works would interfere very little with the various trades unions which cry out so much against the work done by convicts.

It would be well, also, to give the county council power to remit a certain proportion of taxes to those who use vehicles with wide tires on the wheels, as they do much less damage to the roadway than narrow tires.

Power should also be given to the county council, under restrictions, to borrow money for the making of new roads or bridges.

ROAD MAKING AND MAINTENANCE.

SECOND PRIZE PAPER. NO. 35.

BY

DAVID H. BERGEY, B. Sc., M.D.,

North Wales, Pa.

I.—GENERAL CONSIDERATIONS OF THE SUBJECT.

Condition of the Roads under the Present System.—The public roads of Pennsylvania are in a deplorable state. This is their general condition, but the present Winter has been so unusually wet and mild that they are extremely bad at the present time. It was impossible to keep earth or dirt roads in repair under the conditions of weather which prevailed during the past Winter. Some roads required constant repairing to keep them even in a passable condition, and without which they would have been altogether impassable. This has, of course, been largely due to the wet season, yet it shows very forcibly how unprofitable and unsatisfactory is the present system of road making. The need of reform is clearly patent, and reform is inevitable. There is certainly plenty of room for improvement.

The present system of road making by plowing up the ground along the side of the roadway and scraping it into the middle of the road is a vast improvement upon the older system of having the ground shoveled out by a gang of men. It is superior in its engineering and economic features. It saves a great outlay of money, time and labor, and makes a roadway far more passable than under the old system.

59

Objections to the Present System.—This system is objectionable, however, on account of the infirm condition of the
roadbed in wet weather, when the roads are often almost impassable, and on account of their roughness in Winter, freezing
and thawing at intervals, thus becoming highly injurious to
teams. The wear and tear of our roads during the Winter is
enormous, and it is, consequently, highly necessary that we
should have some reform in this matter. Thousands of dollars
are annually squandered in Pennsylvania in so-called road
improvements, and yet these improvements are only temporary
ones, and must be repeated from year to year.

Conditions Operating in Retaining It.—Our present road
law, and the system of working the roads under it, was, no
doubt, the best that could be devised at the time it was formulated—at least, under the conditions existing then ; but we have
outgrown its usefulness, and must, therefore, adopt a better and
more economic system. A number of conditions operated in
retaining the present crude and imperfect system so long. The
rapid extension of railroads, and the facilities for intercourse
and shipment of products which they afforded, operated largely
in retaining it. The use of the navigable streams and the
cheapness of water carriage was also an important factor. The
use and extension of the toll roads, or turnpike system, affording better means of transportation on some of the principal
lines of travel, also operated in favor of retaining the present
system. Besides, the nature of the system itself, and the character and abilities of the men operating it, made improvements
out of the question. The supervisors under the present system, with rare exceptions, were not trained engineers, and
therefore unable to formulate remedies for the defects of the
system. The elective system of choosing the supervisors is
therefore undesirable, because rarely are competent persons
chosen by that method. Another cause which operated more
than anything else in retaining the present system was the fear,

on the part of the taxpayers, that any reform that might be instituted would increase the taxes, and thus increase their burdens, and no reform will be likely to meet with their approval that threatens to increase the taxes. They must be educated to understand the value of the reforms to be instituted. They must be brought to see that improved roads will increase the value of real estate, that the value of farm products will be raised thereby, that the price of commodities will be reduced, and that their social condition will be greatly improved. Unless taxpayers can be brought to see these things, they will object to the adoption of any reform that will be likely to put any greater burden upon them, even for a short time. The strongest objections will, no doubt, come from the agricultural districts, and yet they will be gainers rather than losers thereby. The lot of the agriculturist is a hard one, as evidenced by the exceedingly large number of farms which come into the sheriff's hands every year, and it is important that nothing shall be done which will increase the hardness of their lot. We are all dependent upon the farmer, and it behooves us to foster and protect his calling as much as possible. The gain from improved roads would largely come to the farmer, in that the cost of transporting his farm products to market is greatly reduced, because he saves largely in time and labor. They benefit the farmer, at least primarily, though, secondarily, the towns serving as a market centre are also benefited, and should pay their share toward the improvement and maintenance of public roads.

Objections to Toll Roads.—Toll roads or turnpikes may be considered in the light of monopolies. They were undoubtedly of great importance formerly, but their usefulness will be greatly lessened by macadamizing other roads. They are more frequently in a bad condition than otherwise, and when this is the case the collection of tolls is robbery. The law requires their vacation if not properly repaired, but it is seldom done. They earn, usually, a large dividend for the stockholders, as, for instance, the Perkiomen and Sumneytown Turnpike Company, of Montgomery County, voted a dividend of 7 per cent. to its stockholders last month. Any public enterprise that pays a dividend exceeding the legal rate of interest appropriates its earnings in an unfair manner.

They are also unfair in that they tax the traveling public alone, while they are not the only ones benefited by them. They benefit the towns to which they extend and the farms adjacent to the line. It is, therefore, unfair to tax the traveling public alone, and the tolls on turnpikes are an outrageous burden upon them. If they were properly repaired they would not be quite so objectionable, but they are generally in a wretched condition, and hence the tolls are a real burden. The traveling public pays road tax for the maintenance of the public roads, and therefore they have a right to expect them to be kept in proper repair for travel. They are, therefore, an extra burden on the taxpayers, and frequently on those who pay most toward maintaining the public roads.

In 1857-58 Ireland freed itself from toll-gates ; Scotland, from 1878-83, and England will also be freed before long. We trust Pennsylvania will follow their example.

On these considerations turnpike roads should be abolished and their property revert to the State and county. Where companies do not vacate voluntarily the State should claim them by right of eminent domain. The stockholders should, of course, receive just compensation for their stock. They should be purchased at an appraised valuation. The township and county authorities can maintain them better than the companies and to greater satisfaction.

Value of Different Kinds of Roadway.—The following table from " Practical Treatise on Roads, Streets and Pavements," by Q. A. Gillmore,[1] gives tests made with a dynamometer attached to a wagon moving slowly on the level, and gives the force of

---

[1] Quoted by Professor Jenks.

traction in pounds, with the different roads in fair condition. The weight of the wagon and load was 2240 pounds :

		POUNDS.
1. On best stone trackway,	. . . .	12½
2. On a good plank road	. . . . 32 to 50	
3. On a cubical block pavement,	. . . . 32 to 33	
4. On macadamized road of broken stone,	. . . .	65
5. On Telford road (six inches of broken stone of great hardness on a foundation of large stones set as a pavement),	. . .	46
6. On road with six inches of broken stone on concrete pavement,		46
7. On road made of thick coating of gravel laid on earth,	. . . . 140 to 147	
8. On a common earth road,	. . . .	200

The comparisons of the different kinds of roadway in the following table are taken from a paper on " Resistance to Traction on Roads," by Rudolph Hering,[1] with the calculations of the force of traction required on each kind of road added for comparison with the foregoing table.

From the tables we learn that a team can draw more than four times as much on a Telford road and allied systems than on common earth roads in good condition. This shows the enormous waste of time and draft occasioned by the present system. In a paper on " Road Drainage,", by Thomas Mac-Clanahan, of Monmouth, Ill., the estimate is made that for one-fourth of a year a good load can be hauled ; for another fourth two-thirds as much ; and for the remainder of the year only half a load, or only two-thirds of a load on an average throughout the year.

Systems of Construction Suitable for Adoption.—The only systems of road construction which offer no great objectionable features are the Telford and Macadam systems. From the foregoing table a force of sixty-five pounds is required in the macadam system and forty-six pounds in the Telford system to draw 2240 pounds. From our knowledge of the macadam system we would infer that the test was not made on a first-class macadam, as it seems to us that, if properly constructed, it should offer no

[1] Engineering and Building Record, Jan. 25th, 1890.

Character of Road.	Resistance in Terms of Load.	Velocity.	Authority.	Force of Traction.	Compared with Other Table.
Sand,		Pace.	Bevan.	448 lbs.	
Sandy road,		3' to 12' per sec.	Morin.	187 "	
Loose gravel,		Pace.	Bevan.	320 "	
Gravel four inches thick,		"	Morin.	224 "	140 to 147 lbs.
Common gravel road,			Macneil.	140 "	
Gravel road,		3' per sec.	Rumford.	86 "	
Hard rolled gravel,		12'	Bevan and Minard.	90 "	
Wet turf,		Pace.	Morin.	75 "	
Hard and dry turf,		"	Devan.	280 "	
" " " "		"	"	129 "	200 lbs.
Ordinary earth road,		"	Morin.	90 "	
Hard clay,		Trot.	Morin.	224 "	
Hard and dry earth road,		Pace.	Kossack.	112 "	
Ordinary cobblestone,		Trot.	"	102 to 7 "	
Good (3½ inch)		Pace.	Morin.	280 "	
Good " "			Gordon.	140 "	
Good carriage, with spring,		Pace.	Navier.	150 "	
Macadam, little used,			Morin.	75 "	
Bad macadam,		Trot.	Gordon.	90 "	
Old "		Pace.	Navier.	140 to 97 "	
Ordinary "			{Macneil, Perdonnet, Kossack.	160 "	
Good macadam, slightly muddy, wet,		Trot.	Morin.	112 "	
Best French macadam,		Pace.	Navier.	90 "	65 lbs.
Very hard and smooth macadam,			Macneil.	64 "	
Best macadam,			Rumford.	75 to 42 "	
" "			"	45 "	
" "		Pace.	Gordon.	45 "	
Ordinary stone block,			Morin.	64 "	
" Belgian block,		Trot.	Perdonnel, Poncelet, Minard,	50 "	
Belgian block, Boulevard, Paris,		Pace.	Navier.	49 to 37½ "	
Good Belgian block,		Trot.	Rumford.	32 "	32 to 33 lbs.
" stone "		Pace.		52 to 33 "	
" London "			Gordon.	90 "	
Well laid Belgian block,			Macneil.	56 "	
Good Belgian block,			Morin.	54 to 34 "	
Planked roadway (bridge),			Gordon.	75 "	32 to 50 lbs.
Asphalt,				37½ "	
Iron				130 "	
Granite tramway,				45 "	
Sledghs on snow,				30 "	
3 inches thick, ¾ inch runners,				34½ "	12½ lbs.
Temperature, 20° F.,				26 "	
				50 to 39 "	
				56 to 39 "	
				17 "	
				13¼ "	
				11½ "	
				75 "	

more resistance to wheels than the Telford system. We, therefore, feel safe in saying that in respect to surface resistance the
conditions are the same in both cases. These statements are
also substantiated by the second table, where the force of traction on the "best macadam" is recorded as ranging from thirty-
two to sixty-four pounds. These two systems recommend themselves for consideration on account of their firmness, smoothness, durability and comparative cheapness of construction and
maintenance.

Grading of Public Roads.—Wherever practicable, no road
should have a grade much exceeding 1 in 44, or 120 feet to the
mile.[1] On such a slope a horse can draw only three-fourth as
much as on level ground. It is safe to trot a horse down hill
on macadamized road of this grade. On a slope of 1 in 24,
or 220 feet to the mile, a horse can draw only half a load, while
on a slope of 1 in 10, or 528 feet to the mile, only one-fourths as
much as on level ground ; such grades should therefore be
avoided, if possible. These facts have been neglected in constructing most of our public roads, but they are not neglected in
the construction of railways. Hills of too large size to be cut
through entirely should be avoided, or they should be crossed
by a series of inclined planes of easy grade. This is the plan
pursued by railway engineers in constructing railroads across
mountain ranges, and should be adopted by road engineers in
constructing public roads.

For either the Telford or macadam system the bed of the
road should receive some preparation before the work of construction begins. It should be excavated, leaving a four-inch
elevation or ridge in the middle and gradually slope toward the
edges. This saves some material in the construction of the
road, besides giving the roadway an arched contour. This
feature is a valuable one, especially in thin macadams.

Not all roads should be macadamized, only the principal ones

[1] Appleton's Cyclopædia, on " Roads."

5

leading from one town to another, or, at least, in the beginning. But many are useless and might be vacated without loss to anyone.

II.—ADVANTAGES OF GOOD ROADS.

Good Roads an Advantage to Town and Country.—Good roads are not only a benefit to the section of country which they traverse, but also to the towns serving as a market to those sections. They benefit agricultural districts, in that they improve the facilities for transporting the farm products to the market or lines of commerce, thus saving time in transporting and increasing the amount of burden carried with each load. In this manner they have a great influence on the price of commodities. The price of wheat is increased for a locality having improved transportation facilities. If it costs a farmer $1.00 to haul 100 bushels of wheat one mile on dirt roads, and by macadamizing the roads this cost can be reduced to 20 cents per mile, the price of wheat is raised accordingly; one mile saves 80 cents, ten miles save $8.00 per hundred bushels, or 8 cents per bushel—the increase in price of each bushel—not considering the larger load that can be carried on macadamized roads. The price of wheat is thus permanently raised by improved facilities for transportation; the value of farm land is also relatively increased. The value of farms is increased by the improved facilities for transportation of their products in thus finding an earlier market. As the time needed to reach the market is lessened, the farm is brought relatively nearer the town and its market. If improved roads make the journey an hour shorter, the farm is, relatively speaking, brought an hour's journey nearer the market.

When farmers once see this road problem in its true light, they will not hesitate a moment to consent to higher taxes, if necessary, to bring about the desired improvements. They have come to look upon the present condition of our public roads as a necessary inconvenience, one that it is not possible to remedy, and must therefore be endured. They do not realize their loss in time and labor in hauling their farm products to the market. They do not seem to be aware that a horse can draw more than four times as much on macadamized and Telford roads as on ordinary dirt roads in good condition, and that this is increased to more than ten times as much when the dirt roads are in bad condition, which they are often for more than half of each year.

The farmer also receives a similar benefit in the saving of time and draft in hauling coal, feed and other commodities from the railroad and mill.   The time saved in hauling each load, and the increased burden that it is possible to carry, greatly reduces the real cost of these commodities.   In this section of the State (Montgomery County) nearly every farmer sends his milk either to the creamery or to the depot, and ships it to Philadelphia. The time lost in this manner amounts to a considerable sum during the year.   If the roads were macadamized, this saving of time would represent that much profit on the dairy.   If the loss of time amounts to half an hour each day for half the year—and many farmers lose more—or ninety hours during the year, the loss would amount to $9.00, since the hired help of the farmer costs him at least ten cents an hour.   The saving of time on this item alone would go far toward paying his road tax, and would be so much profit on his dairy.

Towns are benefited by improved roads in that they increase the scope of their market, and therefore a larger area will bring in its products and take away its supplies.

Benefit to the Traveling Public.—The general public, whether traveling on foot, in carriage, or on horseback or bicycle, would also be benefited by the great saving in time.   Improved roads may detract slightly from railroad passenger traffic, because pleasure parties and others might travel by other means more frequently than now, if the roads were macadamized, ; this would, however, be a direct saving of money to them in most instances.

Extend Educational Advantages.—We must also consider the enlarged and improved educational advantages of good roads. They bring us into closer proximity to good schools, to lectures,

and to churches.   They facilitate the more general intercommunication in the rural districts.   In the same manner the moral
plane of a community is elevated and civilization extended.

Saving of Money to Communities.—It is estimated that in
this State $200,000,000 have been spent during the last fifty years
in the maintenance of the public road system.   This would be
at the rate of $4,000,000 per year.   This has certainly been an
enormous expense.   The average cost to maintain one mile of
macadam road is $10.00 per year, while ordinary dirt roads cost
from $30.00 to $90.00 per year for each mile.   If $1,000,000
or $1,500,000 could be appropriated annually by the State
and divided among the counties, it would prove of great value
to the rural districts, and the advantages derived from improvements carried out in this manner would be beyond estimation.
Such an outlay of money would repay itself many fold in a few
years.

III.—THE CONSTRUCTION OF PUBLIC ROADS.

1. *The Telford System.*—This system is very similar to that
employed by the Romans in constructing their great highways
many centuries ago.   It was revived in England during the
early part of the present century, because the promoter of this
revival, Telford, considered it preferable to the system then in
use in England, which had been introduced by Macadam.   It is
still a question of preference with many people.

The Foundation—How Made.—The roadbed in this system
is built up of large stones to any desired depth, set as a pavement.   They are closely packed, and this gives a solid and firm
foundation to the road.   It is preferable to use irregular stones,
because they more readily hold the layer of broken stones covering them.   These small stones will not readily bind on a smooth
surface.   This fact is plainly shown in resurfacing a road built
on this system, and also in placing a thin macadam on exposed
rocky surfaces.

Layer of Broken Stones.—The layer of broken stones covering the foundation should be composed of stones of less than

two inches in diameter. They should be of granitic or basaltic rock, or of limestone or argillaceous shale, because the permanency of the road depends on the hardness of this layer. This layer has to maintain the wear and tear of travel, and it is, therefore, important that the hardness of its material be the primary consideration. This layer should be thoroughly rolled with a ten-to-twenty-ton iron roller, to pack the stones firmly and bind them on the foundation stones. In depth this layer may vary from two inches up to six or more inches.

The Surface Dressing.—The third layer should be composed of fine screenings of sufficient thickness to cover the preceding layer, and it should also be thoroughly rolled, in order to pack it firmly and thus render the surface of the finished road hard and smooth, so as to offer as little resistance to wheels as possible. It should be rolled while wet, as in that condition it packs much better than in the dry state. It may be of the screenings made in crushing the stones for the preceding layer, or it may be of crushed sandstone, shale or slate. The main use for this layer is to bind the preceding layer of crushed stone and to give firmness and smoothness to the surface of the road as soon as possible after completion. The finished road should slope toward the sides, with an elevation of about four inches in the middle; this will afford sufficient slope for drainage.

Objections to this System.—The objections offered to this system are that the surface layers wear away, and thus the large stones composing the foundation are exposed, rendering the road rough and uneven. When this occurs, the entire road must be resurfaced, necessitating a great outlay of money. This objection is an important one, and should be considered in deciding which system to adopt. It is also more costly than the macadam system.

2. *The Maeadam System.*—This system was introduced into England by John MacAdam, about 1816; it is similar to the system employed successfully in France as early as 1760. In a few years more than 25,000 miles of road

had been constructed on this plan. The chief reasons which led Telford to revive the system employed by the Romans, and which is now known as the Telford system, was the defect of the macadam system in that it had not sufficient depth in low places, and had not been employed with proper care. The system had proved more satisfactory in France because the roads had been built more carefully. The depth of the structure is therefore an important consideration in this system for low places.

Construction of the Roadbed.—It consists of a roadbed built up entirely of one-and-a-half-inch angular stones. No large stones are used for the foundation in this system. These small stones must be of the specific size, small enough to pass through a two-inch ring, and should be of crushed granitic rock, or of limestone or argillaceous shale, crushed by a machine designed for the purpose. The hardness is a very important feature, as they must bear the entire wear and tear of travel. This layer may be from six to fifteen inches in depth, and must be fre- quently rolled while wet by means of heavy iron rollers to pack the stones as firmly as possible; this will prevent them from rutting from heavy teams during wet weather.

The Surface Layer.—The surface dressing should consist of fine screenings of the same material formed during the crush- ing process, or of crushed sandstone or shale. This layer requires the same treatment and conditions as the correspond- ing layer in the Telford system, as it merely serves to bind the layer of stones below it and gives hardness and smoothness to the surface of the road as soon as completed.

The finished road should have an elevation in the middle of about four inches, gradually sloping toward the edges. Such a slope is necessary to carry off the surface water and yet will not impede travel.

Objections to the System.—An objection offered to this system is that it is liable to cut into ruts after heavy frosts, and is therefore unsuited for heavy hauling, but this difficulty can be entirely obviated by giving a proper depth to the macadam structure in low, swampy places, and by thorough rolling. A depth of six inches is not sufficient depth in low places to support heavy teams, and is certain to cut into ruts, hence a proper depth will obviate all this and render the road permanent and durable. An arched roadway and proper rolling will also greatly increase its durability.

Conclusions.—From the foregoing discussion, we conclude that the macadamized system is preferable for general road construction, in that it is more likely to be permanent, and requires less resurfacing and repairing that the Telford system. A. J. Cassatt says : "From a number of years' experience with both Telford and macadam roads, I am strongly of the opinion that the latter is the best for our country." Even if it should cut into ruts in some places, these can be filled in with a few cartloads of stones at little expense, thus making the road as good as before, while the same material would not go far toward resurfacing a Telford road. The cost of repairing in the macadam system does not exceed $10.00 per mile each year.

From the cost of Telford and macadam roads constructed by the Friends' school at Westtown, Chester County, we infer that the cost of Telford roads slightly exceeds that of macadam roads.

They had 7300 feet of Telford road constructed, fourteen feet wide, with foundation of large stones eight inches deep, and with a surface layer of one-and-one-half-inch stones sufficient to bring the depth to fourteen inches in the middle and ten inches at the sides. This cost them $4200 or $2.00 per running yard, exclusive of grading and finishing the sides of the road and cleaning the ditches.

At the same time they had a macadamized road 175 yards in length contracted for, to be made of broken stones covered with fine screenings. This was to be fourteen feet wide, eight inches deep in the middle and four inches at the edges, at a cost of 97 cents per running yard, or at the rate of $1707 per mile.

Another macadam road, fourteen feet wide, and twelve inches in the middle and nine inches in depth at the edges, was also contracted for at a cost of $1.45 per running yard, or at the rate of $2552 per mile. The material was close at hand in each case and the facilities for crushing were excellent, as water was used, thus saving the cost of coal.

The cost of the Telford road built by the Westtown school is unusually high, but its depth is in excess of that given to ordinary roads. The macadam contracted for at 97 cents per yard represents nearer the cost of such roads. No high-grade macadam road should cost more than $3000 per mile. Such a road should be sixteen feet wide and twelve to fourteen inches thick.

Prof. Shaler says : " Founded on hardpan or subsoil, it is commonly possible to make a tolerably permanent road by placing upon the bed a layer of from eight to twelve inches of broken limestone, or, what is better, a less thickness of broken shale."[1]

Mr. J. F. Pope, a prominent civil engineer, estimates that "a road eighteen feet wide, nine inches thick at the centre, falling to four and one-half inches at the sides, can be built for $2100."[2]

"Mr. Samuel R. Downing[3] says : "My estimate for a township-built, sixteen-foot wide, ten-inch thick macadam was $2845, and that, further, upon the same basis of calculation, a twelve-foot nine-inch thick road could be built for $1960, or a ten-foot six-inch track for $1066."

IV.—THE RECONSTRUCTION OF PUBLIC ROADS.

In the Telford System.—In this system resurfacing is required more frequently than in the macadam system, because the surface layers wear away and expose the larger stones composing the foundation, thus rendering the surface of the road rough and uneven. When this occurs, the road requires com-

---

[1] Prof. N. S. Shaler, Scribner's Magazine, October, 1889.
[2] Mr. J. F. Pope, quoted by Samuel R. Downing, in Public Ledger, March 20th, 1890.
[3] Mr Samuel R. Downing, Public Ledger. March 20th, 1890.

plete resurfacing to put it in repair. This is necessarily costly, as the two upper layers of this system must be replaced entirely. The road will wear away faster in some places than in others, making it necessary to repair it where the greatest strain is brought to bear upon it. It requires a long time for these new surface layers to bind in with the old road, and they are more easily displaced than the original layers. To completely resurface a Telford road, fourteen feet wide, to a depth of six inches, will cost from $1750 to $2000 per mile.

In the MacAdam System.—In this system the chief difficulty is from rutting, but a few cartloads of stones will fill in many yards of ruts, and these soon bind in with the roadbed and leave a hard, smooth surface as before. The surface rarely becomes uneven, but if it should, a few cartloads of screenings put on in time will save a great deal of expense by keeping the road in good condition all the time. There should be constant supervision of such roads every day of the year. A great deal of money can be saved by such constant attention. If small defects, taking only a few hours to repair, are neglected, they will, in time, require that many days or weeks to remedy them.

Should a complete resurfacing be required in this system it will be as costly as in the Telford system, but from the nature of the roadbed it is not liable to become uneven and rough, because it has the same hardness throughout, and it will therefore wear for a great many years before such a general resurfacing will be required. If the roadbed has sufficient body from the beginning, a great deal of subsequent expense is saved thereby. The macadam system, if properly constructed in the first place, will prove the most economic in the end, and it will pay well to give such a road proper depth, and thus save subsequent expense for resurfacing.

V.—THE MAINTENANCE OF PUBLIC ROADS.

1. *Taxation for Road Purposes.* · *The Labor System.*—Seven States and one Territory, New Mexico, employ this system

entirely in maintaining their public road system. This is a
relic of feudal and slavery times, and is found in use only
in the Southern States. Alabama requires all able-bodied
males from eighteen to forty-five years of age to work on
the public roads of their district for ten days in each year.
North Carolina requires all able-bodied males from eighteen
to forty-five years of age to work on the public roads of their
district for fifteen days in each year, and Georgia, all able-
bodied males from sixteen to fifty years for from six to ten
days in each year; South Carolina, all able-bodied males from
sixteen to fifty years for from three to twelve days in each
year; Mississippi, all able-bodied males from eighteen to fifty
years not more than ten days; Louisiana, all males, not more
than twelve days; Kentucky, all males from sixteen to fifty
years, with no limitation in time. New Mexico, all males from
twenty-one to fifty years for two days.

In Illinois the labor system may also be adopted in any
district upon the vote of a majority of the voters, all able-
bodied males from twenty-one to fifty years of age being required
to work on the public roads not less than one nor more than
three days in each year. Arkansas also requires all able-bodied
males from eighteen to forty-five years of age to work on the
public roads of their district for ten days in each year, and only
levies a money tax when the roads cannot be kept in good condition by the labor of those liable for road duty.

This system is unfair because it recompenses inferior hands
the same as those who are good workers. It brings the best workers down to the level of the poorest. This system compels each
man to work on the public roads for so many days, and the
actual cost of maintenance is far greater than under any other
system, because, though the State pays no money to maintain its
public roads, their maintenance costs its citizens an enormous
amount of labor, which represents so much money to them.
Many sections of the States employing this system complain of
having the worst-maintained public roads to be found anywhere.

This system has no points in its favor and should be abolished wherever in use. We would not for a moment, therefore, think of adopting it here. Who would think of using this plan in large cities? Economy requires that the highways of cities be maintained by money taxation, and the money expended in the most systematic and economic manner possible. The labor system would be too cumbersome for cities. The laborers could not be properly directed. The system is altogether impracticable.

Money, Taxation and Labor Combined.—This system is in vogue in this State at the present time, and, in fact, in all the States in some form or other, except the seven relying on the labor system entirely.

A tax is levied on all real and personal property and on trades and professions. This tax may be paid in labor or money at the option of the taxpayer, but a large proportion of it is paid in labor, whlle formerly, when the dirt was shoveled into the road instead of by means of the scraper, many earned more than their tax, and were paid the overplus in money; this is, however, not now allowed.

Our present system of taxation is as nearly equitable as our knowledge of economic principles would lead us to suppose that it could be made. It makes its demands on all property and on all incomes, according to their several abilities. This is as it should be. The burden of supporting the public road system should be as equitably apportioned as the benefits derived from them will justify. It is the mode of payment that we object to: the payment of road taxes in labor. The payment of taxes in labor has not proved profitable, in that taxpayers thereby shirk their duties and responsibilities to such an extent that the roads have suffered from neglect and mismanagement. By some, the greater part of their time on the road is spent in the telling of yarns, while others, who are more conscientious, do the work that is accomplished. It allows property owners to impose on their township by substituting inferior hands while they draw the same compensation for them as those receive who are ableoodied workers. In this respect it is unfair toward those who possess no property. Such transient labor cannot be as systematically directed as can the labor under a contractor who expects so much work from his men, and sees that they accomplish it.

By Money Taxation Alone.—Taxes should be paid in money, in order that it may be expended as economically as possible. A poll tax in money may not be as easy to collect as one in labor, but taking into consideration the time that is squandered in paying the tax in labor, and the unsatisfactory nature of the labor rendered, and that the season at which this labor payment is required interferes with the regular work of the taxpayers at a most inopportune time, makes a money tax far more expedient, more practicable, and more economic. This is a tax according to income, and therefore represents the ability or faculty of the taxpayer, and divides the burden, as near as may be, according to the benefits received.

No State has this system in vogue entirely. A number of the States have an optional payment in money, but it is expected, in all such instances, that the major portion of the tax will be paid in labor. There is no other provision made to accomplish the work. This system is pronounced, by those who are competent to judge, to be the most efficient, the fairest to all classes, and the most economic. It is the most efficient because the labor most suited to the work to be done can be obtained in this way ; it is the fairest to all classes because it compels those who use the roads most to pay most to maintain them ; and it is the most economic because it consolidates all the money levied for road purposes, and it can therefore be expended where and for what purpose most needed, and in the most systematic manner.

This system is employed in large cities and towns. It would be impracticable to have labor taxation in cities ; the labor could not be applied to any advantage, and it is but natural that this is the only system that should be adopted, whether for town or country. It is the only system by which the public roads of a district can be systematically constructed and maintained. All kinds of property should pay its share of the burden. It should be adopted in this State, and the payment of road tax in labor abolished.

The construction and repairing of the roads, under this system, can be given out by contract to men controlling gangs of laborers, and there would be no objection to employing convict labor upon the roads, as it would not interfere with the daily work of laborers, as their employment in the manufacturing industries and mines so often seems to do.

2. *Raising Funds for Improving the Roads by Borrowing Capital.*—Townships should have the authority to borrow large sums of money by giving bonds running a series of years—say fifty years—wherewith to improve the principal roads. Should they do this, the principal roads of the township could be macadamized at once, while the money raised by taxation at the present rates would be sufficient to keep these roads in repair, and pay at least part of the interest on the bonds. This would entail no extra burden on the taxpayers, and they would have the advantages of good roads while the improvements are being paid for. The coming generations, in this manner, will also be obliged to assist in defraying the expense of improving the roads. This would not be unfair to them, because they will enjoy the same benefits, and should, therefore, assist in paying for them. A sinking fund should be started at once to eventually pay off the bonds. Many conservative persons are adverse to this plan of going into debt to improve the roads, but it seems, from what we have said, especially in reference to the equal benefits derived from the improvements by posterity, and therefore their equal liability, and the great immediate and permanent benefits from improved roads, that this plan is entirely proper, and we feel no hesitation in supporting its adoption.

If each township had the authority, if it desired to make use of it, to borrow $50,000 on bonds, and the average cost of

construction of macadam roads is $2,500 per mile, then the
$50,000 raised on the bonds would be sufficient to construct
twenty miles of road, but it is certain that the cost of twenty
miles should be considerably less than $50,000, and we feel safe
in saying that twenty-five miles is the lowest average that would
be obtained with proper management.

Gwynedd Township, Montgomery County, has, on a rough
calculation, thirty-eight miles of internal dirt roads, besides sixteen miles of township line roads, making a total of forty-six
miles, counting half the line roads as also belonging to it.   It
has also about fourteen miles of turnpike road. By issuing
bonds for $50,000, all but thirteen miles of its internal dirt roads
could be macadamized at once, and this would leave only the
least traveled in their present condition, and a large part of
these could be abandoned altogether without inconvenience to
any one.   The maintenance of these thirteen miles would not
be costly, because they would be little used.

The time and labor saved would represent the earnings of
the borrowed capital.

State Appropriation.—The State should give aid to the
counties to maintain their public roads.   Let the State appropriate $1,000,000 to $1,500,000 annually, for ten years, for the
purpose of maintaining the public roads, which shall be apportioned among the different counties according to their ability
to improve their public roads, and according to the value of
such improvements to the State.   This money should be applied
each year in macadamizing an additional piece of road.   This
would soon lessen the cost of maintenance, on account of the
decreased cost of maintaining macadamized roads.

The improved condition of the public roads would benefit
the towns as well as the country districts, and they should
therefore give assistance, and this can best be brought about by
State aid to the counties.   This aid should be in proportion to
the wealth of the county.   The poorer districts should receive
the most aid if their improvements would benefit the State at

large as well as those counties. It should be left to the State and county road engineers to decide how the State appropriation should be apportioned.

3. *Road Officers.*—In order to secure the best management of the public road system, each township should be constituted a road district, if large, or two small townships, or several townships having but few internal improvements, might constitute a district. Each township should have its board of controllers, and each district should have its road engineer or supervisor, appointed by the board of control. This board should have control of the funds and receive contracts for road construction. There should be a county supervisor in each county, and a State engineer or supervisor appointed in a similar manner to the county and state superintendents for' school purposes. They should be specially trained civil engineers, receiving suitable salaries. Their salaries would be saved every year in the better management of road affairs.

State normal schools should introduce engineering courses, so as to afford cheap and easy means for young men to fit themselves for the position of road engineer. They should receive State aid similar to those intending to teach in the public schools. In this manner a corps of competent road engineers could be trained in a short time, and there would be plenty of applicants for the positions if the salary were equal to that for school principals.

Township Supervisors and Boards of Control.—The township is the unit of government under the present plan, and it seems to be the one which is most likely to give general satisfaction, and should therefore be retained in recasting the mode of road government.

Each township should have its board of controllers or commissioners, say of three members, serving gratuitously, like township school boards, and should have the same authority relatively as school boards have in their districts. They should be elected triennially, *i. e.*, one each year, and should appoint a competent civil engineer as supervisor to carry out their plans. It is highly important that the supervisor of roads be a trained civil engineer. It is a business that cannot be grasped intuitively. The average farmer is not more competent for the position than he would be for that of one of the learned professions. This has been one of the main causes of the wretched condition of the public roads. Supervisors should therefore be appointed by the board of control, and the elective system abolished, as a competent man is more likely to be appointed by the board than if chosen by popular election.

The supervisor should see that the contracts for the construction and repairing of the roads, entered into by the board, are carried out in the best manner, or he may assume full control of the work himself, hiring the men and receiving their pay from the board the same as would a contractor. It is, however, preferable that they should be contracted for, as the best labor can thus be secured. Cities employ this system, and hold the contractors responsible until the work has been accepted as fully satisfactory.

His salary should be in accordance with his position and the value of his services. If he is employed by more than one township, he should draw a portion of his salary from each.

County Supervisors and Boards of Control.—The county commissioners serve as a board in the control of the affairs of the county. They build the county bridges, and thus their duties will not be extended very much in giving them general control over the more important roads in the county. They should be elected as at present, and should superintend the construction and maintenance of the county roads through a county supervisor or engineer appointed by them.

This officer should be a thoroughly-trained civil engineer, competent to give full information to the board on all points in road construction. He should make an annual report to the

State engineer as to the condition of the roads, and the cost and extent of the improvements made, and such other information as would be of general value and interest. He should determine, with the State engineer, the amount of State aid his county should receive, and should apportion it among the several districts by the advice and assistance of the township engineers. His compensation should be in accordance with his professional abilities and the value of his services.

State Road Engineer and Assistants —There should be a State supervisor of roads, with one or more assistants, appointed by the Governor, who shall have jurisdiction over the inter-county and inter-State road matters, and be the head of the road department of the State. He should, with the county engineers, form a State association of road engineers, which should meet at least once each year, and discuss the different aspects of the road question, and formulate new laws whenever required, and present them to the State Legislature for adoption. He should, with the county engineers, determine the amount of State aid which each county should receive. and in this he should be guided by the wealth of the county and the general value and importance of the improvements to be made.

The State engineer should make an annual report to the Legislature, giving statistical information on the general condition of the roads of the State and the number and kind of improvements promulgated during the year. Such a report would be of incalculable value both now and in the future. He should have made a State road map showing the condition of the public roads leading from and to all the principal towns. Such a map would be of great value to the road engineers, to the traveling public, and to schools and colleges.

· 4. *Administration of Roads. The Classification of Roads.*— For convenience of administration, and to divide the work systematically, the public roads should be divided into three classes : First, those local roads in the townships connecting the principal roads, and which are therefore of secondary import-

6

ance and of mainly local value, should be under the jurisdiction of the township boards and their road engineer, and should be laid out, constructed, and maintained by them, chiefly by local taxation, and should be known as township roads. Second, those roads leading from one town to another, traversing several townships, should be under the jurisdiction of the county boards and the county road engineer, and they should decide as to their location, width, and the nature of the improvements to be placed upon them, while the portions in each township are laid out, constructed, and maintained by the township authorities, and the cost of construction and maintenance sustained by the township and county, according to the benefits derived by each. The township should not contribute more than half the cost of maintenance of roads of the second class, and the county the remainder. These should be known as county roads. Third, those roads extending from one county to another, or through several counties, or from one State to another, or forming the boundaries of these, should be under the jurisdiction of the State engineer and his assistants as far as location, width, and nature of improvements are concerned, but they should be under the jurisdiction of the county and township authorities for construction and maintenance, the same as the county roads. These should be known as state roads. The townships traversed should not pay more than one-fourth of the cost of maintenance of roads of the third class, and the remainder of the cost should be paid by the state and county.

This plan would give efficient administration of the public roads of the State, and the burden and duty of one board cannot be shifted on to another. Roads of the third and second class should have a width of twelve to sixteen feet, and a depth of from ten to fifteen inches of macadam structures. Sixteen feet is wide enough for the paved part of most roads, and twelve inches sufficient depth. The roads of the first class should have a width of eight to twelve feet, and a depth four to ten inches, or more, according to the nature of the soil. Six inches is considered by many to be an insufficient depth for macadam roads, but, according to the tests made in Bridgeport, Conn., by Mr. B. D. Pierce,[1] the street commissioner, with four-inch macadams of crushed stone rolled with a ten-ton roller, we would infer that if the roads were properly constructed, according to the best-known methods, that a depth of four inches was sufficient for most purposes. The stone must be one-and-one-half-inch stone, and thoroughly rolled while wet, with several inches of screenings, mdde in crushing the stone, placed on top and also well rolled, to bind the layer below it, and, above all, the bed of the road must have an elevation of at least four inches in the middle, gradually sloping toward the sides ; this will give the finished road an arched appearance, while really the entire roadbed is arched. Such a roadbed will be much firmer than a level one. Bridgeport, Conn., has fifty miles of such road, and it gives entire satisfaction. These roads are considered by Mr. Pierce and members of the board of public works, to be better than Telford roads, and under equally long traffic are as easily and cheaply maintained.

We think, therefore, that in many localities a roadbed of from four to six inches, properly constructed, would answer all the requirements. H. W. Kratz, Esq.,[2] member of the State Board of Agriculture from Montgomery County, says that where the land is well drained, and for ordinary use, six inches is sufficient.

Road Machinery.—The county boards should procure a sufficient number of steam stone crushers to prepare the stones used in macadamizing, and a sufficient number of iron rollers of ten to twenty tons weight to roll the new roads as fast as constructed.

A portable stone crusher, costing about $1000 would turn out about eighty perches of stone per day, and would thus earn, at fifteen cents per perch, $12.00. The wages of three men would

[1] Engineering and Building Record, quoted by Downing.
[2] Quoted by Downing.

be $5.00, and $7.00 would pay for rent and coaling a thresher engine, making the total cost of crushing fifteen cents per perch, while a perch of stone hammered by hand would cost $1.00, a saving of eighty-five cents on each perch.[1] A stone crusher would provide stone enough for three or four townships.

A good steam roller six feet in width costs $5000, but it is better than a horse roller. It may not be necessary to provide one for each township, but one for every two or three townships, according to their size. These rollers may range from ten to twenty tons in weight. It may be desirable for the township boards to procure several horses and carts to do all the hauling on the roads. It would be cheaper for each township to own several teams to do the hauling for repairs. The original outlay for this machinery should be met by the county.

Laying out Roads.—An important question which will require the most careful study from road engineers is the laying out of new roads and the determination as to which roads should be improved in our present system. In our present system there are many lines of roads that could easily be dispensed with, and their maintenance is therefore an entirely unnecessary burden. The point that must be considered primarily is how best to afford a means of communication for the largest number of people, with the least amount of travel. This can only be accomplished by taking some large town as the centre, and letting the principal roads radiate from it toward the more important towns surrounding it, in a straight line, if possible, and next by connecting these smaller towns by the shortest routes possible.

This sketch[2] shows how much more serviceable such a road system would be as compared with that which is often found, or than in a system in which the roads run North and South and East and West, as they do in the newer States, along the section lines. There is no system whatever in the manner in which our

---

[1] Samuel R. Downing, West Chester, Pa.
[2] Sketch omitted as unnecessary.

roads are laid out at present, at least some of them. They are often the remains of the original Indian trails or the bridle-paths of our forefathers.

It is necessary, therefore, that in the improvement of the public roads, those roads which are of the first importance shall be improved first, and if possible their course changed so as to make the finished road as serviceable as possible. It will be found that if such a system is adopted, that many of the roads now in use are useless and may be reclaimed, and the ground used for agricultural purposes. This would assist somewhat in defraying the expense occasioned in acquiring territory for new and more direct routes.

Repairing Roads.—Bridges and ditches must be constantly watched and repaired. All ditches should be kept open so that the water may have free passage and not damage the roadbed and bridges.

Any roughness of the surface of the roads, or ruts, should be at once filled in, and thus avoid greater expense. This work will keep several gangs of men with horse and cart busy most of the year in each township. This repairing should be looked after by the road engineer, under the supervision of the board.

5. *Conclusions.*—From the discussions of the subject we draw the following conclusions as being the most desirable and most economic in the construction of the public roads and the maintenance of the public road system:

First.—That either of two systems of road construction now in use in many places might be adopted, viz.: the Telford and macadam systems. Of these the macadam system seems to us to be the most desirable, in that, if properly constructed, it is likely to be more durable, and hence need less repairing than the Telford system. It also costs less than the Telford system.

Second.—That toll roads or turnpikes should be abolished, because they are monopolies in the hands of a few stockholders, and are only an extra burden on the taxpayers obliged to use them.

Third.—That for the maintenance of the road system the most desirable plan is that by money taxation, and that the system of working out road taxes should be abolished.

Fourth.—That funds be raised in the different townships to macadamize the roads, by instituting loans on bonds running a series of years, and that a sinking fund be started to provide for the payment of this loan, and that the State give aid to the different counties, according to their needs, to assist them in maintaining their public road system.

Fifth.—That each township elect three road supervisors or commissioners, who shall appoint an engineer to construct and repair the roads. That in each county the county commissioners shall constitute a board of control, who shall appoint a trained civil engineer to carry on the work of construction. And that the Governor shall appoint a State engineer or supervisor, with assistants, if necessary, to superintend the road affairs of the State, and who shall constitute the head of the public road department.

Sixth.—That the roads of the State be divided into State, county, and township roads for purposes of administration, and that a road map be made, giving full information as to the nature of the soil and condition of the roads of the State, for the use of travelers, road engineers, and for educational purposes.

ROAD MAKING AND MAINTENANCE.

THIRD PRIZE PAPER. No. 25.

BY

JAMES B. OLCOTT,

South Manchester, Connecticut.

Nothing good is new in road making except through more perfect understanding of localities, materials and implements. But as we are born ignorant, and liable to deceive ourselves, or be cheated, fresh studies of the situation are always in order— even to hold what we know already for daily practice.

The common road problem before the American people may be stated briefly in this way: With hastily constructed cities and exhausted agricultural districts, to make the best wheeling possible for every citizen.

A republic, for such a task, must have all its energies, mental and physical, in hearty sympathy with the enormous labor. Its roads are the grandest concern of a nation.

Comparing the body politic with the human organism, it is as if the ducts of the system were to be reconstructed of fresh substance by slow processes of healthy assimilation. Or as if the redundant railway life of the nation were now being strenuously injected into every common road fibre of the country. Shall we longer waste our lives in varicose practices in the urgent road question of to-day.

The argument of this paper supports stone, broken small, as the cheap, native flooring for the best common roads; all spaces to be filled solid with the same material, roof tight and water shedding over dry foundations.

It will maintain that a layer of clean sand or clean, fine gravel is better and sometimes cheaper than broken rock for

87

firm foundations on thoroughly drained clay, or upon thoroughly drained earths, that are liable to move by water and frost like clay.

It will urge the use of broad-tired carts for delivering fresh road metal upon itself, as the readiest, indispensable and common sense method for compacting a highway to a feasible finish at once.

It will permit surplus rock filling in the roadbed of any size or shape, provided the coarse material be laid below all chance of wheel friction and is immovably bedded in sand, gravel, or the equivalent as regards water and frost.

It will point with scorn at the old and new absurdity of stuffing bottomless holes in the road with broken stone, under the plea of "maintenance," as one of the howling disgraces of American engineering, and endeavor to show how to do better.

The whole tone of this paper is a protest against our general ignorance in the art of common road making, and a plea for popular education and special training.

Much road legislation would be premature, and large highway enterprises unwise till something like public faith is established, invisible assurrances, that *the best*, not merely better, roads' can be built on a small scale in the first place. By best roads we mean the best for the cost, materials and circumstances.

Little or nothing of surveying or formal engineering is attempted in this paper, because it designs to be fullest in regard to the internal structure and security of road material in the highway. Nice and exact details or forms to be fit must be strict local affairs in each case. All the States need topographic surveys and maps for the better guidance of all the people. Governments are too ignorant to govern properly. Good road work cannot be made by the yard at some grand centre for transportation, but must be done to measure on the spot. We shall be very fortunate if we can convey better ideas of road making to all the people and set them to thinking for themselves.

In beginning our inquiries, it is pertinent to ask if our railway education has not had much to do with our common road thoughts and practices? What must be the effect on the rising minds of the nation of laying thousands of miles of iron and steel roads upon wooden sleepers? What else is it but an extravagant example of building for the sake of speed on rapidly decaying foundations? Punished with the running expenses of those transient roads, why should we shudder at the cost of stone roads of an imperishable character? And why dare we not think of steam traction on the best stone roads? Let us take courage and look the facts of our time in the face as our fathers did before us.

Accurate calculation and elaborate plans—on paper—go for nothing, while the actual handling of road metal and laying it in the highway is left to unwitting and careless men whose only stake in the result comes from the nearsighted notion or general "principle" that botched jobs for a misguided public will insure them continuous employment. Road making suffers, now, in the hands of real estate speculators, political managers, street contractors and semi-pauper laborers armed with votes instead of their own road tools and technical training, as play acting suffered while honors and profits were consumed by one or two star performers, and the all-important details dragged in the hands of beggarly supernumeraries.

Perfunctory formality is the ruin of much of our road making, while improvements of form in our rural districts are undeniably needed. The huge four-horse road-scrapers, dragged through the country, are doing grand educational service by teaching the American people the inevitable lesson of form. They give practical demonstrations, and cultivate the popular eye as to what the proper grade and shape of the highway may and must be. The view formerly held that gutter-wash makes desirable wheeling when ridged up for open winters, is gradually yielding to the missionary work of these effective machines.

Ideas of fitness, relative cheapness and durability of various substances in the roadbed, are later developments in the con-

sciousness of society.   Every citizen—like the farmer in the old
reading book, who found a boy in his apple tree—will be glad to
try the virtue in stones after he has fully proven the insufficiency
of turf.   Yet it should never be forgotten that grass can be
made very useful in shedding water and preventing dust and
mud along the sides and gutters of a highway.   Statutes are
about the last thing to show that *comfort* is good law for men
and animals.

The science of roads grows out of the industrial earth
during long evolutionary periods.   We who believe in stone for
heavy traffic, must be patient with communities trainea from
father to son in throwing every stone out of the loam road.
They can't be expected to reverse that process and put hard-
earned money into pulverized rock in a minute.   Earthen roads
are great luxuries to tender-feet horses, and invalids find the
rumble of stone rather wearing, or positively injurious.

Some of our wealthiest rural districts are yet struggling
with compromise notions, mingling earth and stones together,
not thinking that these might be nicely served separately on
parallel sides of the highway ; or that a perfectly smooth, rotund,
solid rock road can be dressed with loam for the Summer season.
What is meant here by the word solid will appear later.

The sorry mistake is too often made of ridging up gutter-
mud in the vain endeavor to build a solid road of rough broken
stone on top of that.   Remains of crude country adulterations
often show in venal or ignorant city and village practices.   Rock
roads, in the first dawn of urban intelligence, seem chiefly ambitious of being rough enough with cobble-stone pavement, to
multiply the rattling, roaring echoes of growing business.

Ages of road wallowing and shirking over frozen ruts are
required to teach the whole of any stick-in-the-mud generation to
unite in thorough work to better themselves.   Results in cities
are nowhere so lovely as to give the country entire confidence in
city engineering.   We are not yet done digging arts and laws
from the mistaken foundations of ruined empires and copying

them! That is like sending our business circulars to the list of advertised letters! When shall we learn that every seedling generation of wise parentage has a right to vary and become happier in its circumstances? When that the epitaph of every defunct nation may be : "Killed by its government." In their eagerness to bring all traffic and labor within their own limits, municipalities have not seen clearly that the maintenance of roads depends altogether on how they are built to begin with.

There is no question but the best roads would double the value of farms as fast as we can agree to build them right. But farmers who have seen their landed property depreciated by the over issue of securities, till impoverished land has become, North and South, East and West, like the wild-cat money nobody wanted—will not be enthusiastic for roads they alone are to be taxed for. Go show an old farmer your cities—the very brightest and best of them—and then go with him and let him show you the sources of city "prosperity" in the country. 'Twill take long journeys to find the whole of it, but the facts are manifest. For every dollar of permanent city value you have exhibited, he will shake his whip at country places robbed of two, five and ten dollars since we took the land from the Indians. Let there be no Ananias and Sapphira, his wife, in the new legal arrangements for road making. *Common roads are the visible bonds of the Commonwealth. They are of and for the State, as much as the State House itself; are not so local as that is, and should be paid for by the State, as that was.* Where else so level and just can the doctrine of eminent domain come in?

The idea that a road needs a foundation as firm, in proportion to the weight and thrust of vehicles and the business done upon it as a house, is one of the last to enter our calculations. We accept stone-road work for heavy traffic, and the wrenching gauge of loaded wheels, that no reputable builder or careful farmer would take a linear perch of to under-pin a pig stye. We have required millions of failures on every hand to make us see the futility and waste of our road work. The constant fact that every particle of settlement in the bottom of a road produces a corresponding dislocation of the finished surface, is very slow to lodge in our minds. *Do our friends, the wheelmen, really know that yet?* Every woman and child in the land should have the fact explained to them at once.

The other and cognate idea, that to make roads wear smoothly even when foundations are solid—the substance of the road, ever to be exposed to friction, must be of one uniform texture and quality, thoroughly compacted, is not appreciated, even in engineering circles. Stone and wood and stone and brick roads are too often commended. Cape Cod sand furnishes smooth wheeling in the bottom of its ruts, because of its uniform quality.

A third conception, equally vital to the integrity of the best road work in any climate, grows naturally out of the two foregoing ideas as stated. With an unyielding bottom and a superstructure of homogeneous crushed rock, leaving no crevices or particles not in solid contact, we may have a rounded surface practically impervious to water. Shutting out water, the great destructive element, fluid or in the form of ice, lessens immensely the cost of maintenance.

If there is such a thing as chemical adhesion in the substance of a well-built road, surely all chance of that desirable consummation will be lost if it is made, as we often see it done, so as to be only a percolating arrangement for all the water falling upon it.

Ideally perfect stone road construction is rarely or never reached. We have not been looking in the right direction for that in recent years. Only by accident, or after considerable periods of time, by re-surfacing and patching (never so perfect as original work may be), is here and there a chance for closer observers than ordinary to correct their theories of construction by actual facts. *Our many blunders involve the disgrace and ill-repute of broken stone roads with chronic disgust or lack of desire*

for questionable street improvements among those who might other-
wise be glad to pay for them.

How often have we told somebody, with ineffable sapience, that "to dry up your mud and water on a road you must have some even-sized stone dumped or spread upon it?" Dare we convey that "principle" into the kitchen or laundry as a remedy for sloppy floors? Or tell it to the "marines" even, who are not supposed to realize the rotundity of ships' decks and the use of lee-scuppers? The smallest urchin knows now that a glass of water will hold a tumblerfull of nails, and French engineers decided generations since that a cubic yard of "even-sized stone" would hold half a cubic yard of water!

Again, look at our frequent "nice" recipes for laying up a highway with strata of stone in different sizes, growing smaller and smaller toward the top. Our theory of these layers of stone in *diminuendo*—if we have any—must be that they will shut together solid with a sort of telescopic effect, when we come to load them. In practice these different strata of "even-sized" stone, each layer smaller toward the top, do "telescope" under the concussions of wheels, as trains of cars "telescope" in ruins when they come in collision. Friction is too excessive to make the telescoping satisfactory, and a segment of the moon to roll the stratified road stone could only pulverize or crush it into mud all the sooner.

By the negligence and unfaithfulness of stoneworkers themselves, who build roads that are penances to travel on, far more costly and less durable road materials have been' foisted upon confused communities, damaging true engineering science in popular estimation. The worst counterfeit is the closest imitation of the genuine metal.

Whenever we have constructed a water-proof road, or one that directly becomes so by the attrition of travel, we find we have done away with a part of the need for under-drainage, or rather, *insured against faults in that very important particular.* In crowded communities sanitary considerations must enter into road construction. We don't want street filth leaching into cellars. A highway that sheds water perfectly—instead of leaking like a riddle—is rid of its worst enemy, and has the cost of repairs reduced to the lowest terms. The wear of surfaces will depend, then, on the amount and kind of travel and the nature of the material composing the road.

There is no reason, except in our minds and ways of thinking, why we can't have water-shedding roads of broken stone. A rock-crusher would smile grimly at the difficulty of furnishing coarse and fine material together in fit proportions, to puddle solid under water. "But that would shrink our measure," it would say. "You'll have to talk with the boss about that." It would laugh at the notion that it can't bite rock fine enough to fill its own interstices. The only obstacle is in the way we have made it screen and assort road metal, while laboring under the too easy mistake that "porous" stone road work is desirable.

Right here let us moisten our subject and ease our minds by considering drainage. It is the first law of road making. Let us hang up to ridicule all the authority in the land for not obeying it.

A certain eminent engineer was talking with B—, of L—, concerning the road bottoms of the latter's native town. "Our roads," said B—, "look as innocent and quiet as a pan of milk with the cream on just now. My grandfather said they changed pretty quick after the hemlock roots rotted out of the ground. There was a long loop of road going around — Hill, which sagged, stump fences and all, more than four rods from the original survey, without making a break in the land anywhere. In Spring this very same nice road we are on acts as if it were all afloat, in great junks like rafts, five feet deep. The water in the ditches and in every puddle will wink, the bushes will nod at you and rails tumble out of the fences with every step of your team. The whole highway dangles like a slack rope or a hammock swinging. It's going to take something more than figuring to fix this road solid. When it is all jelly in April it will swallow forty thousand loads of stone to the mile, without leaving a sign of where they went to, except by shoving the adjoining turf a little !"

Here was an arable soil of the finest quicksand, several feet deep, based on the toughest blue clay ; both, when sprung by frost, capable of holding immense quantities of water. The ancient road cut, deepened by wearing, acted as a sluice for adjoining fields and hills. The old plan for navigating that sort of a road in Spring, when the legs of horses and oxen are in the way, and something of the stone-boat order of vehicle, with a team of wriggling amphibia for draft purposes, would naturally be suggested, was to use brush upon it, as Capt. Eads curbed the Mississipi River with brush, or else thorough drain the whole broad highway, laying what is not stoned down to fine grass. An engineer worth his salt, seeing that road shaking in April, would advise applying the alder and maple bushes from the abundant hedge rows as the most scientific temporary measure, precisely as that farm community had relied on brush for generations to carry them safely over the worst places.

But as populations increase, grow wealthy and impatient of wise rustic proceedings, some cheap botch who doesn't think, gets a cash job under stupid contract from the public who don't think, to drain that shaky road with tile or stone. After the money is gone with the brush and the handy men who made light work of applying it, somebody discovers that the so-called drainage is no good, for the tile or stone drains are packed choke-full of that most insinuating clay and quicksand silt. Energetic authorities, with more muscle than brains, often have such jobs done several times over without odium, before any one—perhaps a woman who thinks—happens to hear of the trouble and suggests vegetable fiber (from stopping her leaky dish-pan for the nonce with a shred of rag) to pack the tiles in ; then civilization moves on, using marsh hay, eel grass, forest leaves, waste cotton, or peat moss imported from Germany, to cover the joints of the tile carefully laid on plank. A line of tiles beneath the bottom of each roadside ditch, and one or two parallel lines draining into the others from the body of the highway, may be the cheapest first step for the improvement of roadbeds that are sure to be quaking quagmires at certain seasons. It might be the height of foolishness to let such jobs to the lowest bidder.

Stone men, from the time of the stone ages, will not live up to their present opportunities until they rid themselves of the utterly vicious conception that leaching water through their finished road work is permissible. That is bastard drainage— blind drainage—the kind that would try to pump the sea dry with the water running back into it.

If we will not see the danger to health in crowded populations by the washing of infected filth against the foundations of dwellings; if we do not see the certainty of our work being shaken by frost over a saturated subsoil, then we shall be made to see and *feel* the competition of our enterprising brethren of the asphalt persuasion, who in theory and practice roof their foundations water-tight, and make us pay dearly for no risks in the above vital particulars.

Stone road work, no matter what name we give it, must be made solid and impervious to water and frost, and remain so throughout the year. We crush stone, not for the purpose of providing porous drainage layers in the roadbed, but for the convenience of handling and laying the unequally granulated rock clean and solid as rock again, in the desired form and place of the stone highway, then to wear smoothly and only from the top, for indefinite periods of time, like the tire of a wagon, the iron of railways, or the original rock itself.

The rotund portion of a broken stone road should be capable of wearing handsomely and without ruts or roughness, till by the slow friction of travel and the crushing of loaded wheels it is worn flat and *dishing*, and the dust of it is blown or washed entirely away as arable soil, fit for the uses of tillage. Then, and not till then, should come the labor of renewal in precisely the same manner in which the road was first built, unless by that time the chemistry of rock making is better understood. We ought to rediscover the not long lost art of chimney-top mortar. Mortar making, except in the plastic stages of mud in the highway, is so little known in engineering science now, that flying brickbats from crumbling chimneys make a considerable difference in death rates. Ordinary farm builders used to do better. Once let the nation conceive the idea of solid rock roads for everybody, and by the scientific use of fit minerals they will become more and more common everywhere.

Having so adapted machinery to the road business that highway metal to fill its own interstices can be procured in any quantity, and so instructed and equipped labor as to supply all deficiencies in the grain of the material, our next care in this paper is to show how it can be consolidated in the roadbed. In this respect current science and mechanics are deplorably at fault, and taxpayers, blinded by surface finishers, stupidly see little or nothing of the costly and insulting jokes played on them by quack road contractors and engineers.

Before we proceed, however, let us consider a few words from one of the old masters, whose language is by no means obsolete, whose name has become one of our most familiar parts of speech in connection with our subject, but whose ideas, in their purity and exactness, are rarely or never applied to road making.

John Loudon MacAdam, after spending some part of his youth in the United States, returned to the place of his nativity in Scotland, and, turning his attention to making good roads, shortly became famous in his own country, and afterward all over the world. It is said that of the 30,000 miles of roads in Great Britain five-sixths of them were reorganized in his name during his life. He saw the opportunity of his time. British roads had been stuffed for years, by local authority, with all sorts of stone, dumped in roughly and often unbroken, till traveling with comfort was no longer possible at any season.

He declined being called an engineer. (*"Are you a professional engineer?"* *"No."*) He was a road maker, developed in time of great need. Instead of three-fourths team-work, as had been, his bills showed three-fourths labor. We can guess what a row that change would raise. But he revolutionized the whole business of road making, by showing anybody—even women and children, who could pick the rough stones out of the road, break them, and lay the fine fragments back again nicely—how to make the best of wheeling—sometimes with half the old material. *We*, by the force of false profits and so-called "civil engineers," with "prize essays" and much obsolete stereotyping in "patent insides and outsides," are actually copying the old road bottoms MacAdam (compelled by the penuriousness and jealousies of his time) left behind him. We are like the too literal Chinese tailor, who reproduced every patch on the commodore's sample trowsers in three dozen pairs of new breeches! MacAdam's methods—or what were said to be his—spread like wildfire, however, and, doubtless, much was done, not as he would have it, then as now. Hear him and weigh his strange words well. After insisting upon draining the roadbed, wherever that is necessary, he says :

"The broken stone *is only to preserve the under road from moisture,* and not at all to support the vehicles, the weight of which must be really borne by the native soil, which, while preserved *dry,* will carry any weight, and does, in fact, carry the stone road itself as well as the vehicles upon it."

Again : "The stone is employed to form a secure, *smooth, water-tight flooring,* over which vehicles may pass with safety and expedition at all seasons of the year."

And again : "Its thickness should be regulated only by the quantity of material necessary to form such a *flooring,* and not at all by any consideration as to its own independent power of bearing weight."

The offices of the stone are *to endure friction and shed water.*

And still again : "The erroneous idea that the evils of an underdrained, wet, clayey soil can be remedied by a large quantity of materials has caused a large part of the costly and *unsuccessful* expenditures in making broken-stone roads." [1]

Evidently, there were parties before MacAdam's time who found their account in furnishing "large quantities" of stone to dump on the highway. Can we doubt, if he were among us to-day, that he would order up much of our work to be broken over and relaid, solid and clean, on a dry foundation?

This MacAdam was essentially a teacher. He had purified his language by conversation with simple-minded people whose words must be few and well chosen. He set hundreds and thousands of needy laborers at work—entire families of cottagers—right at their doors. No doubt, he learned much of them. How could he be expected to teach an old laborer that hammered stone, at ten pence per ton, would furnish the sharpest kind of gravel, fit to rust and cling into rock when once every particle is well set and bedded solid in a road? British labor, at that time, was born to that knowledge, and the secret of MacAdam's popularity was that he understood it better than its recent masters, who were being taught, rather against their wills, how to make a road.

Every wayside in England was a school for the English middle and upper classes in those days, and there are signs in the literature of that period that many would-be-leaders hated this man MacAdam who presumed to come between misguided labor and themselves. They took honors and emoluments by prescription. He would not accept a baronetcy, and until old and impoverished by his patriotic exertions he refused the £6,000 voted him by parliament. Too well known to be hung for disputing the doctors, the heroic face[2] and life of this great Scotchman are singular appearances in the world's road history.

---

[1] These extracts appear in Gillespie's " Roads and Railroads," 1858, and are either adaptations from MacAdam or taken from some essay this present writer has not seen.

[2] See Harper's Weekly of August 10th, 1889, for portraits of MacAdam and Telford.

His good work wore out after awhile.   His few and brief writings were never reprinted in this country.   Not much that he said is ever mentioned—or is covered with elaborately spun sophistries—and the art which McAdam left so simple that no one, even though an engineer, might err therein (with intelligent labor watching), has become so abstruse that nobody understands it.

One who has been sampling foreign roads with a bicycle[1]— and perhaps with his head and shoulders—says there is not a foot of well-kept public road in all England.   Iron roads have taken the attention of British managers since MacAdam set the common people to engineering their own roads.

A single sentence of the great road maker is often quoted but never explained and probably never understood:

"The stone must not be laid on in shovelfuls, but scattered over the surface, one shovelful following another, and spreading over a considerable space."[2]

Applied literally to our machine road work that saying would be nonsense.   Our road metal is of a uniform quality of rock, is broken and screened in uniform sizes.   There would be no sense in spreading that assorted rock carefully from the cart like manure, yet that is precisely what you see going on.   If you say anything you will find that you have touched an "ark" of the craft that has survived long after its general usefulness has passed away.   The gosling engineer found it in his textbook, his tutor did not explain its old significance in handicraft and heterogeneous rock breaking; the American workman finds no one appealing to his reason or better common sense; the slow spreading motion suits his chronic complaint, and is retained as a part of the grip of the "Old Man of the Sea" astride of our necks to-day.   Like master, like man in road making.

Every motion MacAdam made grew out of facts in his expe-

[1] Mr. Pennel, in Harper's Weekly of August 25th, 1889.
[2] Loudon's Cyclop. of Agriculture.

rience.   His rocks were not uniform, but of all qualities as
gathered from adjoining fields ; boulders and pebbles, rounded,
of quartz, flint and sandstone ; tough, "greasy," hard-heads,
rejected of wall building ; limestone, slaty and laminated rock,
harder or softer ; everything which generations of thoughtless
people (treating their highways as rubbish holes as we have
treated ours) had turned upon the public, and all must suffer for
MacAdam had to contend with in the old roads he ravelled, shred-
ded and knit over again—or the gangs of workpeople he organ-
ized did—and left consolidated in a new, smooth fabric behind
them.

He said reject the soft stone.   He would have no more clay
or loam in his work than a mason will have in his mortar.   If
he ever condemned fine stone it was because of the liability in
his practice of its being mixed with earth.   But how could he
control the doings on 25,000 miles of highway ?   Some ambitious urchin—a great engineer in after life, perhaps—would catch
up his mother's hammer while she was gone to get dinner or
supper and break the soft rejected stone into a tidy pile for
measurement.   Who would stop him ?   And it would be a hard-
hearted boss, one who had never heard the text about "little
children" who would fail to tally the lad a penny for his enterprise.   Indeed, it may be presumed that soft stone if well
mingled with harder ones, by shrewd and rapid workmen—none
too honest then as now—were continually winked at as inevitable.   But *each shovelful should be scattered widely so that no
lumps of soft stone could be deposited together.*   So our labor and
our text-books are burdened with the more trivial pains of
MacAdam when the circumstances that caused them are obsolete, and while his weightier matters that ought still to be in
force are forgotten.

How long shall the American public be imposed upon by
"systems" too absurd to bear a particle of analysis—that have
proven themselves no better than road ruts for laziness and indifference to jog along in ?   When Ruskin threw his " Seven

Lamps of Architecture" into a "system," he was candid enough to say, in excuse for the temporary arrangement, that he might have had eight, nine or eleven "lamps" in it. Systems are like the ruts of which a good road maker is ashamed. Few of them will bear keeping over night ; time itself and the magnetic needle constantly vary, while men should remain true to the shifting situation, for no road system can be carried across the country without constant adaptations to local exigencies. Fashions, too, often change without improvement, or we should have road paragraphs in every school reading-book like this one of MacAdam's :

"*In every road I have been obliged to alter the mode of management, according to the situation, and sometimes according to the finances.*"

No pastry cook will try to mash raw sugar—if she can get any—with a rolling-pin, while knife, fork, spoon, flour-duster and paste-cutters lie in the way on her moulding-board ; but something very like that is what we see trying to be done every day—"*street closed*" by the dignified countermarchings of the steam roller over open-work bridges, formed by rocks of all shapes, cornering together, helter skelter, in the bottom of new city street work. No possible weight on such "rolling-pins" can ever make that cobbled up material solid. Only by passing this stupidity as a sacred "system," thoughtlessly from hand to hand, (*like the big stone to balance the grist of olden times*) could the foolishness be perpetuated. The ordinary broad steam roller cannot be trusted to roll twelve or fifteen inches of the finer mixed crushed rock specified in this paper, water-tight. The tread of these roller-mills is too wide. · It is not roller-grinding that we need for loose stone, but tamping, treading and narrower rolling in the process of settlement.

Ask a caulker, a steam piper, the dentist who fills our teeth, or the laborer who properly packs earth and gravel beneath a railway sleeper or about a post in the ground, and see what tools they use for stuffing and solidifying the filling of crevices, and we shall know more of the demands of rock-road making, where thousands of interstices to the cubic yard are to be made solid.

Skilled workmen, quick to notice any redundancy or lack of fine or coarse stone in the texture of the metal as delivered, with lithe [1] stone hammers, handy as whips, for cracking a few stone upon occasion, and pull forks adapted to the shifting and reassortment of small quantities of material, will be ready when the science of rock-road making is fully understood.

Whenever a wide-awake public makes water-tight stone roads imperative in cities, pipe water will be at hand to wet new work and facilitate packing, but will be used by experts with caution, to avoid carrying rock dust downward faster than it is needed, or before the tread of broad wheels and the stirring of the feet of teams, delivering the crushed stone, have done their appointed work in thrusting the particles of the whole body of material into their fit places in the roadbed.

Narrow tires have no use in road work, except the fill is deep, and a place of deposit for rubbish. The sulkies of the State surveyors general should be shod at least four inches wide, merely for church going, and to bring the good fashion into vogue.

Dump carts with broad tires are much the best for depositing stone in road work. *Three shafts for two horses is an old and well-tested rig in some iron mines. With all-leather harness, this constitutes the shortest and most comfortable strong team in existence.* Four-wheeled dumps, for one or two horses, are much used in certain sections, but these are long and cumbersome. A single horse cart should have at least five-inch tire ; two-horse dumps six to eight-inch tire. Wagons, with scantling bottoms, for dropping broken stone through their bodies, if admitted— which is doubtful economy—should have rims at least four inches wide.

There is nothing new about broad-tired carts except that we can build better ones than the world has ever seen. It is nar-

[1] No need to harden our joints with stiff handles.

row tires which are comparatively new and were ordered by the skinflint calculator, one-and-three-quarters inch wide, to cut inside his neighbor's two-inch ruts. Broad wheels, sawn from logs, are much the oldest, quite as scientific, and recommended by the oldest masters of agriculture and road making. Rome governed and skinned the known world with broad-wheeled ox carts. MacAdam was perfectly familiar with vehicles of six-inch tread, but had small use for team work, as the heft of carting was already done for the botched stone roads he amended. He ridiculed the pretensions of certain clumsy sixteen-inch wheels built in his time—*conical*, half dragging mechanical monstrosities, full of spikes—as unworthy of favor by turnpike tolls. But he approved the *level* tread of broad tires.

When the public gets sick of seeing its roads cut to pieces by heavy freighting on narrow tires, disk-harrow wheels will be driven out of use by more intelligent and scientific fashions. Less road law would be necessary if our legislators had even seen the best possible roads, or the tools to build them.

Whatever the road is made of, or patched with, the rolling weight of the carted material should always be used to harden the new work. This involves beginning at the end nearest the stonebreaker, or other source of supply. MacAdam's quarry was the old road, and he broke his stone at the side of it.

Our boys and girls go abroad and return much enamored of the frequent little depots of broken stone piled neatly, and with men in attendance, by the roadside, in foreign parts, ready and waiting to pounce on any defects in the wheeling. Would this "system" be such a lovely addition to American scenery that we need to hurry about transplanting it, with all that it implies? Either European roads are so ill constructed that they need patching too quickly, and too constantly, or the suspicious preparations are needless. Our business is to make roads so good as to excite the curiosity of our own globe trotters, and of travelers from abroad as well, to come and see how we do it and help pay expenses. Ten thousand times more American money is spent on foreign roads than is well spent upon our own.

Instances are not rare of miles of fair country road being destroyed by narrow tires in hauling the material for a quarter of a mile of new road that proves a disgrace to all parties when it is done. Still there are those who wish to be continually in authority when such things are going on !

The changes indicated in running-gear for road making are all such as would be better for farming and gardening districts and all freighting also, aside from their particular application to highway work. If a road teamster can't haul loads over his own fills, how can the public be expected to do it ?

When once the material for the best stone road is in place, the sooner it is trampled and rolled solid the better. It is because broken rock needs so much manipulation—shaking rather than grinding—to bring it down to its bearings, while the fresh fractures of the material are in the best condition to stick and hang there, that road teams must be vigilant and constant in this service—never following each other's ruts, but covering every inch of the new work, going and returning, with their most salutary pressure, *which does not crush the metals.* A driver with a good team who shirks this care will make ruts wherever he drives. Several years' apprenticeship to the best road making would be a very fitting introduction to general team work, hack driving and private coach service, for it is our teamsters and drivers who will make or mar our roads ; and with due study out of these might grow our best road engineers.

Except for the broad tires, giving lighter draft over the new material, it might be impossible for the strongest teams to furnish their indispensable assistance, especially when the new road runs up hill. The alert steam-roller man may be willing to acknowledge here that by utilizing the power of teams, now worse than wasted, with narrow tires, we are preparing fields for far other than sham exploits by his machines, where they may win substantial and permanent credit in the last triumphant polish of what is almost solid. Broken stone takes so much management to force, coax and inveigle the unwilling particles of it together that we must impress every pound of team work into the service, while steam rolling, if to be had, will apply later.

Softer places and ridges are covered by the wheels of nicely driven teams returning empty. In practice there is no difficulty about this team rolling method. It applies perfectly everywhere. Horse owners and feeders find that broad tires more than pay for themselves in saving oats and corn. Animals and men soon grow skilled in their work, and good teamsters take honest pride in the road making which constantly appeals to their reason and judgment, leaving all but the latest two or three rods of its product in fit condition to speed a horse or run a bicycle upon. The public may enjoy this kind of street work even while it is going on.

Whenever this method of cart rolling new road work is seen to be in exact accord with highway science for the whole people, then we shall have the wheels of steam rollers cut narrower and breaking joints in accord with it, thus making their pressure *more searching* and *effective*. *If it is possible to make a dint in his road anywhere, the road-maker himself is the man to find that out by proving his work in actual use and rigid test as he goes along.* With new narrow-tread steam rollers as aforesaid, and force enough, it will be possible to lay down, finished and ironed to perfection, long stretches of solid rock road in a day, or in the night, when necessary for public comfort. Current calculations of the broad pressure and packing effect of the common steam roller, based on the effect of its superficies, are enough to make a horse laugh, when compared to the punching tread of the road cart tire with a ton on each wheel!

In the country, the value of occasional showers will be felt in road making, and secured by every nice workman in putting the finishing touches to his job. As it is, it is possible that a sudden heavy rain on raw work may wash fine rock, filling dust down too fast, in spite of the best management. So it is possible, as such places will show plainly when the sun comes out, to supply the little fine material to make good the deficiency. The practice of robbing the internal structure of a stone road of its full proportion of intersticial matter for the sake of dressing the surface, is vicious in both ways. Filling and packing should proceed contemporaneously. As soon as these points are thoroughly appreciated. and the minds of inventors are fixed upon them, we may expect a development of patent compounds designed to facilitate the union of broken stone work and now impossible by reason of rude and dirty ways of working. Lime and iron were suggested by road engineers many years ago.[1]

Road stone differs materially in different sections of the country. In controlling these differences, when otherwise they would go against us, more opportunities for skill and dexterity will occur than can be put in any essay or book. Some persons live long and useful lives and die very much regretted, without having learned at all stages of temperature to spread butter on bread handsomely. It is highly probable that some few people, even if they try hard and are well paid for doing so, will never succeed in finishing a road perfectly and with dispatch. Tom Hood's old florist, who was "too dry" or "too wet" herself when her plants were suffering, might have been the mother of road makers, sufficiently sensitive to know how their work was going on without being told of it.

After a road is done, and about as hard as it ever can be, when loads of stone and the best improved narrow-wheeled steam roller fails to make any impression on it, when we know that all the inside of it is one coherent mass, when it actually does shed water, even then a road artist, proud as the skilled modern surgeon, of healing the fairly glazed rock surface by "first intention," may wish to give a color of age to his work. How can he best do this ? By adding the least top-dressing— not a fourth of an inch anywhere, for it's only a coat of mineral

[1] Engineer Walker, in MacAdam pamphlets.

paint—of tough, fine, earthern gravel to suit his complexion. This is but a varnish. Perhaps only fleet trotters and bicyclists, willing to save their rubbers from sharp grit, will thank him for it. This is the way to give age at once to a bit of new road. *It can well be omitted*, for this is all the excuse there ever was in the best stone work for outside "binding material." The apparent need of that follows from the foolish stealing away of stone chips from the body of the road.

What is said here of dispatch in making stone road work solid, applies to all material used in road making; whether of sand, turf, earth, loam, gravel, brickbats, cobblestone, old mortar, coal ashes, furnace slag, sawdust, tanbark, shavings, village and city garbage and refuse, stable-manure, brush, poles, round or cleft logs (all more or less in use by this civilization, as cuts in city streets testify), the sooner a road is compacted and smoothed over the better.

> " If it were done when 'tis done, then 'twere well
> It were done quickly."

Pauper labor and chain-gangs—the offspring of learned craft and studied proletarian ignorance—cannot well be the raw material of the best road making, except they are warmed over and renewed by the touch of divine charity and human fellowship. The best roads will be engendered in the thought of the best artisans, and these will be most familiar with the nature of all things. Have we seen the quiet gangs of men engaged in artificial rock-pavement around our national buildings? Where every man is a master tradesman, and it is impossible to tell who the boss is, so closely do all mind their business? Those are working models of applied sciences. Let us begin road making in that way, and trust imitative human nature to follow us. It would be cheaper than our present half-civilized methods, of choosing a new road-mender every year.

Take such a common matter as coal ashes from a mill, for instance. Those slaty pieces and ragged clinkers, if uniformly distributed in the mass, are indispensable to the life of the road. But we usually see them ground to powder in a loose condition by the narrow tires of ordinary travel, instead of being rolled and trodden solid at once, as delivered on the highway, by scientific teams, teamsters and workmen. Every bit of slate broken, and every rough clinker pulverized, makes the road more mealy, the substance of it shorter, less coherent and less able to endure the grind of hoofs and wheels. Coal-ash roads are not half as permanent as they might be if these directions were followed strictly, and without a cent's additional cost in laying. Polished particles cannot hang together in a road-bed, yet we often treat road metal on a highway, by allowing it to be run over in an unfinished condition, suffering the thrust and crush of wheels and hoofs, forcing every particle of it to polish its neighbor, very much as rough castings in mills are whirled in tumbling-barrels to polish each other.

When we call to mind the wear and tear of vehicles and horses, stumbling along some avenue new laid with big contractor's "macadam," it must be conceded that the method is anything but scientific, and nothing that MacAdam himself would have agreed to. Only case-hardened authority and "system" will be guilty of such things.

Wherever an attempt is made to mitigate the roughness of partially-broken stones, by doubling over them unctuous street clay, or by hauling on greasy mud scraped from other streets and avenues, or by bedding the stones in gutter scrapings[1]— what name can we apply to such filthy practices ? and how shall we describe the condition of communities enduring them? Would you transplant these dirty steam-roller tricks into the country ?

A road or street so top-dressed is not a pleasant matter for contemplation, all the way down through it, except to the resolute community and its master workmen, who have decided to

---

[1] "'Cyclop. Britannica" mentions "street scrapings" with "sand and gravel" for binding stone.

go to the bottom of the trouble with a stone-breaker and do the work all over again, as herein described. That is MacAdam. There are thousands of miles of execrable stone road that will pay better than any road stock we have for re-working. Bad road work will out—like murder. This labor would give scope for a new style of machinery; traction stone breakers, with narrow roller tenders, working nights, perhaps, in crowded cities; or in dull seasons, handicraft, with improved tools, might be revived by an enterprising people, who will have their streets perfectly clean. *A stone road, rutted and mixed with clay, is no better than so much dirty raw material, to be quarried free of cartage.*

The nature of the soil beneath a road has much to do with the cost of its construction. Sands and gravels which never hold water afford the cheapest and most secure foundation, and in all the gradations of sand, gravel, hard-pan and clay, the degree of water-holding capacity, in a climate where the action of frost must be considered, furnishes a close index of the comparative cost of making an absolutely permanent and smooth road.

The best road making in many populous and naturally thorough-drained districts, is complicated by the practice, for many years, of attempting betterments of clay, hard-pan, or gravel containing much clay or loam, or other material which has destroyed the drainage of the roadbed that formerly existed and increased its water-holding capacity. In such cases it may be cheapest to select a new line for the proposed solid-rock road. Or, if sand is plenty, and there is room enough in a rural street, let the artificial mud be scraped entirely away to grow grass upon, down to the original sand, to which other sand may be added, and on this, well trampled by turning teams, may be built the best stone road. Many years of travel on simple sand will grind that to mud in wet weather.

Sand, for a foundation, has been injured—unwittingly, perhaps—in public estimation by clerical commentators. In drying winds, or where water can wash it away ; or where rats, bank-robbers or jail-breakers will find too easy digging, there should be caution ; but pure, dry sand, well settled and down deep in the earth, never budges. We may build church steeples or mill chimneys on it.

We must have sand appreciated in engineering schools and in popular comprehension, because it is well worth hauling long distances, sometimes, to cover and qualify clay beneath the best stone roads. Every old street pavior knows the value of sand as a permanent cushion for stone. It will give and take just so much, kindly, in the road bottom, but no more.

Here, for instance, is an extreme case in actual street prac-tice, but not an uncommon one. It well illustrates thousands of miles of the road problems now staring us in the face for solu-tion. It is a causeway, built high up, street wide and mostly walled in, of clay strong enough for bricks. It has been covered and recovered with stone, roughly broken, and mingled with mud, without ever a thought of making a water-tight floor roof over that causeway.

In mild Winters and Spring thaws these stones are thrust down into the saturated clay, causing that to ooze and float upon the surface, often creating such a public outcry that more rough stone are added, to go downward in due time like the others. This process has been going on for generations as the regular conservative thing.

The interesting performance is variegated in cold Winters by frost entering the elevated roadbed of clay and stone deeply, and swelling it gradually, so that every few years long stretches of the "retaining walls" are sprung off past their centre of gravity and have to be rebuilt. It is *vigilant and astute "engin-eering"* that twigs the walls before they actually tumble into the meadow. These slow movements add to local "industry," of course, but constitute a serious item in the "maintenance" of calculations that were worse than useless in the first place, because a sore public nuisance is created and road stupidity

generated by wholesale for a century throughout a broad district
of country.   No end of children are born, marked—greatly to
the injury of the State—by the hopelessness of that hoary old
"system."   The "Slough of Despond" will occur to the vet-
eran reader in this connection : " *Yea, and to my knowledge,*"
said Helper, " *here have been swallowed up at least twenty-thou-
sand cart loads, yea, millions of wholesome instructions !*"

What is the scientific remedy for such a flagrant breach of
the peace as that *common in lesser measure, perhaps, wherever
clay is ridged up between retaining walls of turf all over the
country ?* In this case sand is cheap and convenient, while stone
must be brought long distances. What else can we do but plant
a rock crusher on that causeway, lift the stones and break them
fine enough to fill their own crevices, bedding them solid and
water-tight on sand enough to keep the clay still ?

It is believed there is double the quantity of stone on that
causeway, when they are cleaned from mud and broken fine, to
build a perfect rock road. It is as good as a quarry, and represents the accumulated savings of generations of superficial
thinking about highways. With a solid stone floor roof and an
edging of turf over them, those retaining walls will stand for-
ever.

The relative value of stone, sand and clay varies immensely
in different districts. Ten loads of either respectively, in places
that need not be specified, would willingly be given for a single
load of either on the spot in time of need. Railways have a
duty to themselves as well as to the people in making fit ex-
changes possible.

Somewhere in our road making we must have a place to
use refuse stone, brickbats, and so-forth, or our methods will
never be popular. It will be scarcely worth while to play
"Telford" with these substances, and set them up on end, if
the fill is deep enough and sound packing is plenty. Several
noteworthy authors admit the shoddy material without specifying precisely what shall be done with it. Hence, in city street

diggings for water, gas, sewers, etc., old rubbish, once thought
to be buried, is continually coming to the surface to the great
astonishment of bystanders; and is carelessly tumbled into
ditches and holes, to the frequent injury of the roadbed. This
is a matter wise city fathers should see to. Every town or
growing village should keep a street prophet who will beware of
the loss by burying rubbish where it will have to be dug up
again.

It must be allowed that where clay has been covered with
six to twelve inches of sand and there is still room enough in the
roadbed to put refuse stone, brickbats, etc., where they can
never come to the wearing surface, these rough materials, if
trodden air tight and well covered with better substance, may
save all their bulk in choice road metal. A roadmaker will be
too squeamish who can't find some safe place for almost anything, if he has due notice of it—except a porous sub-structure.
That should be forbidden by law.

When solid rock road is to be built across an exclusively
clay country, don't let us fail to make the best of what we have
got for a foundation. Clay is the hardest and heaviest of soils,
and will hold up anything if we keep it dry. Reject loamy and
mucky portions for the bed of the road. Make that high enough
of the crude aluminum. If a central drain is needed, with outlets
into side ditches, or, under drains parallel with the road, make
them the first thing. Where the side ditches must be deep and
open, dig them so, and with well-sodded banks, fit to mow, where
neatness is desirable—as where is it not ?

To fill across a clay marsh or swamp is one thing—a road
over arable clays is quite another. Here a wider excavation for
material, with gentler slopes, and under-drainage of parallel side-
ditches may be possible. Where it is seen that a love of beauty
is worth cultivating—even in road-menders—and that fine turf
has an appreciable cash value in keeping the shoulders of a road
dry, preventing gutters from washing at the eaves, so to speak,
of a solid roof-road, then the side ditches will be well-planned

and constructed beforehand as a legitimate part of the work. Usually the fever to get somewhere prevents much thought of road borders.

Wherever water, with or without frost, is liable to render the foundation of a road insecure, provision must be made against it. There are perennial springs that anyone can see, and basins of rock, hard-pan or clay, which become springs in wet weather, that few will see beforehand. These are very apt to cause trouble where cuts have been made for roads. The chances are too numerous for specification in an essay. Simple land drainage of clays will improve lines of highways in frosty regions. Three inches of sand along the line of a wet meadow under drain furnishes a dry foot-path ; and when it is overgrown with grass-thatched, *roofed*, as it were, with grass fibre, frost never softens that sand, and we see illustrated the effect of solid stone floor roofing upon a ridge of drained clay highway.

Drainage should be done separately from road work, and months before it, unless extraordinary pains are taken to ensure the earth's settling. But as part of the filling on clays, exposed to water and frost, let it be repeated that coarse pit sand, or fine, loose, dry gravel, are better than broken rock to lay the best stone road upon, because they pack easier and hold as well. Herein so many mistakes have been made that we need line upon line and precept upon precept.

Let us beware, however, of trusting to gravel that is part clay—or that will grind the clay inside of a road. Esquire R. R. Bramley, whose slow English came out before MacAdam's nervous sentences, and contained the same road principles, cautions us against using stones with clay in them: *They make a saponaceous, greasy mass*, he says. Clay mingled with water is a. very insidious and slippery thing. Chemists have difficulty in separating some forms of clay from water. We want no manner of it mingled with the bottom or top stone of a road that we design to be frost proof, because of its great water-holding capacity, and because it acts as a lubricant in preventing the fractured surfaces of broken stone from clinging together. The really acute roadmaker will be as shy of having clay in the interstices of his stone work as the vigilant mason is of having clay in a brick or stone wall. Wherever unburned clay goes there water will stay if it gathers, and then frost may expand it with irresistible power.

On top of the best finished road in use much vegetable fibre is constantly dropping ; fine dust, also, is making continually, and these greatly assist in rendering the best stone road roof-tight. Even if the road is frequently swept this will be so. Whoever has strained fruit juice or filtered water will not dispute it.

But at the bottom and inside of his work the roadmaker wants no clayey, loamy or vegetable matter, nor any washings of such leaching down among his porous stone in process of construction or hardening, to be swollen and shocked by water and frost at some later period.

If we bed large stones on clay alone, without the utmost faithfulness of fine grit packing (for which sharp sand may be cheaper and better than crushed rock), up will come the dilute clay whenever the road is used in a rainy, freezing and thawing Winter. Even with ideal vigilance on the part of authority there is still danger from the insidious clay, *unless every man engaged upon the work knows wherein the danger consists.* It is not enough that surveyors general and county surveyors know how to make our paths straight—that should be taught in our commonest schools.

Cover that clay with a thick blanket of coarse sand, or fine dry gravel, free from earth and clay mixtures—though in some places fine crushed rock may be cheaper—and the best road making may go on above in perfect security.

Except within four inches of the wearing surface of the road—or that which after a long time may become so—the sand filling is mechanically as serviceable as the most costly road metal. Experience will prove that a finer and more lasting superficial finish, as well as a smoother wearing road, can be built on the sand substratum than over a solid rock bottom. This is because the sand yields kindlier to the finishing above it than rock will while holding its place faithfully, and keeping the clay below in its own place, too. We don't care about planing both sides of our roads. It is the top side we want always smooth. If sand does not belong, geologically, above clay, it is inclined to stay above it in road work, unless exposed to mechanical mixing. Observe the trouble the brickmaker has to work sand into clay with his many-spiked pug-mill.

After an open Winter or two, and when laborers and con-tractors are out of employment; when tax-payers have become critical and the people generally grow uneasy; wheelmen very sensitive and sensible about rough roads; carriage makers see-ing their rolling stock shaken to pieces, begin to ask questions; local and social feeling long swamped in mudmarchings; gover-nors blushing for the hard roads they have to travel; farmers further from home markets, though but ten miles from a city, than though they lived up the Mediterranean or in Japan; capital seeking profitable investments or driving across the country after sunken money; institutions of learning ashamed of their own graduates; political partisans hunting live issues; when all these forces join the public press and legislatures in hurrying up road making in districts where the soil is largely composed of clay, it is time to make the sign of caution. Look out then for quack remedies. Let us go slow and sure, or in the excitement and enthusiasm of many voices, bad work is certain to be done, even with the best of intentions.

Here is a current sample of the "greedy" way stone road work is going on now. It looks like a move to palm road machinery on the obfuscated sense of publics who don't know how to use it :

CRUSH STONE FOR GOOD ROADS.

The town of Sweden, Monroe County, N. Y., owns a stone crusher and hires men by the day to run it. Last Spring the town appropriated $2,000 to crush stone, and, to make a rough guess, I think the $2,000 crushed stone enough to make five miles of perfect road. They set the crusher near stone, which is donated ; the town pays for hauling stone to the crusher and pays for crushing it ; the road districts go and get the crushed stone and lay it. Each road district and individual is greedy to get the stone, and I think that money thus expended goes ten times as far as any other in making highways. In the last three years the town of Sweden has made about twenty miles of road, so good that a team can haul as large a load in this open, muddy Winter as in Summer. The land is clay, and the roads not laid with stone or gravel are simply fearful. It would pay a person to go a long distance to see what has been done to the roads in the town of Sweden. When the roads are all made with crushed stone and the fences removed from the bleak places where snow drifts, the millennium will not be far away.—*Semi-Weekly Tribune*, January 10th, 1890.

D. A. BARKER.

It is easy enough to build good-looking stone roads over clay which will pass any early inspection that is liable to be given them ; that will please superficial students of the slow geologies of road making who have never known a really good stone road ; that will win such exulting paragraphs of praise from the press as the above ; and yet in the bitter end disgust everybody who rides over them, because they do not wear smoothly, owing to the slow but constant sinking of the bottom stone in the clay subsoil.

Whoever has ridden over one of these hastily built "better roads" knows the history of the country it is in ; has seen the road knocked to pieces, remembers well when the original mud beneath it was a notorious terror during wet weather and open Winters, or in Spring, will have learned that sharp, angular broken rocks, rammed in confusion into the clay by a few years' use, and inextricably mingled with it by struggling teams may become a bottomless road-horror when the clay is churned to batter. Soft slab mub, simply, however deep, is nothing to the new arrangement for pulling off shoes, laming horses and wrenching and cutting the running-gear of vehicles. Only the entire force of our census bureau, reorganized upon fresh economic principles, can estimate the cost for "maintenance" of such aggravated wrong beginnings of roads as that. It may be cheaper to abandon them entirely.

When once the lower stones of a road—no matter what their size is—have gone wandering, varicose, sidewise or downward in the saturated clay—opened by frost and thaw to swallow them—the stones next above continue dropping under the weight and thrust of teams, all cohesion in the superstructure is lost and no man can tell where the bottom of that road will bring up.

Even in Southern England, where deep frost is not expected, we are told now of roads four feet deep of broken stone, presumably where railway labor, such as we import from countries that have enough of it, is used to unlimited material; where nobody exists like the frugal patrons of husbandry who helped MacAdam in a period of agricultural depression, but where street contractors and roguish or ignorant city authorities, in collusion with those who sell stone and promote heavy jobs, have their wicked way with road affairs, unsustained by a wise common-sense and economic or social science. This mass of stone—an enormous "drainage layer"—whether lubricated by commingled clay or not, will move, by slow "glacial" action, for many years, while trembling under the mighty traffic of a great city. Rough stones piled together and subject to racking pressure soon slip at points of contact and lubricate friction with their own fine material. Acute angles wear off; but while the incoherent body of rock is constantly shrinking, it never becomes solid.

One of the vested interests, and great but neglected local industries of cities, consists in scraping up the mud which oozes through the interstices of badly-constructed rock roads. This is contraband of health and good policy, besides being ruinous to the integrity of street work and society. It looks as if we meant to keep laboring people sickly, as well as poor and ignorant, the easier to govern them.

Corrupt examples of metropolitan engineering are certain to affect all rural road making unfavorably and in more than one way; for if the city is taxed all or more than it can bear for bogus street work, the citizen is less able to buy and pay for honest productions of all kinds, and countrymen are less able to equip themselves with tools and machines for road making. Hence the whole country is impoverished, and entire States fall into decay.

The absurdity of open-work foundations of stone on clay, or on many grades of loam—even sandy loam—that become *quick* or quicksandy when acted upon by frost and water, is so common—stalking unblushingly abroad in the land—that the warnings given here may be considered silly, hypercritical and incredible by the large portion of the community who have not looked into these things.

Since MacAdam's time the proportion of people who have little or no *intimate* acquaintance with the ground—the earth—and the crude material of which the crust of it is composed, has vastly increased and is increasing. They have pens, ink and paper and a facility for using them well calculated to deceive the unwary. They are trusted to make newspapers, magazines, text-books and cyclopædias, jumping boldly into subjects where the most skillful specialists tread with caution. One who knows well even but a thing or two of roads, by experience, will not be deceived by these mere bookworms, who subsist chiefly upon each other's borings. But the reader who knows nothing of road matters—since special educations are developing special ignorances as well—is very liable to be cheated by the prints that are made to sell and catch the flying pennies of the day. One of our "cheap" cyclopædias [1] has this definition of the word "MACADAMIZING. (*Engin.*) A method of road making charactericed by breaking the stone so small that they may form, when covered with a layer of earth, a smooth, solid mass

[1] Zell, Philadelphia.

—so named after the inventor, *Jas. MacAdam*, a native of Scotland, 1756–1836."

This statement is less injurious to the studious, because it is brief and the proportion of blunders to the square inch is *so large*. But the Committee on Better Roads will find that this definition is as good as the average mind about stone roads.

Public misconceptions are the more to be deplored during a period when we are spending hundreds of thousands in shamelessly poor road work where we are paying a dollar for really expert study and advice, and while we find no remedy in the literary authorities that have already tainted our minds with error.

For instance, here is a "respectable" cyclopædia[1] saying under the head of "Roads," that MacAdam rejected all fine material and "splinters" of stone. Where is its authority? Indeed, there is none, and the writer has the good sense to doubt his own statement in the following sentence; for if MacAdam rejected the finer bits of stone, how could he make water-tight roads?

But the cheating story had gone abroad before that writer's time, and his bread and butter may have depended largely on his *not* contradicting it. It has cost the nations untold millions of money—that fraud of cubic measurement for broken stone that is *half air*, has. In the feeble beginning of machine stone-crushing, perhaps the cheat was needed, but now, gentlemen—for shame! In this day of judgment, when we want the whole people to join us in honest road work, let us have done with it. SELL YOUR STONE BY WEIGHT *in proportions fit to make solid road.*

No doubt we did get the sham measure by way of Mac-Adam. But how? By the way his women and children cobbled up their conical heaps to be measured by the yard. It is the superannuated old device of the decayed woodchopper (who is permitted to spend more time piling his wood in "every sizes"

[1] Appleton, recent editions.

to make it measure more, because he is old and feeble), surviv
ing among great corporations.

This worse than thimble-rig swindle permeates all our road
writings, measurements and labor. It is the father of all the
slimy stone roads we have to contend with. It gave us our
crumbling open work, "drainage-layer" foundations, which never
can keep a smooth surface. There is no end to such a fraud as
that till it is run entirely into the ground.

When we contract for six, eight, ten or fourteen inches of
stone road work, what do we expect to get—stone or air? Nobody seems to know, at present, but people of judgment will
know before they will be taxed to make the best stone roads as
common as they ought to be.

About the size of his stone, this was what MacAdam told
the Parliamentary committee:

"If you made the road of all six-ounce stone IT WOULD BE
A ROUGH ROAD, but IT IS IMPOSSIBLE BUT THAT THE GREATER
PART OF THE STONE MUST BE UNDER THAT SIZE."

Stone of even size will make a "rough road" because they
are half air. In making up their little piles of stone to be measured, MacAdam's families of workpeople must have seen that
their chip stone added little to the measurement (as our bully
rock-crushers have seen), but no doubt all the clean stone chips
went on to the pile, while fine fragments and dust, if with a
suspicion of dirt, remained to make a walk beside the road.
MacAdam hated the dirt that was unavoidably lifted with his
stone, no doubt, and took every means to be rid of it, and with
others talked of *washing* stone and gravel. He could have had
no other reason for rejecting small bits of stone.

We are giving too little, rather than too much, space in literature to these low-down and neglected, but most essential,
truths of road making, for the common people, taken together,
who will never see this essay, are always wise beyond what is
printed, having learned all these things by tradition and personal contact, as their would-be leaders should stop to think.

Theirs is literally the all-seeing eye—let us not attempt to deceive it; whipped by road and street taxes for generations, resulting in nothing from father to son but sites for more road taxation, the kindlings of faith and confidence in the hearts of the people wherever they occur, must be treated with rare sincerity, or our last state will be worse than our first.

It is necessary that we should quote some of our bogus "engineering" to precisely show what we are driving at :

> The true principle of roadmaking[1] consists in giving every road two component parts ; one the foundation—to be solid, *unyielding*, POROUS, *and of large material;* the other—the top surface—to be made up lighter material, bound compactly and evenly over the rougher foundation.

This writer of a "prize" paper—through the Massachusetts Board of Agriculture—widely commended in "engineering" circles, is Mr. Clemens Herschell, of Boston. He further ventilates this honeycomb doctrine for roads, so there can be no mistake about it, as follows : " *The point never to be lost sight of is that this foundation course must remain porous, must be pervious to water, so that all water that shall soak through the top covering will find through it means to escape to the ground underneath."*

Mr. Chauncy B. Ripley, of Union County, New Jersey, is described in the *New York Times* as now making roads "*according to contract, rigidly, in all cases,"* where, in the rough bottom layer, "*each stone stands an inch or so away from other stones,"* to provide for the water of the surface, "*which percolates through the stone"* of the top structure.

No child, properly experienced in its mud-pie stages, can possibly grow up to have faith in this cob-house arrangement of stone remaining in place as stated, in the crush and grind of a roadbed.   Yet this road making is going on at a cost of "*about* $10,000 *per mile,"* while the same journal says of the same county in New Jersey, "*roads that have been considered of the first class, and that have cost enough to make a solid and durable*

[1] From newspaper page (in plates $1.50) of the "American Press Association," with offices in all the principal cities.

highway, have been so softened by the wet weather that they have
succumbed to the strain of ordinary teaming, and are cut to pieces
and seamed with dangerous ruts."

With such theories and such work dominating the country, it was high time for a National "Committee of Better Roads."

In case radical repairs are proposed on an old stone road that is full of ruts, holes, frequent low spots of considerable area and badly out of regulation shape in many places, what shall be done to make the best road of it?

First consider the significance of the depressions. What do they mean? Are they *worn*—ground by the friction of travel into softer portions of rock that was unequal in quality? Do they each one indicate some old "porosity" or honeycomb arrangement of texture that has caved in? Or do these signs all show defective drainage—some trouble at the bottom, and a road structure that always leaked like a riddle? That good stone have sunk in a yielding subsoil? Let us make no mistake in this investigation—thorough and positive knowledge is of the utmost importance to a correct diagnosis of all these chronic cases. If these marks show that the road has gone down into the mud with us many times—like a broken-kneed horse—it will go down with us again. For all such muddles the only radical reform is to lift the good stone, break them smaller if they need it, drain the road and relay, roof tight, on a bed of clean sand or fine gravel that will keep the subsoil quiet.

In flush times, when labor is dear, and machines can make money for enterprising parties, it is generally thought cheaper to pile on more stone and sweat taxes out later from somebody's labor for maintenance.

Ninety-nine times in a hundred the fault in old broken stone roads will be found in the subsoil, which was never drained or covered with the stone-floor roof prescribed by Mac-Adam. That soil either boils up through the stone, making mud or dust in their seasons to fly in the travelers' faces, and wash into side ditches, or blow into the windows of houses or upon adjoining lands. Not rarely the side ditches are closed by bulges, caused by frost and travel and the settlement of stone at the side of the water-soaked highway. Citizens of the ditching persuasion smile when they observe citizens of the engineering persuasion providing labor of this kind. Would they be better satisfied if the profits of the swindle were equally divided? Some fear the burden of these foolish transactions in cities tends now to the survival of the filthiest.

The mere grading of the surface with broken stone can be but a temporary amendment of the track which is constantly falling away at the bottom.

In districts long subject to the sinking of stone, the use of sand suggested here may be bitterly opposed by those who have found their account for many years in supplying the subterranean market described, as observed merely from the surface demand. Millions have been sunk in that worse than useless way, as a few careful experiments or cuts across streets will show. From this point of view some old city streets are as full of undeveloped road industry as British turnpikes were in MacAdam's time.

A perfect road—let us repeat—can be built on clay by using sand in place of a large portion of the bottom stone, with a much less depth of both than is supposed necessary of loose, coarse stone alone.

Marshes covered with a strip of sand, where no frost ever enters, will float solid, water-shedding stone road intact under the heaviest travel, as a pontoon bridge, rising and falling across tidal waters, would float the same well-constructed stone road (flexible at the ends next the land), if only a substantial bottom is provided for the stone as good as the sand will give upon marshes free from frost. The value of sand in stone road making is so little known in some sections that repetition will be excused in explaining it on paper. Many illustrations of the general truth of what is here stated will be remembered by unbiased and thoughtful workmen.

Give them stone enough and our steam-roller brethren can crush them in thin layers into'the earth they have already consolidated with their tremendous pressure. Given a rock bottom, and no doubt a fifteen ton roller will grind a thin layer of "even-sized stone " to powder upon it. But this is too much of a good thing. It is a waste of time and material to make roads in layers with all that superfluous energy. And the awkward fact remains that the body of stone we want on a road, if screened, assorted and applied at once, will be porous. No matter how heavily it is rolled, it will be continually crumbling, crawling and wearing in its thousands of shackling internal joints. While shaking beneath the load it carries, it will be constantly settling in every part of its loose substance, but never well settled together. Nature hates a hole anywhere, and taxpayers are learning to despise the roadmakers who contrive holes in the highway. If left to her own devices, nature will keep trying to fill the holes in a porous road with something or other. In her function of earth maker she would like to fit city streets to grow grass. But the good road man will aim to stop that. He knows that ice will form in any interstices he leaves and make mischief with his work. Saturated and frozen-thawed clay of a molasses consistency will gush up from below into all these drainage layer contrivances, whether called " Telford " or " macadam," and when the clay comes up the stone is bound to go down to fill its place. So instead of remaining as rigid as a rock, the porous stone road is constantly working, roughening and getting out of shape with every change of climate, like poorly tanned leather or inferior wood or metal. The only way to prevent this is for the road maker to roll his well-filled material solid with his own cartwheels, and never trust the public to do it.

In dry weather porous road work is too dry, and so wears the faster and dustier; having no solid seat on the soil and no capillary connections, it fails to receive that modicum of moisture from below needed to prevent its getting dead dust dry in hot weather. But for the "drainage-layer" little or no artificial watering would be needed, and none at all to preserve the road. The idea of capillary moisture for roads may be new to some people. A dry brick set on end upon the ground will show in a few minutes how capillary moisture rises. Whatever of damp-ness a *solid* rock road will imbibe from the earth or air and hold, is an undoubted benefit to its constitution.

Mr. Macadam failed to tell the committee of Parliament all he knew about roads, because it did not, *and probably did not know enough to question him closely.* In his instance of the swamp road between Bristol and Bridgewater, where broken stone was proven to wear longer than over a bed of dry rock, a part of the difference was, doubtless, due to the uniform condition, as respects moisture, of the broken stone on the marsh road. A certain amount of moisture, to *remain* in it, may be said to be necessary to the *life* of a stone, as it contributes to its weight and solidity.

Our philosophy of stone road work has been entirely wrong. Building on hundreds or thousands of three-legged stools, set side by side, would be no worse in theory than our reliance on a bottom of loose "macadam" or "Telford" stone, certain to settle into the ground sooner or later. Judging our faith by our actions, we have believed that if we only kept piling on stone enough we should some time touch hard bottom, and till then there was no use trying to smooth the surface of a constantly sinking road. Once in a while a street gets a coat of small stone, ironed, but the spots that went down before soon go down again, like the foundation legs of the stools aforesaid, which have merely been lengthened at the top.

Could we look under an old stone road and see the loose material disconnected and hanging there (like the ragged edge of the milky way), only waiting another thrust from above in the Spring of the year to go down still lower, we should see how these things are, at once. Indeed, the stones in many cases will settle of themselves (like plums in a custard pudding)

unless we drain the clay and put something there to stop all
movement by preventing the earth from rising.

Common road business is no more a State than a National
affair. The grand principles of it apply everywhere alike.
Barring frost—which acts little upon rocks, nor on the best artificial stone floor roads, that are also roofs over their own foundations—local road conditions in city and country, North and
South, are very much alike, and transcend all State lines. The
State right, as well as the town and individual right, to go blundering in such a universal concern as roads, is already denied in
the minds of thoughtful men. The road doctrine really fit for
Pennsylvania will be far better than any we have yet formulated
for any other State in the Union. MacAdam in his time was
the great British consolidator of little road trusts to secure
efficient management.

Private road making should not pass without sharp criticism
here, for its sins in construction, "reconstruction," care and
maintenance add vastly to the general confusion. The amateur
road maker, around his own house, in lawns, parks and in ceme-
teries, belongs to one of our dangerous classes. He should
learn right away that the water which destroys his roads and
walks would fertilize his grass. Also, that a narrow, rotund
water-shedding surface is its own protector, and that nice rock
road will need no raking, nor the raw plowman's mark of cut
turf edges, and only while new an occasional stone picked up.
Private roads are worn out a hundred times more by needless
surface water and the pernicious garden-rake than by all the
use they get. Public mismanagement of highways would not be
so widely prevalent were it not nursed in the wealthiest private
places, so that the eyes of children are blinded to the most
staring highway evils. The boy who sails his first boat in the
gutter walk to his mother's front or back door will grow up
accustomed to the guttering of earth roads. Common roads
were always a Slough of Despond, and so they must continue to
be. We have a larger nomadic population than the Turkish

empire has, bred from earliest childhood to be regardless of good or poor roads. Is it not worth while to say that deep cut private roads and footpaths are survivals from the landless times when small suburban proprietors played the old gardener's trick of sinking the legs of the spectator to enlarge the apparent extent of the grounds?

Earth roads go to ruin everywhere in lack of surface drainage, and ready appliances for securing that, at all commensurate with the need or the ingenuity and mechanic contrivances fitted to a hundred concerns of far less importance.

There are iron pipes enough for steam, gas, water and sewage. Cement and clay pipes also—but nothing—absolutely nothing—in this age of mechanics nicely fitted with silt basins and heavy convex iron gratings for conveying water neatly and completely from grass to grass beneath a walk or road ! Even for city parks there is nothing but some clumsy, costly, laborious, and frequently not durable, effective or convenient adjustment of stone and brick to unfit iron grates and some kind of paving. If from any misfit or change of plan the masonry is moved, the expensive structure tumbles into a heap of ruins as if it were only an earthen water bar.

Here, certainly, is immediate and profitable work for the pattern maker. Stone culverts are too bulky for many of the occasions for cross-drainage beneath highways. The low, rough broad conduit is much more liable to choke with silt, rubbish and ice in a frosty country than the cheaper smooth iron pipe would be, near the surface, where it can feel the warmth of every thaw as snow and ice does. Let us cordially invite iron men into our stone road councils. We can't get along without them. It is well known that in foundries many pieces of pipe perfectly strong for road work go to the fire again because slight defects are found under steam pressure. With the proper fittings—inlets and outlets—(patent rights being reserved to this new road movement)—there is not a thriving town in the United States but would buy a hundred of these indestructible conveniences as soon as they learned the use of them for surface drainage of highways, and save money by it.   As for individual trade—no housekeeper who can afford a teakettle and prizes a clean doorstep will be without samples of the smaller sizes as soon as they can be introduced.

Cement and vitrified pipe are used with success under roads and railways, and would be more used, even for conveying considerable streams, if it was thoroughly understood how reliable they are when immovably packed in gravel, sand or coal ashes, so that frost cannot disturb them.   Enclosed in a perfectly unyielding matrix, they are able to support all needful weights.   It is difficult to get two of a trade to agree, but the suggestion here is quite in order, that if the different kinds of earthen pipe were made to match, the public would be better served.   In the use of earthen pipes for roads sales would be larger, also, and those of iron as well, if inlet and outlet pieces of iron were made to join with earthen pipes and take the end and outside friction.   Two long iron bolts between the iron ends would hold the whole together under many a highway.

During recent dark ages, while we have been locating and grading country roads, using the many forms of road scrapers for that business, ambitious machine drivers, seeing the power of moving dirt they could control with a little finger, have made the tillable surface of the road too wide in many places— only enlarging the area of mud and dust.   With the use of broken stone and narrower roadways in many country places, for good wheeling, grass for gutters and slopes of the road will naturally come in.

The children of prairie settlers do not bear in mind how well the wild sod once upheld the wheels of travelers, and a mistaken notion has been imported from less sunny climes than ours that trees always injure a highway.   Some varieties of trees, on the contrary, both drain the road and help hold an earthern surface together by their root fibres.   Here is a branch

9

of road science quite neglected—North and South, East and West.

Those who have observed woodland roads closely know they are *dry* except when below the general grade of the land or actually swamped with water. At any point of temperature a tree, even in Winter, and without any leaves upon it, is evaporating moisture from its twigs, branches and trunk. It must freeze very deep to prevent all root action, and whatever moisture roadside trees may draw from the roadbed will, by so much, prevent the tendency to muddiness in any loam road well filled with tree roots. In private road making the writer applies bonedust heavily in the concave roadbed to encourage the root drainage of avenue shades.

Beside the draining and drying effect of tree roots, the fibres given to the soil by some kinds of trees (well known to plowmen in all countries) have a most salutary effect in holding the earth together. If the soil be rich, the whole substance of the raised and rounded roadbed may be completely filled with horizontal stitches, as the housewife darns and runs the heels of stockings, thus trebling their ability to resist friction. Roots in the surface soil are better than brush to hold up travel when they are alive and pumping water out of the ground. If we are looking for economy, nothing can be cheaper than the way a maple, elm, cottonwood or white pine will fill the surface of an earth road with fibre. The chestnut, hickory, ash, black walnut and beach may all be thought of in this connection, but only the close student of nature, and the adaptation of trees to soils and situations, will succeed in this branch of road making. Yet the nation has many thousand miles of muddy highway where no other improvement seems possible.

There is a use for the overhanging branches of trees in Winter. They shade the road and permit it to freeze or remain solid when, but for the shadow, the road would be softening in the sun. The branches work in this way to prevent and protect their roots from being cut in pieces. The traveler and his weary team, swamped in thawed earthen roads, are glad to reach the frozen track on the North side of a bit of woodland. And the man who would cut away roadside shades so as to let all our earthen roads thaw out and settle together, is very much mistaken.

Time, rather than money, would be required to make a perfect tree road across a tract of black soil, and while the travel was light and the trees small, grass and tile-drainage would help greatly in preserving the integrity of the rotund highway, made narrow and with deep ditches. The best grasses would be the natives of the country. Panicum virgatum, andropogon provincialis and chrysopogon nutous are three good ones, with national reputations. Agropyrum repens and poa pratensis would be bottom grasses if the soil was deep, moist and rich. The extreme Southern States will have better grasses of their own. These would hold till the trees, by their roots and shade, begin to take possession, and with proper management and not too much travel in softening weather, never will quite give up the land.

The writer has so little hope of being understood in these purely rural particulars, that he begs the attention of naturalists, and the privilege of telling a story of the London school-girl, Mary Cooper, who was asked to explain the word " turf," a thing she could not have been familiar with among London pavements :

[1] " But Mary had plenty of determination ; she felt that her very life almost depended on giving an answer, and she lost no time in exercising her little brain to the utmost for some sort of definition ; and just as the inspector was saying, ' Well, never mind, child, I will pass on,' she eagerly exclaimed : ' Turf, Sir, is grass and clean dirt stuck together by God.' "

This definition gained the " highest mark " of the British School Inspector, and the saying of little Mary Cooper, of London, who only knew turf, probably, as described by her mother

[1] " Very Original English," Jarrold and Sons, London, 1889.

or grandmother, will not be taken amiss by the road surveyors of broad America. And now we may go to our stone roads with fresh determination to understand them.

A single instance of private enterprise will show how the engineering profession suffers for every caper cut in its name, and worse in the country than in town, because farmers are sharper critics of earthworks than city people:

A certain country gentleman resolved on having the best possible roads around his house, and secured a trusty man, as he supposed, out of a metropolitan city, to construct them in a scientific manner. There was no rock crusher to be had then, but the best of road stones were quarried in a difficult place at a considerable distance and carted without stint. Following his city "system," this so-called "engineer" had the rock all cracked small enough "to throw at a dog," and screened and assorted into four or five different sizes, *a la* rock crusher. These were placed like eggs in flat layers, each size separately and growing smaller towards the top, in the flat excavation, without ever a wheel or a foot touching them—planks being used for barrows—till the top was rounded with the finest stone, and the whole was heavily rolled by hand till everybody was tired of it.

The first team to try the new road happened to be a loaded four-horse furniture wagon, when, in the words of an eye-witness: "Hurroo! squash goes our Summer's work! knocked into smithereens!" Ruts, with excruciating rock edges, were the marked characteristic of that road for many years, or till it was covered with ordinary gravel. Stone road making got its quietus in one considerable section for a quarter of a century by that unfortunate beginning.

The whole arrangement by which road stones are assorted in too finical manufacture at the crusher, and divested of all fine filling material for the body of the work, is entirely wrong. It defeats every good purpose, is worse than useless, killing to the life of the work, and should be changed at once. Where

do the engineers, who are teaching that rock screenings adulter-
ate road metal, get their authority?

Coarse and fine stone in fit proportions to make solid work
should be delivered on the road together. If the proportions are
right in each load there is no harm if an occasional stone is too
large for the top of the road. With proper hooks, as the loads
are dumped *above grade on top of the verge head of the fill,*
the large stones are readily drawn toward the bottom next the
sand filling, if that is being used on clay, leaving portions of
every load ready to spread with shovels to the required cross
section. The form of the raw road metal—the unfinished mass
before it is overrun much—will constantly look "too high,"
because it must allow for settlement. The shape will vary with
the width of the road, the quality of the metal, the location, the
nature of the travel and the prejudices of people. The busy
end—the extreme end—of a new broken stone or gravel road
while it is being fabricated should not have a slope of more than
two or three feet, except when it is left nights at a more gentle
incline for the safety of travelers. So every objectionable particle can be tossed forward and buried. But the good road
maker will judge on the spot better than all the rules we can
write for him.

The directions that are constantly given for applying two
or more inches of chips and rock dust to the top of new stone
road work are all wrong. If we were not so ignorant and unre-
flecting we should see how that is adding insult to injury.
When the body of stone below has its sufficiency of fine material to fill its interstices, any surplus of chips and dust on top
of the road will be wasted. A hard surface to endure friction
cannot be made from the fine rock. *A mass of small stones
filled in, bound together and thoroughly well supported are what is
needed to make the road wear long and smoothly.* It will be the
faces of stone as large as we can use that will give the durable
surface to the road—not the rock dust by any means—that is
worn out already; except while clean, for the purpose of pack-

ing. *The more stone and the less dust the better so we make our work solid,* and by the shuffling tread of teams and broad wheels help *as many small stones as possible to bed and fix themselves in the surface.*

In difficult regions for making stone roads solid and permanent, owing to a slippery soil and doubtful drainage, the necessity for filling the bottom and the whole substance of the work tight in every crevice is all the more imperative. *In that case the bottom of the road must be made impervious to the soil or the top will never hold a polish*—no matter what road "system" we are working under. For every particle of soil that works up the equivalent bulk of stone will go down, and the surface must be wrinkled and pock-marked accordingly. Unless we get that idea under our hair we never shall make smooth roads of broken stone. To be rid of hopeless "macadam barnacles" many cities are driven into asphalt.

It may as well be remembered for our comfort, all the while, that *the smooth stone roads we are advocating will cost no more than rough ones*—not one tenth part as much, really, when the whole story is told, and we have all learned our trades—as the abominable stone roads we are now making. These alone are fit to demoralize a nation.

Does any reader think we are criticising American road work too severely? If a knowledge of daily blunders in city streets were as current as cheap food is, there would be no need of this criticism. Our editorial brethren can't afford to meddle with anything that looks like "business" in the time of it ; but they do slam stable doors with great noise after the stock is gone!

For instance : "Toronto has spent more than ten million dollars macadamizing streets which become seas of mud after a few hours' rain. Yonge Street must have had a full million dollars of macadam put upon it. The roadway has been a wretched failure all through its history, and now *is to be paved with cedar blocks.* It will actually cost the inhabitants thousands of dollars to get rid of the macadam and put themselves in the favorable position they would occupy if there were only a dirt road to be dealt with."

It is to be feared the writer of that paragraph lost his situation for telling what was "*too true*." Toronto used limestone. The item is quoted in Bayler & Co.'s "Asphalt Pavements," Springfield, Mass. *Homestead* confesses (March 22d, 1890), to spending several hundred thousand dollars in carting "red gravel," that "in wet weather is as wet as clay would be. . . . But it was in 1855 that the graveling craze was at its height." Springfield is not built on a soil of stiff clay, but many streets are now supplied by "art" with the "red gravel," which is as good as clay for producing mud and a fine penetrating dust. Now, however, the same enterprising city authorities are going into what is called "macadam," to be reported on later. What are these but slow "confidence games," wasting the substance and energy of the people?

It is impossible to feed open spaces in the bottom and centre of new screened stone road work effectively by applying chips and stone dust upon the graded surface. Jagged fragments will not run into the open necks of rough rock orifices like sand in an hour-glass. Let any person try putting five cents worth of Epsom salts into the smooth neck of a quart bottle, and the difficulty will be manifest. Pea sizes and shelly bits of rock, which along with the dust make perfect matrices for the rough stone (ever to remain rough, tough and solid in the body of the road, till called to endure surface friction), will never rattle, work or wash down from the top, except in the shape of fine dirty silt, and this will destroy the coherence of all the stones it touches. A macadam road maker will prevent that peristaltic action.

Let us repeat that the proportion of finer filling to be determined by experiment with each kind of rock, and perhaps for each treatment and locality, must be seen to at the crusher, as every cart is loaded, and by experts at the busy end of the new road. When the road is used there will be no lack of fine matter upon its surface if the structure of its body is not made like a filter bed. These directions are applicable to any "automatic spreading machine" that is built to make a highway as MacAdam would have done it.

Wherever sufficient fine-rock filling for the inevitable crevices between broken stone is not furnished with them—taking into account all settlement by carting and rolling—the presumption is that the job is being robbed of its dues either by ignorance or roguery. While we must continue to assert that modern engineering and the greater part of our road literature have been criminally careless in this vital particular, yet the stuffings of earth and mud we often see being used by misguided workmen, either regularly or furtively, to cover and mix with rough stone, may be a pitiful sign that common labor knows something ought to go among those rocks, rather than of total depravity. *Is it not a modern case of making bricks without straw?*

In the common stone road work we see going on no pains are taken to provide fit packing for the internal and bottom parts of it. Stick-in-the-mud roads are anticipated. It is expected that a large proportion of the stone will at once sink in the mud. *Steam-roller circulars say: "Never mind the mud; slap on the stone, and put our roller to it." Shall we blame the ignorant machines, or their masters, who promote, buy and set them at work?*

Because nature abhors a vacuum, the proper packing of a rock road is often left to take care of itself, with some feeble-mindedness about "drainage layers," which has been noticed in this paper before. But all such half-finished work on slippery earth foundations is a foreordained failure. *Tongues of clay thrust into the bottom of a stone road, to be swollen by water and frost, are the entering wedges of certain destruction.*

MacAdam told the committee of Parliament that in reforming British roads, gorged with rough stone, he raised but four inches of them to break again. If this was his scant practice over tenacious clay bottoms and under heavy travel, it is the weakest point in his whole story. No doubt, some of Mac-Adam's old road foundations, mended too superficially, have been sinking ever since. But we may well question whether his sterling principles had a fair chance even'in his own time. All the sly frauds in England were against him.

Fine chips and rock dust are in great request for private walks and roads, and the reasonable inference is, when there is none to spare for ordinary streets and highways, that influential parties are being favored, or that long lines of streets that have been scamped, to increase fees for maintenance, are howling for temporary repairs and easements which cannot be put off any longer.

The old masters of road making tell us that the surface of ancient highways must be roughened with picks to' produce a bond for resurfacing. We might have a machine made for that business—we already have a very cumbersome one—but retired modern contractors will describe, after dinner, *a much easier way for them. Lay on a coat of rough stone for the public to drive over.* When we see a mile of stone about as big as our heads laid out for us to bang at, we may understand that the contractor thinks it is *our* business to dent each one of those rocks into the surface of the old stone road for him. When that is faithfully and patiently done, by the wear and tear of our teams and vehicles, *then* the valuable contractor will proceed to put on his finer top-dressing! These are the highway robbers of the nineteenth century. Never were worse maggots in the hive of industry.

Schools of engineering have gone blundering. Professors of economic sciences, who have tested their own powers on bicycles, declare, "*It is mud, not grade, which makes common-road transports cost a hundred times more than by railway.*" Our very text-books are evidence against us. Compare any of them with MacAdam's essays, and we shall see how they have kept us on hoary old precedents, degraded by topsy-turvy evolution in the peculating minds of public and private servants, who have studied most for their own mistaken interests.

It would be a curious and amusing, but not profitable, labor to show how, from Telford's craft (did he get it from Mac-Adam's old English four-inch-deep, left-behind road bottoms!), of setting cobble-stone paving roots upward, to leak, beneath his "macadam," we have been led by generations of thieving contractors, through shingling in reverse with flat stone, to catch water, and random rip-rapping of roadbeds on dry land, in view of "porosity," to dropping stones, or anything we can pick up, into holes—like Mark Twain's bluejays—for the pleasure of hearing them rattle! It is high time for a change. But if we catch the least hold of the foundation truths of road making, and study for the whole of them in practice, we shall find that the fathers, here and there in ages past, knew them all better than we do.

We say little or nothing here of the grade, shape, slope, width, depth, or *length* of roads. In our view, these points are not of the first importance. Nor do we enlarge upon the history of road making. The encyclopædias are dry as dust with all that. History can be written in different ways; but what boots it to prove that the original lay-outs of highways in the older States were opposed in every way to centralization? Or that steam transit got its first popularity because it offered to let everybody live where they had a mind to—presumably in the country? Or for road mechanics to spend time arguing that the cheapest and strongest form in which road stone can be put on a highway, is that of a flattened ellipse,[1] while the internal structure and coherence of substance is utterly neglected, common practice about as far as we can from sound principles, and daily theories of road fabrics crazy as bedlam?

Let us quit for a moment, the eternal laws of road metals, and

---

[1] In a short, accompanying paper, the author gives reasons for a concave bottom. A narrow road that will stand, is better than a wider one that will break up and prove a waste of time and material. The Roman Empire did not die of its 8 x 10 feet roads.

consider the forms of statute law proposed in several States. These agree in allowing *city votes with country influences*, to induce rural townships to bond themselves in $4000 a mile, more or less, for a network of *State roads*. Then, according to current notions, contractors are to sally out from cities with huge teams, consisting of traction engines, ten to twenty automatic stone-spreading machines and steam rollers, in one continuous train, and build said roads at magical speed. But are these machine roads to be of the same detestable quality as to roughness and costs for maintenance that cities now groan under? And when the promoters of these schemes have strewn the country with good-for-nothing highways, absorbed town bonds and made sure of all the money, what then? In a time of general depression, with the people begging work and bread, shall we be looking for the second coming of MacAdam to teach us how to make the best of jobs by overhauling those roads, as he taught the engineers and governments of former times? Let it be respectfully suggested that *now* is the time to learn how to make the best roads, before we have disgraced ourselves any more.

There is a view of the social and individual life of a people, the life that lies at a foundation of lasting State and National life (the life our fathers taught and warned us against losing eternally), which must not be forgotten in connection with road making and road legislation, and especially in regard to the way road law is executed. That view, including country highways, we get a practical glimpse of in the *New York Semi-Weekly Tribune* of February 25th, 1890:

GENEROUS RIVALRY FOR ROADS.

After studying the question in every possible light, I am of the opinon that the most feasible way to keep roads in condition would be to hold each person responsible for that portion which extends through or alongside his farm. There would be much more road-working than now, and with better result. I have conversed with several farmers, and they agree unanimously that this would be just the thing to do. A generous rivalry would spring-up between those who possess any enterprise to see which should maintain the best piece of highway. The road commissioner could direct what should be done, and if anyone neglected to perform what is required, the officer should have power to do it himself and charge cost to the delinquent. Extra work could be done by the towns, as now. In any disputes as to divisions of sections where different persons own on opposite sides of the road, the commissioner's adjustment should be final. Being responsible for a certain section would be an incentive to each to study ways and means to keep his portion in best condition, and he could do most of the labor at odd spells, and scarcely feel it. Nobody seems to be responsible for the roads now ; what is everybody's business is nobody's, and all who travel suffer the consequence.

GALEN WILSON.

Instead of being governments for and by the people, our governments are slowly drifting toward being chiefly for themselves. The writer above quoted shows us how we may adopt our road laws, in executing them, so as to revive public spirit, abate inequalities and make every rural district a nursery of road makers.

While we have been forgetting and subverting the road principles of MacAdam, we have also forgotten and perverted the wisdom of the fathers in making every citizen a statesman and a pillar of the republic. He is a traitor who would wean the people from the care of their State highways. State roads, like national marines, must grow out of the hearts and lives of our men and women, and he will be our saviour who will lead lawmakers back by slow and painstaking methods to the care of rural byways and highways. Though he might never use it again, General Grant, when elected to the presidency, suggested to a committee of his ambitious townsmen, who wanted to do something, that they might fix his old walk to the post-office !

Why should we look to foreign examples instead of working out our own safety, with the immense means and all the time there is on our hands ? What country road models has England, for instance, to offer us ? Here is Richard Jefferies' last book saying :

. "The farmers in New York State and Massachusetts can grow apples, pack them in barrels, dispatch them two thousand eight hundred miles to Liverpool, and they can be scattered all over the country and still sold cheaper than the produce of English orchards. This is an extraordinary fact, showing the absolute need of speedy and cheap transit to the English farmer if he is to rise again. Of what value is his proximity to the largest city in the world ? Of what value is it if he is only ninety miles from London, if it costs him more to send his apples about ninety miles than it does his American kinsman very nearly three thousand ?"

Richard Jefferies is dead. It is said he was allowed to starve because he would write things as he saw them in real life rather than as they appeared some time ago in books. For truth is a relative thing, and as Jefferies would hold the glass to actual British back hair, mere bookworms and readers of journalistic echoes could not appreciate his finest points quite at once. He may be quoted yet as an advocate for steam traction on common roads—an excellent thing in fit places, no doubt. But he didn't know all the circumstances of that apple trade. He didn't know that those " cheap " American apples were stolen by one of the confidence games, that when played on a large scale pass for commerce. Jefferies didn't know that the American grower and packer barely received in return enough to pay for the shingle nails used in heading his barrels.[1]

Slow stone road making, like slow agriculture, to pay must be guided by the rising fixed stars of trade, rather than by the occasional comets and meteors that dash across our paths. Man is everywhere alike in preferring to be blundered out of a hundred dollars rather than cheated out of a cent. The American orchardists who " co-operated " in making sweet cider cheaper in the streets of British cities than at their own doors, will bear the fact in mind for generations. The kings of American commerce should know that our agricultural peasantry of the future, selected and manufactured from the alert of two hemispheres, hunted and haunted by all the tricks of trade, are destined to become, and are becoming, the keenest rural residents that ever stood on earth. Local truth only will do for them.

[1] See Secretary Gold in *Connecticut Farmer*.

We do not allow ourselves to be rattled by the lunacies, mistakes or frauds of a period of general confusion. These are simply calculated to try men's souls, as well as their roads, and show the stuff whereof both are made. What we want is easy and permanent wheeling. This depends, first : on the material of the road, the way it is put together, and how it is supported. But if roads are to be treated originally merely as a basis for repairs, patches, and continual taxation for maintenance—the everlasting presence of a standing army of pottering road-menders—we neither want them nor their work. Both are nuisances to be abolished, rather than necessary evils to be endured.

The infinite pains, care and cost given to the maintenance of surfaces on stone roads, whose bottoms are continually settling, may be likened to the expense and trouble of puttying and plastering cracks in the walls of edifices whose foundations are constantly sinking. Who can take pride in either?

The idea most generally accepted at present about stone roads among ordinarily studious people, seems to be that the mysterious going down of bottom stone into clay is unavoidable —perhaps "unknowable." Daring investigators, intellectually, say these wandering stones have about the same effect in anchoring a highway that the driving of piles through quicksands into the deep hardpan have in steadying a building. To such among others this paper is respectfully dedicated.

We don't want the country governed by its ignorant streets as cities are, but by its intelligent people, hence there must be a diffusion of knowledge as to the texture and structure of highways.

Those who will have the substance of a road essay reduced to the brevity of a telegram or a newspaper scrap to stick in their hats, will find the gist of this one in the following sentence:

The best stone roads will have thorough drainage, and a bottom impermeable to clay, covered with a smooth, water-shedding, floor roof, of pure, hard, crushed rock, rolled solid by broad-tired carts, delivering stone fine enough to fill its own interstices, and large enough to endure travel.

ROAD MAKING AND MAINTENANCE.

HONORABLE MENTION. PAPER No. 13.

BY

EDWIN SATTERTHWAIT,

President Cheltenham and Willow Grove Turnpike,
Jenkintown, Penna.

As there has been already enough written and published on the subject of road making and subjects connected therewith to make a respectable-sized library, and as all of these are more or less valuable, and most of them within reach of all who may desire to gain information on the subject, it would seem as though about all had been done in that direction that could be done to further the greatly-desired object—of improving our roads. Road making cannot be learned wholly from books. Like every other mechanical art, the only way to learn how to do it is to do it. There are, however, some questions of vital importance which continually present themselves in the practical operation of the construction and maintenance of roads, which, though they have been discussed by the most renowned experts since road making began to assume the dignity of a science, cannot yet be considered as satisfactorily settled, and which can only be solved by the light of observation and experience; and there is much information needed of a local nature, such as the relative value of materials required that may be within reach of a given locality, as well as the best mode of using these, and I shall endeavor to confine myself to such questions of a practical nature as I have gained information upon from personal observation and actual experience.

As to our common dirt roads. Bad as they are, and difficult

as it may be to make them much better than they are, they will
have to be for a long time, with a few exceptions, the only
obtainable thoroughfare for all country districts. It is only in
the immediate neighborhood of large cities that the means can
be obtained for the making and maintaining of a high class of
artificial roads. It is, therefore, of the highest importance that
whatever can be done should be done toward the improvement
of our common roads. There is, perhaps, no subject that has
more perplexed our legislators and all public-spirited citizens
than this. A vast amount of what has been lately published
about roads has been in relation to this branch of our subject,
and any amount of suggestions (many of them rather vague
and indefinite, it must be confessed) have been sown broadcast,
but, unfortunately, with no practical results. No clearly-defined
practical means has yet been devised to put a stop to the shame-
ful manner in which money is squandered on our country roads,
and no good results obtained. Almost every State has, I believe, a different system of road laws, but in all, I believe, the
complaint is the same. Much money is spent, and very little
to show for it. I have very little to propose in the way of legislation. I am afraid the trouble lies deeper. What is wanted is
more honesty. If we could have supervisors honest enough to
insist on having a good day's work from every one employed on
the road, the same as if working for themselves, and men honest
enough to do as good a day's work when working on the roads
as when working elsewhere—that is the only thing I can see
that would remedy the evil. If, instead of the present system
of a dozen or twenty men doing what three or four could and
should do, the supervisor would keep two or three good men,
who understand how and would do a good day's work, constantly employed in going over the roads of the township
making repairs as soon as they were needed, this, with the frequent use of the road machine, would keep the dirt roads in
good condition for less money than is now spent on them. I
believe that all are now agreed that the "working out of taxes"

should be abolished, and that the supervisor should be allowed to employ whom he pleased, and none but good men. It might also be a change for the better to elect the supervisor for a longer term than one year, as one great trouble now seems to be that it keeps him busy all the time looking out for his election for the next term, and the fear of losing a vote is apt to be a stronger motive than the desire for the public good. With these two changes our present system in Pennsylvania, of two supervisors in each township, with the entire charge of the roads, is perhaps as good as any other. It is frequently suggested that the roads should be, in some undefined manner, under the charge of State or county officials. I cannot see any good that could result from this, except the creation of a host of good fat offices to help run the political machine.

I am aware that in some other countries (notably in France) they have a far more perfect system managed by the State with admirable results ; but until we shall succeed in purifying our political atmosphere very greatly such a system would not work successfully here, and it would be the height of folly to attempt it. In the vicinity of large cities and in the thickly populated country districts, where the amount of traffic is so great as to make a better class of roads a necessity, the case is different. And I think it might be well to authorize, by law, such townships as might decide to do so to borrow money sufficient to grade and macadamize, from time to time, their leading and most traveled roads. They have such a law now in New Jersey applicable to counties, which seems to be very satisfactory ; but here in Pennsylvania it would be better left to the townships.

In considering the subject of improved artificial roads the first question that suggests itself is that of the ways and means, as these improvements are very costly, and much money is required somehow to be raised. And the first thing to be settled seems to be, shall all roads for the future be free from tolls, or shall we go on, as heretofore, forming chartered companies, and have the roads maintained by the tolls collected from those who use them? Notwithstanding the unpopularity of this system, and the horror that most people seem to have of paying toll, this seems yet to be the most feasible plan, as far as it can be done, and is certainly as just and fair in its operation as any other scheme of taxation that could be devised. Good roads are expensive to construct and maintain, and there would seem to be no fairer way of obtaining the means to do this than by those using the road paying in proportion to their use of it. I think, therefore, that until some better plan can be devised, legislation should be in the direction of encouraging the formation of stock companies for making improved roads, rather than the opposite policy, which many seem to favor. That good turnpike roads are of more advantage to the public who use them than they are generally to the stockholders, there cannot be a shadow of doubt. In the suburbs of large cities I know of no way in which capital could be invested to pay a better percentage to the public than by the construction and maintenance of the best class of artificial roads in the place of such dirt roads as are common, say in the immediate neighborhood of Philadelphia. I am tempted here, in illustration of this, to give a little experience of my own which occurred within a few months past. I happened to have some hauling to do (a boatload, thirty-five tons, of salt hay) for a distance of seven miles, four or five miles of which were over dirt roads in the city. This, over fairly good macadamized roads, could have been done with ease, with the teams employed, in three days, at a cost of $50. But on account of the condition of these city roads—being hub deep in mud, so that the empty wagons were a load for the teams—it took two weeks to do the work, at a cost of $200, and the horses were then nearly used up. This was more than the whole thing was worth, and, of course, put a stop to that business. These roads, remember, were in the city of Philadelphia. I feel satisfied that the loss to the community from the bad condition of these roads during the past year, in the loss of time and extra wear of horses and vehicles, and the loss from business that had to be abandoned altogether on account of the state of the roads, would make a sum of itself sufficient to macadamize many miles of them. And I will here make a suggestion : Let the city borrow, say a million dollars, which would make a hundred miles of the very best Telford road, and use it on the most traveled roads of their suburbs. These roads could afterward be maintained in perfect order with the money that is now annually spent on them, and the increase in the value of property from this improvement would at once bring an increase in taxes more than sufficient to pay the interest on its cost, and the rapid and permanent increase in all suburban real estate which would follow, and the increase in taxes, would soon doubly repay the city for the outlay. I know it will be objected that the exigencies of machine politics are such that if this was attempted and the money appropriated, there would soon be little to show for it ; but I happen to know that there are parties engaged in the business, who are in every way responsible, who would contract to Telfordize in the best manner one hundred miles of Philadelphia's suburban roads for the sum named ($1,000,000), and would contract to keep them in perfect order for a long term of years at a very reasonable cost, probably less than they are now costing the city.

This subject of road making and maintenance, I suppose, is only intended to apply to country roads, and not to street paving, and when we come to speak of improved or artificial roads only those surfaced with broken stone need here be considered. Gravel has, it is true—where that is easily obtained, and for want of something better—been very much used, and to great advantage in improving roads, but I believe that even in those parts of New Jersey where gravel roads have so much obtained, these will, before long, be superseded by the use of that best of all materials, trap rock, of which the State possesses an inexhaustible supply, and which is now being developed so extensively for road-making purposes.

On the subject of constructing stone-surfaced roads so

much has been said, and all the details are set forth so volumi-
nously in the many valuable works that have been published
on the subject, that it would be folly to speak of it here except
on a few points, which are still controverted and would seem
to bear further investigation.   One of these disputed points is,
whether the material used in surfacing a road should be all
broken small and of uniform size, or should have a foundation
of larger stones covered with those finely broken.   The first of
these systems, called macadamizing, has derived its name from
one who has, perhaps, done more than any other who ever lived
to enlighten the world on the subject and give an impetus to
the improvement of roads.   Stoned roads, before the time of
MacAdam, with a few exceptions, were made without any pretence of scientific construction, and were composed of stones
thrown together promiscuously, and though making a surface
over which horses and vehicles could clamber without actually
sticking fast in the mud, were described by writers of the time
as the most horrible of inventions that could be conceived.
MacAdam, though not the first to discover the advantages of
having the surface of a road covered evenly with stone broken
small and of uniform size, was the first to bring this system
into prominent notice, and, being very energetic and persever-
ing, he succeeded in creating a complete revolution in road
making, not only in Great Britain but in the civilized world.
The peculiar system of MacAdam consisted in having all the
stone on the roads he constructed broken quite small—six
ounces in weight being the largest limit—and after the road
was properly graded, so as to insure perfect drainage and a
slight convexity of surface, these were spread over the ground
evenly at a depth of from five to ten inches, without any admixture of earth, gravel or anything whatever, and nothing to be
laid on the clean stone on pretence of binding, and never with
any stone or anything else by way of foundation.   He persist-
ently insisted that clean broken stone will combine by its own
angles into a smooth, solid surface that cannot be affected by

vicissitudes of weather or displaced by the action of frost. MacAdam always contended that stones laid in this manner would, with the travel over them, become bound together so firmly and compactly as to become entirely impervious to water. And this, he contended, was the whole secret of road making— the great object being to keep the earth dry, the only use of the stones being to form a roof for this purpose; for he says that, after all, it is the ground that is the road, and must bear the weight of the stones as well as the vehicles passing over it. And he says nothing can make so good a road as dry earth, and that the thickness of the coating should only be regulated by the quantity of the material necessary to form such impervious covering, and never by reference to its own power of carrying weight. And he further contends that the wear of the road, from the travel over it, is very much greater where the surface coating is underlaid with an unyielding substance, as on a rock, than when on a slightly elastic foundation, such as dry earth. And for this reason he always objected to a stone foundation of any kind, and insisted that these tended to let in the water to the earth below, which was the destruction of the road. He says that he had always considered such a foundation as a useless and unnecessary expense, but experience had proven it to be positively injurious. And for the same reason he never allowed any clay or other substance mixed with the stones, as he said it tended to make the coating more pervious to water. Mr. MacAdam goes so far as to assert—and he proves it, too, by the strongest testimony—that he has constructed miles of road on this principle over bogs and marshes without any foundation whatever, and they not only maintained the travel and lasted well, but that the wear was much less than on the same road where it passed over hilly and rocky ground.

Perhaps the most astonishing thing which MacAdam claims for his roads is the small depth of the stone he considered necessary. This road over a bog was only from seven to ten inches thick, and he sometimes speaks of four and even three inches being sufficient in some situations. I can only reconcile this with my own experience, on the supposition that in England the roads are not near so liable to be injured by deep freezing as in this country, though MacAdam insists that if the water is rigidly excluded from the ground below, the frost will not harm the road. Though the system of MacAdam, which I have briefly described, is not now generally practiced, and may not be the best for this country, it is impossible to deny but that it has great merit. With slight modifications, it was generally adopted in France, where they have the best roads in the world.

The Telford system of road making, which is now the most common in use here, differs from the MacAdam in having a foundation first made in the shape of a roughly-laid pavement of stone six or eight inches in depth—this being covered first with stone coarsely broken, and then with a coat broken quite small, and this covered with a coat of gravel or screenings from the breaker, and the whole compacted with a steam or other heavy iron roller. It is the common practice to mix some clay with the broken stone in making this kind of roads, to help combine the whole into a solid mass. A road of this class, when carefully constructed and of the proper materials, may be considered the perfection of a country road. In considering the relative merits of these two systems I have been led to the conclusion that for most situations in this country a road on the Telford plan would be the least costly and answer as well or better. In this climate, where frost is liable to penetrate very deep, I doubt whether a covering of the depth that MacAdam specifies would be sufficient, and where a depth of a foot or more of stone is necessary, if one-half of these may be of unbroken stone and of a cheaper quality—as is allowable in a Telford road—a considerable saving may be made in the cost ; and it does look reasonable to suppose that a foundation of large stone, if properly laid, would better resist the tendency of heavily loaded vehicles to press them into the earth and form ruts on the surface.

I can only reconcile the theory of MacAdam, that a mixture of any kind of refuse with the stones is unnecessary and positively hurtful, on the supposition that his experience was not with stone of the hardest and best quality. I consider it most probable that in his experience, which consisted largely in lifting the stones from old roads, and having them finely broken and properly replaced, that much of this material was of a kind that soon ground up with the traffic over them and afforded material for consolidating the mass. My experience has taught me that when the material used is not of the best quality it will consolidate more readily than that which is harder and better. It was demonstrated in making the roads in the New York Central Park—where the hardest and best of stone that could be obtained was used—that no amount of rolling would compact it, when this was tried according to MacAdam's theory of carefully excluding all dirt and other foreign substance. The experiments on these roads were very interesting, and the result quite important, as they prove, beyond all doubt, that very hard broken stone will not combine by its own angles into a smooth, solid surface. The experiment here was pushed to the extreme of wearing out the stone by abrasion, and had to be abandoned.

I think it may now be considered as settled that where the best material for road making is used, such as good trap rock, or even the best quality of furnace slag, the screenings from these or some other substances must be used to help consolidate them. And, again, when we consider that the interstices in a body of loose broken stone comprise one-half the bulk of the mass, and when pressed as solid as it is possible to get them, the open spaces comprise one-fourth of the bulk of the mass, it is hard to conceive how this can be impervious to water, as MacAdam says it will be, unless the crevices are filled with something.

As regards the maintenance of a road of this class, it seems hardly necessary to say that the way to keep it good is never to let it get bad. In nothing is the old adage of "a stitch in time" more applicable. Every Telford or MacAdam road should be watched over by a careful superintendent, with material always at hand to level up and smooth over all inequalities as they appear. This is not only the best, but it is, by far, the most economical method of keeping a road in repair, for there is nothing more clearly demonstrated than that the wear of a road increases in a geometrical ratio as its condition deteriorates. It will, however, sometimes happen, where the travel is very heavy and continuous, that the road will become so worn as to require a complete resurfacing. It is recommended in that case that the surface of the old bed be slightly loosened up with the pick before the new material is spread on, so that the whole will combine better and form a solid mass. There are now machines in use for doing this, in the shape of a steam roller with a pick attachment, which are said to do the work better at a great saving of labor. The advantage of compacting a road with the roller before it is used for traffic is so obvious as to require nothing more to be said on it. If not done with the roller, it must be done by the travel, which is bad for the road—as it wears away rapidly in the process—and bad for those who use the road to be compelled to do at their own cost what should be done by those having charge of the road.

The questions of the materials to be used, and how to obtain them, are of the greatest importance in road making, and are often difficult questions to determine. It would seem to be a common notion with many who have essayed to enlighten the public on this subject that stones suitable for road making are obtainable on every farm, and that all that is necessary to do is to encourage farmers to have them properly prepared at their leisure and delivered on the roads. On the contrary, though there is an abundance of stones on most

Pennsylvania farms, those suitable for making a first-class artificial road are quite uncommon. Stones gathered promiscuously from the surface of the fields, though they may do very well to patch up a bad place in a mud road, are mostly very unfit to use even on the poorest kind of a turnpike. Even if generally of good quality, they are sure to be mixed with soft and worthless ones, which spoil the whole. Even where there are quarries of hard stone they are, for the most part, of stratified formation, with layers of different degrees of hardness, and, even if generally good, are devoid of that uniformity which is so essential to make a good road. And, besides, a quarry of road stones, to be worked to advantage, must be extensive enough to warrant the erection of a breaker, and must be situated very near to a railroad, so as to have a track so convenient that cars may be loaded direct from the crusher. Breaking stone by hand will soon be a lost art in this country. Stones for surfacing a road should not only be of uniform hardness, but must possess the greatest possible degree of toughness. Perhaps the best measure of the quality of stone for this purpose is its power of resistance to crushing force, though it appears, from experiments that have been made, that the qualities of hardness and toughness are not always the measure of the resistance to abrasion or the wearing away by the contact of horses' feet and the wheels of vehicles. In the selection of the materials to be used these are the qualities to be desired. Those possessing these qualities in the highest degree that I have had experience with are the trap rock from the Orange and Bergen hills in Northern New Jersey. These quarries are now being rapidly developed, and so great is the competition in the business of crushing this rock for road purposes that it is likely soon to become the cheapest as well as the best material now obtainable in this neighborhood—the vicinity of Philadelphia.

Granite, though excellent for paving blocks, and very much used for road making, is very variable in quality, and is mostly,

I think, far inferior to Bergen Hill trap rock for macadamizing. Where this may be considered too expensive, a good substitute is found in furnace slag.

Having, during the last eight years, had charge of a road on which many thousands of tons of this material were used, I have had good opportunities of judging of its value, and of comparing it with the various stones in use. The first thing to note about slag is that its quality varies almost as much as stone, the slag from some furnaces being next to trap rock in value and worth double that from others. I refrain from naming these because I suppose it was not intended that these papers should be the medium of advertising anybody's business. It is a common belief, however, that where slag is cooled when it comes from the furnace by throwing water on it, it makes it brittle and destroys its value for road making. Where slag of a good quality can be readily obtained, its cost is so much less than that of the best quality of stone that I do not hesitate to recommend its use, having used much of it with good results. I could name, as an instance, the main street in a town where the traffic is great and much of it with heavily-loaded vehicles, was coated with slag, which, though too coarsely broken to make a perfect road, made a good road, on which, for five years, there was no perceptible wear whatever. It was then resurfaced with finely-broken trap rock, only to make a more smooth and pleasant road for driving on. In the borough of Norristown they have used slag for many years on the streets in preference to any other material, and with good satisfaction.

Limestone, such as is common in this vicinity, though it makes a nice smooth road for light driving, has no enduring qualities for heavy traffic, and I have not found it as lasting as the poorest slag. There are, however, harder limestones of the older formation that are excellent, and it is claimed for them that they are superior to any trap rock. There are some very extensive quarries and machinery for producing road material of this stone on the Hudson. I have had no experience with it, but, from samples I have seen, I have no doubt of its value.

A gentleman in the road-making business who has a very extensive plant on the Hudson, and who claims to turn out one thousand tons per day of crushed stone, says of his stone: "It may be said, without fear of contradiction, that one hundred square yards of this stone answers the purpose of one hundred and fifty yards of any other stone, not excepting trap rock. True, trap rock has hardness, but the grinding of constant travel disintegrates it, and then it returns to its elementary principles—mud. Trap rock is virtually petrified earth, and, after dissolution, becomes soluble matter. The Helderburgh limestone takes equally as long, if not longer, to disintegrate, and when it does it settles into a cement as firm as any metal can be."

We all, of course, know that every one considers his own the best, but I give this gentleman the benefit of this statement, because, if true, it is very important, and is certainly well worth looking into.

It may be well to give a little idea of the cost of these materials. Most of the iron furnaces now have machinery for crushing slag for roads, and the price delivered on cars varies from about fifty to seventy cents per ton in large lots. Trap rock costs all the way from one dollar to one dollar seventy-five cents per ton on the cars. To these prices, of course, must be added the freight, which, on slag from the furnaces along the Schuylkill Valley to Philadelphia and vicinity, is about one-half that of trap rock from the Bergen Hills, making the whole cost of this just about double that of slag. But as the cost of each in carting and placing on the road is the same, there will not be so much difference in relative cost of the finished road. A mile of road already graded, that could be built of trap rock for ten thousand dollars, would cost from six to seven thousand built of slag.

In this connection it occurs to me that there ought to be

within the reach of those interested in such matters, some means of testing the resisting power of different road materials. I imagine that a simple and inexpensive machine might be contrived that would test, with sufficient accuracy, the resisting power, or the amount of pressure per square inch, a substance would bear.

Just here I desire to say a few words upon the intimate relations that exist between the railroads and road making. So far as artificial roads are concerned, almost everything depends upon the facilities afforded by the railroads in hauling the required material at a moderate cost. Without this can be done, the making of first-class roads would, in general, be out of the question. And I believe there are many liberal-minded railroad officials who are far-sighted enough to see that the prosperity of their business is largely identified with the prosperity of the country contiguous to the line of their roads, and who know that there is nothing that can add to this prosperity more than the improvement of the roads, and who know that the common roads are the natural feeders of the railroads, and who are disposed to aid all they can in their improvement. But I am sorry to say that this disposition is not as prevalent as I think it should be. As an instance in proof of this, which occurred quite lately, I was informed by a gentleman in the business of furnishing road material that a prominent official of a great railroad refused to deliver material for him at a point on their road where it would have been a great convenience to have had it, and gave as a reason that they did not wish to accommodate the turnpike company that wanted the material, as their road was too good already, and was competing with the railroad to the injury of their business. If such a contemptible, short-sighted policy as this was to obtain in railroad management, it must put a stop to all road improvement, as good material cannot now be obtained in most localities except by rail.

I have mentioned the great quarries of Northern New

Jersey and on the Hudson, because these are now being so extensively operated, and not because there is not an abundance of as good material in our own State and within easy reach of this vicinity; but I know of none in operation of much extent. But I am satisfied there are great bodies of the best quality of hard stone on the lines of some of our railroads that might be and would be utilized for road making here if the railroads would encourage the enterprise, as I think it would be their interest to do.

There is a point connected with the making of all kinds of artificially-covered roads that cannot be too much insisted on; that is, that no surfacing should be done until the road is well graded. For it should never be forgotten that while a road is left to its natural state there is a constant tendency to improve the grades of itself, the hills being washed down and the valleys filled up with every rain; but when once the covering is placed the grades are fixed for all time, and can never be improved except it be at very great expense. No road should ever be graded to a perfect level, on account of drainage—this is not desirable—but the hills should be reduced to within two degrees, or about one in thirty, at least, where that is possible. A great advantage resulting from this is that in cutting away the hills and filling up the valleys, places that are liable to quagmires and quicksands are elevated so as to free the road from this danger.

As so much is now said—and very properly, too—about the inferiority of the roads in this country compared with those of Europe, it may not be amiss to say a little on this subject. When we come to look fully into the causes which have produced this disparity, I do not think there is any cause of discouragement; for besides the advantages there of cheap pauper labor, it must be remembered that centuries of civilization have given those countries time to accomplish very much that there has not yet been time for here. And there are other things to be taken into the account. Before railroads and steam navi-

gation were invented all the mails had to be carried by stage
coach over the common roads, and where there were no water
communications all merchandise traffic was by common roads;
so that for centuries road making had been a most important
department of governmental care in those countries. For
example, as early as 1816 there were in England and Wales
alone twenty-five thousand miles of turnpike roads, and this
was just at the commencement of scientific road making. By
that time the work of carrying the mails alone had become
immense, and this required the constant oversight of the government. And a great deal of the time of Parliament had to
be devoted to the ᵈdepartment of roads and the transportation
of the mails. And so it happened that before railroads were
invented all England had become a network of good artificial
roads, and the whole nation had learned what good roads were,
and had become accustomed to them to such a degree that they
had come to consider them a necessity that could not be dispensed with.

This country, on the other hand, had scarcely emerged
from a wilderness state when steam navigation and transportation by rail sprang into existence, and soon claimed the bulk
of all the traffic in the conveyance of persons and of merchandise of every description. The great revolution in the business
of transportation thus created put a check for the time to the
progress of road making, then only just in its infancy in this
country, and from which it is now again just emerging.

Had steam navigation and railroading been deferred for
another half, or even a quarter of a century, we would have
been vastly further advanced in the science of road making.
But it was not to be expected that in a country so vast, where
the temptation is so great for the population to spread over an
immense extent of territory, that it would be possible to make
roads through it all, such as would be looked for in densely-
populated countries, where they have had centuries to do this
work. So that we need not be discouraged. We are now, at

least, making a good beginning, and when once the example is set, and our people learn what a really good road is, it will not be long before they will not be satisfied without them, and law-makers and supervisors and all concerned will have to give heed.

We have in this part of the United States, at least, the material in abundance; we have learned something of what a road should be, and we have those who possess the skill and ability to do the work, and there is no longer an excuse for the lack of means, which should be forthcoming. For every other form of enterprise and public improvement capital is put forth in abundance, and it is universally admitted that there is no way in which money can be spent that would afford a better return than this in its beneficial influence to every member, from the highest to the lowest, of the community.

ROAD MAKING AND MAINTENANCE.

HONORABLE MENTION.   PAPER NO. 16.

BY

CHARLES PUNCHARD,

1223 Hollywood Avenue, Philadelphia.

IN the construction of highways it will be found, on referring to the records of history, that the first place must be given
to the Roman Empire.   Upon its subjugation of a country
almost the first practical improvements introduced were good
roads.   These, when laid out, were more for military and
strategic purposes than for the immediate benefits that might
accrue to the inhabitants of the districts through which they
ran.   The main principles governing their construction were:

First.—To run them in as straight a line as circumstances
would permit, and also sufficiently wide to allow an unobstructed
passage for traffic.

Second.—To have as low uniform grade as the country would
permit, which in some cases would necessitate the levelling of
hills and filling up of valleys.

Third.—To keep the water outlets clear, and the hedges or
fences on both sides of the road at a height which would enable
both sun and wind to act upon its surface.

After the elapse of centuries many of the roads constructed
by the Romans are still in existence, showing most conclusively
that the principles adopted were sound at the start, and that
despite the vast improvements in the way of steam and machinery in modern times, we have not advanced further in the main
principles of the construction of good roads than were practiced·

(160)

by them.   Probably the nearest approach to them has been in the
countries where the highways are now operated under legislative and municipal ordinances, as in England, Germany,
France, and part of the United States.   The immense impetus
toward the improvement of the English roads was given by the
introduction of the so-called *Highway Act*, passed in the
House of Commons in the year 1862.   This act completely took
away the construction and maintenance of roads out of the hands
of the parish officers known by the high-sounding title of
"Parish Surveyors," who, in the majority of cases, were men who
could hardly have answered any simple question upon what
constituted a good road.

   This act, which completely altered the old system of parish
supervision, provided for the establishment of a "Highway
Board," the members of which were made up of one or more
persons from each parish, according to the size or number of
miles of roads.   The highway boards were called upon to appoint
professional surveyors for the districts over which they had
jurisdiction.   They were required to hold meetings at least
once a quarter, to receive reports and other details from the
surveyors, for paying accounts, receiving estimates, and awarding contracts.   Annually they were to publish in the local press
a full report of the state of the highways under their charge,
together with the expenditure incurred during the year.

   The practical working of the act soon showed better roads
at less expenditure, together with a more equitable system of
assessment for the maintenance of the same.   The Highway
Act, from its improved system of equitable assessment, was the
means of attracting the attention of the several Poor Law
Union Boards, and resulted in the introduction, within a few
years, of the Union Chargability Bill, by which the parishes of
the said unions were amalgamated and placed under a similar
system.

   It may not have passed unnoticed, that of late several paragraphs have appeared in the Pennsylvania press from the pens

11

of tourists as to the excellent roads of the "old country."
With such facts as cited above, it may not be out of place to
consider whether such a precedent could not be followed in the
State of Pennsylvania. As it comes directly within the spirit
of the papers desired by the donors of the University of Pennsylvania Road Prizes, it will be again referred to, after the matters relative to the construction and maintenance of roads are
fully considered, and the following subjects have been fully discussed : *What constitutes a "good road?" Engineering Features ;
Economic Features ; Legislative Features ; Summary.*

WHAT CONSTITUTES A GOOD ROAD ?

In the construction of a good road, it will be necessary to
take into consideration the following : *Climatic influence ; Geological formation : Material ; Drainage ; Traffic ; Location ; Elasticity ; Cost and Maintenance.*

CLIMATIC INFLUENCE.—It is a well-known fact that many
roads which have been laid with really sound materials and
apparently fairly constructed, have signally failed in their purposes, owing to the negligence of their constructors in not taking
into consideration the climatic influences of the district in
which such roads are laid. Severe storms, intense frosts, low,
humid atmosphere, sudden, hot drouths with occasional heavy
wash-outs, entail severe strain upon the best constructed roads,
by removing the lighter surface material and converting it into
mud, breaking up or disintegrating the cohesiveness of the
heavier material, and so displacing the sectional divisions of the
road strata. For want of immediate attention to its repair, a
road is left in a weak condition; consequently its usefulness is
gone, necessitating a heavy expenditure to restore it to its original state.

The often serious results of these climatic influences can
be materially lessened and their damaging propensities modified.
Against severe storms and wash-outs there should be provided
properly constructed water outlets, clear, open drains or gutters

and a well-made grade falling from the crown of the road.   These
protections will reduce the force of the surface washings.
Severe frosts are also often injurious in their effects upon roads,
especially in the Spring season.   Care, therefore, is necessary to
see at once to the water outlets, relevelling places upheaved,
ruts in roads which are subject to frequent traffic on them of
heavy vehicles, raked back, and the keeping of the surface to
the original grade.   From an economical point of view, a few
dollars spent at the right time may save hundreds of dollars at
some future period in restoring the road to its proper condition.
The full action of the sun and wind upon the road surface is
another important factor, it being one of the means of keeping
it dry and hard.   Trees should also be kept well trimmed, fences
maintained at a low height, and thus encourage these beneficial
helpers.

GEOLOGICAL FORMATION.—Geological formation is an
important factor, and roads should not be constructed until a
well-drained and solid foundation has been secured.   Many
roads have been made without much thought or care having been
bestowed upon the strata and beds upon which their foundation
materials were laid, and which is shown by the surface of such
roads losing entirely all uniform appearance, and causing constant outlay for their maintenance.

Outside of certain districts and of rocky places, the strata
upon which roads are constructed in the majority of cases will
come under the following classes of soils and sub-soils, viz.: *Silicious, calcareous, clays (both light and heavy), marls and loams
(including swamps and morasses).*

Silicious soils of a silex or flinty nature, and *calcareous soils*
having properties of lime, present no great difficulty in securing
a firm, dry and solid foundation for the construction of roads.
On soils of a *clayey* nature, either light or heavy, it is absolutely
necessary to secure perfect dryness of such beds, which can
only be obtained by a perfect system of drainage, both at bottom
and surface.   *Marls and Loams:* Soils that vary considerably

in their natural properties, classed as rich and poor earths, in many places are intermixed with a large proportion of flint and other hard materials, the component parts of which are generally small. Other marls are softer and hold moisture tenaciously, requiring a thorough system of drainage to enable the roadbeds to be properly made. *Swamps and Morasses*, being of a soft and spongy nature, better known as low, wet grounds, under the name of marshes, fens and bogs, present the greatest difficulties in highway construction, and in several places have entailed heavy charges for their proper maintenance. Such localities demand perfect drainage.

MATERIALS.—In the construction of a good road, it is absolutely necessary to have materials in each of the sectional divisions of good, sound and durable quality. The sectional divisions are now commonly placed under three heads, viz.: *Upper, middle, lower* vertical sections, being the combined principles of the standard authorities, such as McAdam, Telford and Law. It is necessary that each separate section of its construction should be laid in the gradient form of the proposed formation of the road, from the fact that the traffic is more upon the centre than on either of its sides, and helps to keep the cohesiveness and component parts in more compact form and elastic state, preventing displacement of its materials. The materials of which the several sections are formed may be described as follows :

LOWER SECTION.—Solid broken rock, rough cobbles, iron slag, slate refuse, shale and similar heavy substances from the various quarries. As such materials can be obtained in almost any district in which roads are required to be made, in more or less quantity, constructors should be guided, of course, in the selection of the material by the facility with which it can be procured.

MIDDLE SECTION.—Materials of a porous and yet durable nature. These qualities are found in burnt clays, stones taken from silicious or calcareous soils, broken rocks, or similar hard and durable substances, which should be broken to a size that would pass through a two and one-half inch screen or ring, and of either cubic or angular shape. Here, again, constructors should be entirely guided by localities.

UPPER SECTION—Lighter and smaller materials of a strong, dry and durable nature, not easily disintegrated, which will retain their solidity after severe tests of sun and frosts, or sudden change to either high or low temperature. These qualities are found in small broken rocks, crushed stones, from out of silicious soils, stones from sand or gravel pits ; cinders, also, are at times used where the traffic is light, and in such cases are useful, but on roads over which a large amount of heavy traffic is constantly passing, are not recommended. The size of the material should not be larger than would pass through a one-inch screen. The immediate surface of this section should have smaller material, such as gravel or heavy sand, that would pass through a one-half inch screen.

It may be well to define what is meant by the term "burnt clay," as its introduction for use in road construction is of comparatively recent origin, and, as yet, has not been extensively used, but may, ultimately, come into general use. The use of burnt clays, or ballast, is limited to districts that are known to have subsoils of white or blue clay, and, as a matter of economy, in the construction of roads through such, it is found to be as cheap and as desirable material as can be obtained. The *modus operandi* is as follows :

Take a road that has to be constructed through a heavy clay district ; one of a medium width—say a local road twenty feet wide. In Summer weather, or during the hot season, the soil in the proposed road should be cut out to a depth of two feet into large spits and laid roughly one upon the other and left in that condition for about ten days. By that time the sun's rays will have evaporated the moisture held by soils of this nature. So soon as the spits are dry, they are submitted to the action of fire in the following manner : A circle is formed fifteen feet in

diameter, surrounded by a wall made of the roughest and largest
spits, two feet high ; in the enclosure thus formed, straw or
other light combustible material is laid ; faggots or small pieces
of wood are placed on these, and over them are placed other
spits, so as to form a cone or pyramid, the whole structure to be
about eight feet high.   Fire is then applied to several parts at
once, due care being taken to see that the spits sink evenly
until the whole mass is well alight.   After being well banked,
the mass is left for a day or two, and as soon as it attains a good
red appearance, is drawn down, the wall broken, the spits are
thrown on top, and others added as required, from day to day,
until all the earth dug has been submitted to the same process.
In a length of 100 yards of road thus served, it would take about
six fires to burn the 12,000 cubic feet contained therein ; the
cost of labor would probably be twenty or twenty-five cents per
cubic yard.   The burnt earth is then, after cooling, relaid upon
the road and forms the middle section, and now, being of a
thoroughly porous nature, settles into a good, dry, solid layer,
and will last for years.

DRAINAGE.

Drainage is one of the principal features in the construction of a good road, often sadly neglected, and, in many cases,
beyond a few outlets made adjoining the surface edges, no other
facilities are provided to carry off excess of water.   *It is apparently forgotten that the natural cohesiveness of materials will
allow them to contain moisture equal only to their capacities, and
that any excess of the natural absorption must be injurious and
ultimately ruinous to their durability.*   A properly drained road
consists of one that has all surplus water, whether upon the
surface or in the body of it, beyond the natural capacity drawn
off, and this is secured by adopting such of the various means
of drainage as are suited to the locality.

The several methods of draining a road are as follows : Clear
surface outlets in the shape of a gutter or open stone drain on

both sides of the road; a proper grade from the centre to the sides, and in wet or stiff land districts it is necessary to have underdrainage in the shape of a pipe or stone drain on one or both sides. These should be sunk to a depth of one foot below the roadbed, laid with earthen pipes two inches in diameter and twelve inches above the pipe filed with rough stone. Or drains may be laid to run transversely or diagonally to the road section every fifty or sixty feet. One great desideratum must not be neglected—an outfall must be obtained to allow the water from the drains to have unobstructed egress. The size of the pipes (terra-cotta preferred) may vary from two to three inches in diameter in light land districts. Where the land is heavier, pipes of four inches diameter may be required, and in the case of a drain built directly under a road, carrying water from adjoining lands, and where, for obvious reasons, a wooden or, even, brick culvert would be objectionable, iron pipes of a suitable size should be used. Great care must be exercised in the case of roads in swampy or low wet lands. In such instances it becomes imperatively necessary, in order to effect proper drainage, that the land should be drained on either side of the road for a considerable distance.

TRAFFIC.

Roads and streets inside of cities and boroughs are regulated by city and municipal ordinances. Highways are generally divided into two classes, viz.: Main roads or pikes and cross roads, known as common roads. The traffic, as a rule, is very heavy upon the main roads, and such are subjected to severe strains. For example, a carriage, the wheels of which have narrow tires, and loaded heavily, will cut and grind deeply into the surface or upper section of the road, often displacing the material, and other vehicles almost invariably follow the same track, thereby forming ruts which, after a storm, form impromptu gutters, and if left alone for a few days before being repaired, cause great injury to it.

The wear and tear of traffic upon roads leading into towns, etc., is at times heavy and well calculated to test the strength of the best constructed highways, hence, for careful maintenance, require constant looking after, and material should be kept at places easily accessible to the sections of the roads that are subjected to such usage. The bad effect of heavy traffic upon roads not properly drained soon becomes apparent and should have immediate attention to prevent heavy expenditure for reconstruction. It is also of considerable importance to keep the surface of the road smooth, which can be economically done by occasionally repicking, that is, loosening the surface by means of a mattock or pick, and raking to its uniform grade. This will tend to keep the traffic distributed evenly over the entire surface, and which is what a good constructed road, and one kept under proper maintenance, should have, viz.: a uniform wear and tear upon each and every square foot of its surface, which prevents displacement and assists in keeping it in a proper, elastic condition.

LOCATION.

The location of roads has arisen from accidental causes, more especially from the necessities of earlier settlers than from any well-defined plan, except where the lines of the old Government surveyors have been adhered to. Roads in new localities have been necessitated principally owing to the juxtaposition of railroads and the springing up of new towns in consequence, and it will probably be due to such like causes that will determine the location of other roads. It appears unnecessary to deal with the question of future location of roads, which may be called for by the growth of towns and the extension of the railroad system of the country, our present purpose being to deal with the highways now in existence.

ELASTICITY.

Another great feature in a properly constructed road is its elasticity. Uniform traffic upon the surface tends to distribute the wear and tear of its component parts, so that they offer equal resistance, and enable the road to keep its solidity, cohesiveness and elasticity. Roads retaining these properties cause less friction and shaking to both vehicles and pedestrians. Such qualities are only to be obtained by exercising proper precaution in construction, compactness and cohesiveness being thus assured. This may be illustrated by noting the different effects in driving or walking upon asphalt roads compared with those constructed of hard stone and like materials.

COST AND MAINTENANCE.

The cost of constructing a good road depends greatly upon its location and convenience to materials, the latter being a very heavy item of expense. Geological formation and drainage are also to be taken into consideration as important features. It is difficult to give approximate estimates without plans and specifications. As a general rule the cost will average from $4,000 to $5,000 per mile, this varying with the proposed width of highways; on main roads the width should not be less than thirty feet, and where they lead into towns it may be necessary to extend the width to fifty feet. The vertical sectional divisions of roads upon those of the main roads should not be less than fifteen to twenty inches in depth, those on crossroads from twelve to fifteen inches. These sectional divisions would increase upon nearing places where traffic is heavy.

The present system of maintenance, as practiced in many townships, by which the supervision is entrusted to a road supervisor, elected annually, and is not responsible beyond having his accounts audited, is altogether unsatisfactory. His chief interest is to keep upon the best terms possible with the constituency which elects him, rather than in keeping his highways in a first-class state of preservation. He is in constant fear of exceeding the appropriation for his district, has to contend with the many suggestions of self-interested taxpayers and the threat of others that unless he moderates expenses their vote will be withheld for his appointment in the ensuing year—all these place him in such a position that, however skilful he may be, he is deterred from fulfilling any well-devised plan that may be suggested, and the effects of such supervision are invariably shown in the inferior roads of that district. This state of affairs is substantially the same as existed in England before the introduction of the "Public Highway Act," and calls for immediate reform, the subject being discussed further under the head of Legislative Features, and which has a direct bearing upon Road Making and Maintenance.

The most important rule of maintenance is to keep the road to its original surface formation, and to secure this must receive careful and constant supervision, the amount of this depending on the traffic. Where that is of a heavy character the maintenance is, of course, proportionately large. Keeping ruts raked down, hollow places filled, surfaces kept to the original formation, water-courses kept clear and materials accessible for repairs, are direct necessities. Where traffic is light there is only need for occasional supervision. The cost of maintaining a properly constructed road should not, for the main roads, even when subjected to heavy wear and tear, exceed $100, and may not exceed $75 per mile; that of crossroads should be from $25 to $50 per mile. These figures apply only to properly constructed roads, and include cost of both labor and material.

The direct methods of maintenance come under two heads :

First.—Labor required.

Second.—Contracts for materials.

The carrying out of the work is under the control of the supervisor, but contracts may be for both labor and material. No contract should be entered into for a section exceeding twenty-five to fifty miles. Practical experience has shown that, under such contract system, highways can be more economically maintained than under the present system.

The Bureau of Highways (or street commissioners) of large cities at times labor under great difficulties, and are unable to keep the cost of maintenance to a minimum, owing to the constant tearing up of streets for the purpose of laying gas and water pipes, electric conduits, enlarging of sewers and the laying of street railway tracks, but the treatment of such hardly comes within the scope of this paper.

PATHS.

Pathways or sidewalks usually adjoin the main roads, and become a direct connecting part of them. The introduction in recent years of bicycles and tricycles has led to a demand for better supervision and maintenance of both roads and sidewalks. Special attention is necessary in the vicinity of towns and other thickly populated centres. The usual method adopted hitherto has been to make them either of wood, flagstones, brick, asphalt or other prepared ingredients, besides the ordinary materials used upon the roads. Wood has been freely used for many years, but, owing to the now greater difficulty in obtaining it at a moderate price, other descriptions of material are fast taking its place. Flagstones of various widths, generally about two to six inches in depth, are commonly used in such parts where the traffic is heavy. These, however, are gradually giving way to such materials as are of a more elastic nature, the public preferring the elastic to the heavier material. Bricks are occasionally used. These, however well laid, are affected by climatic influences, which have a tendency to soon destroy their surfaces, and the wear and tear of the traffic pulverizes them, so that practically they are soon broken up. Asphalt and other prepared ingredients, such as concrete, have of late years come into more general use, and as yet have held their own, both on roads and paths, and bid fair to come into very general use. Paths are made of the same material as used for the roads. Which is the best procedure to adopt will depend more upon the localities and traffic than on anything else. Paths should be raised higher than the centre gradient of the roads they adjoin, have a level surface, and the edges of both sides secured by curbing of heavy material.

SUMMARY.

Having now considered the details required in the construction of a good road under the various heads of the effect of climatic influence, the importance of the geological formation in securing a solid foundation, sound, durable materials, proper drainage, the effect of traffic on the surface, location, elasticity, and the important features of cost and maintenance, we will proceed to consider the

ENGINEERING FEATURES.

The engineering features of construction, reconstruction and maintenance of highways, with the advantages of thorough *scientific treatment*, are described under *Scientific Highway Engineering* and *Practical Highway Engineering*.

Scientific construction of a road requires some estimate of its probable traffic to arrive at the ultimatum of " *What is the greatest weight a road is capable of resisting without displacement of its sections or disturbing its angle of repose?*" A properly constructed highway would easily withstand a pressure of ten tons on every square yard of surface. So far this hardly applies to common roads, but to those of cities, from the vicinity of which heavy castings, locomotives, etc., are sent, necessitating special attention, and this point is worthy of consideration. An experienced observer will have noticed how frequently this application has been practically ignored, and, as a direct consequence, such streets are constantly entailing large sums for maintenance. Many streets, when first constructed, have the appearance of having been properly formed, but owing to one great feature ignored, viz.: the want of a solid concrete bed upon the foundation, to enable the upper section, composed of heavy stones, to resist the force of heavy traffic by proper support of its own weight, soon shows its weakness, gets quickly out of gradient and entails heavy charges for maintenance. This can be avoided, and where streets are subjected to heavy traffic it is a direct necessity that they should have their upper section upon con-

crete of not less than fifteen to eighteen inches in depth. When
properly performed, the only maintenance required is the occasional use of sweeping machines, the upper section being such
that it would last for thirty years or more. It may not be out
of place to mention that concrete laid by the Romans in some
parts of France is still in existence, and the only changes in
these original roads have been the renewal of the surface of the
upper section from time to time.

SCIENTIFIC TREATMENT of the question of the traffic upon
common roads would require statistics of the average number
of vehicles daily passing to and fro, under the following heads :
Vehicles which weigh from   8 to 15 cwt.
      "   "   "   "   15 to 20   "
      "   "   "   "   20 to 40   "
with the important consideration of the width of the wheel
tires. A heavy strain is often thrown upon the road by heavily
weighted vehicles whose width of tires is not in proportion to
the weights carried, consequently a deep incision is made in the
surface, and in some cases the component parts of the middle
section are displaced, resulting in heavy cost for repairs.

SCIENTIFIC TREATMENT demands that roads upon which
there is heavy traffic should have daily supervision. It would
also require a change in the method of hauling heavy timber,
and prohibiting its being dragged directly upon the surface,
thereby displacing its sectional parts. Without exception, heavy
timbers should be hauled on suitable carriages.

SCIENTIFIC HIGHWAY ENGINEERING (excepting special
requirements beyond those already mentioned) is rarely needed
upon the local or common highways ; it applies more directly to
cities and municipalities under the supervision of highway
bureaus, who have to deal with many changing measures and
with large and growing centres, calling for the application of a
higher class of engineering.

PRACTICAL HIGHWAY ENGINEERING.—In the construction
of local highways, it is first necessary to have carefully prepared

plans of the location, details of the geological formation and
information as to climatic influence, quality of materials that
should be used, approximate estimates of the traffic, etc. A
practical highway engineer should be competent to deal with
any of the ordinary bridges, culverts, or side abutments called
for in a local road, and prepare plans for bridges over rivers or
streams. When it becomes necessary to open up communication with roads over a river of say from 100 to several
thousand feet, it may then become necessary to have plans and
specifications prepared by a competent civil engineer.

A practical highway engineer should possess the ability to
make all ordinary surveys and estimates of the cost of materials
to be used ; also thoroughly understand the proper placing of
the sectional divisions, and see that proper drainage is effected
to secure a dry bed before laying the road. He should also
have a good knowledge of the durability and other properties of
materials, and should make himself well acquainted with the
geological formation of his district.

RECONSTRUCTION.

It may be well to state that the following directions apply
more particularly to the reconstruction of roads that are now in
existence, the majority of which have been laid without much
scientific or practical knowledge of what constitutes a good
road, rather than to such as have been properly constructed.

First, it is necessary to remove all dust, mud and soft
materials from off the road.

Second, to bring the road to its proper gradient, this being
done by either of the methods known as *lifting* and *loosening*.

LIFTING is adopted where the road is found to warrant the
addition of material without disturbing its lower section. The
present material upon it is removed for a depth of four inches,
all large stones taken out, broken to size of two and one-half
inches, then adding other material as necessary, resurfacing
to its full gradient.

LOOSENING is adopted when the road only requires resurfacing. It is done by simply picking it about an inch or so in depth, adding material as necessary, thus enabling the new and old to fully incorporate. In reconstruction it may be necessary to see that proper drainage is given. On old or worn-out roads it may be judicious, if the materials are almost wasted away, to remove them and proceed as in the formation of a new road.

WASHOUTS frequently necessitate the reconstruction of the greater portion of a road. It is important, therefore, to provide, as far as possible, against a recurrence of them. To take up a road and relay it in some adjoining locality is merely a question of labor properly applied. Such of the materials from the old road as are suitable, and could be reused in the lower and middle sections, should be thus dealt with, entirely new material being provided for the surface.

SCIENTIFIC TREATMENT OF ROAD MAINTENANCE consists in holding to one rule, that a properly-constructed road should have its uniform gradient to keep it in such condition as to have its surface and under sections retain their uniform state, thus reducing its wear and tear to a minimum. Scientific treatment *tells this*, but here it requires the *practical* highway engineer *to see that such details are carried out.* One other important factor in maintenance is that the traffic upon it is so regulated as to subject the whole body of the road to an even strain. A road well macadamized, such as are seen on first-class turnpikes, with a uniform fall of grade, is the least difficult of roads to keep in repair.

The practical highway engineer takes care to have immediate attention given to the repair of any broken places, all ruts carefully raked over, and no hollows left in the road to form receptacles for water. He will also see that all materials have had proper exposure to atmospheric influences before using. This is a matter which is often overlooked. The practical advantage is that all materials being subject to abrasion in moving, exposure to the air removes the soft encrustments, so that only hardened materials are used. A roaa, when regularly looked after, will require less raking and expenditure of time and money than one which receives spasmodic attention. In the first case the mud and softened materials are at once removed, in the latter they are left to accumulate. Another important feature of maintenance is the proper use of the material raked from the surface. In many cases the accumulation is put into heaps, left to dry, and, after a time, is used to fill hollow places. The practical highway engineer acts differently ; his course is to pass the surface rakings, when dry, through a one-quarter-inch screen and use only the heavier parts. Of later years the introduction of machinery specially adapted to road construction, such as traction engines, automatic stone spreaders, stone crushers, steam rollers, sweeping machines, construction wagon trains—these being used separately or in union—has provided road constructors with such facilities that a new road can now be expeditiously made, and with far less trouble than formerly.

ECONOMIC FEATURES.

ECONOMY is as applicable to highways as to public or private expenditure, and the golden rule of "The maximum of benefit at the minimum of cost" should be the leading idea in road construction. The progressiveness of the age demands the better education of the people to the necessity for a high standard of roads and the immense advantages of good over imperfectly constructed ones. The economic benefit of a good road can readily be seen by: *Its cheaper maintenance; greater and easier facilities for traveling; less cost for repairs to vehicles; corresponding relaxation of strain upon animals drawing same, and consequent saving of time ; ease and comfort to those driving over them.* It is well known that a horse will draw a much heavier burden over a good road than over an indifferent one. From the experience gained in recent years the advantages just stated are so apparent that it should excite no misapprehension of the fact that the time has arrived when the people are inclined to appreciate them, and are determined to have them, on the ground of economy. The most important factor of maintenance is the question of cost. The charges are reduced by the fact that a properly constructed road requires less maintenance; the charges for materials are also lessened, and when, from any cause, reconstruction is necessary, the economy is demonstrated by the reduced expenditure required. Economy in expenditure will be shown later on, under the head of "Legislative Features."

Increase in the value of property adjoining first-class roads follows their construction, as is proved by the rise in price of land having the advantage of proximity to macadamized or turnpike roads. The necessity of presenting a tabular statement of the economy of good roads may be saved by quoting an adage well known to those versed in highway principles, viz.: "It is cheaper and easier to maintain a good road than an indifferently constructed one." The economy of maintenance depends entirely upon the system employed. The present system, under which the greater number of township roads are maintained, is not of an economical nature, and it is absolutely necessary, for the sake of greater economy, to place their control under a more skilful and liberal management, and this point is also dealt with under "Legislative Features."

LEGISLATIVE FEATURES.

HIGHWAY LEGISLATION is attracting attention from the fact mentioned in the last annual message of the Governor of Pennsylvania, in which the subject of better roads was mentioned, resulting in the State Legislature enacting a law providing for the appointment of a commission to revise and consolidate the statutes relating to the construction and improvement of roads, and to consider the question of further State assistance for same.

12

GOOD ROADS, WITH EQUITABLE TAXATION FOR THEIR MAIN-
TENANCE, is the great point and leading feature for legislative
enactment. Equitable taxation means the gross assessment of
a district to be used for the equal benefit of such area, and not
as in the present system, under which each township is separately rated and has to maintain its own roads. For example,
some townships have in them many taxable properties, besides
farm lands, while some adjoining townships, with the exception
of farm lands, possess no valuable industrial interests, but, at
the same time, they are expected to maintain their roads to the
standard of their more fortunate neighbors.

HIGHWAYS, as a rule, are *pro bono publico*, and such legislative features as are hereinafter stated will tend to place each
township on an equality with its neighbor, so far as the burden
of maintenance is concerned. One of the best arguments for
legislation on this subject may be illustrated by the following :

WHAT WAS THE ORIGIN OF TURNPIKE TRUSTS ? Under the
old system of highway maintenance, each parish took charge of
its own roads and bore the cost of such repairs as were necessary. They naturally spent as little as possible, and receiving
no aid from outside sources, the roads were in bad condition.
Roads leading directly from one large town to another, and upon
which the traffic was heavy, demanded that something should be
done. Turnpike trusts were established, possession of the
direct roads given them, which were at once put into good order
and came under proper maintenance. The public was charged
a fee for vehicular use of same, which was readily paid. These
trusts, controlled by legal enactment, were of great benefit in
educating the people to the necessity for legislative statutes
that would place all other highways under the same benefits.
The introduction of good macadamized roads under the Turnpike Trust attracted attention and public recognition.

Another illustration in favor of State legislation would be
to cite the effect of the *English Highway Act*, as mentioned in

the early pages of this paper. Prior to the operation of that act, the cost of maintenance of roads was upon an average £12 to £20 ($60 to $100) per mile per annum. They were, as a rule, kept in a bad state, and under the control of incompetent persons, remained so. Within three or four years after the introduction of this act, the roads were very much improved. The contract system for either labor or materials for twenty-five or fifty miles of road became popular, and economy in expenditure, as already mentioned under economic features, was quickly shown. The former cost was greatly reduced, and with this remarkable difference, that for a cost of £8 ($40) or £10 ($50) per mile per annum (at times even less) the public had good roads at a much lighter cost. In the proposed enactment empowering a commission to revise and consolidate the present highway statutes of the State of Pennsylvania, these statutes having a local rather than a general application, it might be advisable to repeal the same and formulate a new statute covering the construction and maintenance of highways of the whole State.

It would be advisable that counties, precincts or districts be formed into highway bureaus, having charge of an area of say 400 or 500 miles of roads, excepting cases of counties, precincts or districts, where it would be more convenient to join one or more small counties, precincts or districts together if the mileage of each is small. These bureaus would be composed of representatives from each township in such county, precinct or district, and their number would be regulated by the mileage, say one member for each twenty or twenty-five miles. They would meet at stated periods in some centrally located place, as may be selected, and would have brought before them all estimates, contracts, reports of the local civil engineer and all other necessary business.

The appointment of a practical highway engineer; and his remuneration would be in their hands. He would hold office as long as he faithfully preformed his duties, which would consist in personal supervision of all roads in his districts and seeing that all contracts were properly carried out. All orders for labor and material would be made out and signed by him and countersigned by one member of the board, then passed by the whole board before the treasurer paid the same. He would make an annual report embracing the state of the roads, the amount of expenditure, and should include an estimate of the following year's outlay.

The members of the board would be non-salaried, but would receive an allowance for mileage and personal expenses attending meetings. The secretary and treasurer would be paid officers. These boards should be under government inspection. The government inspectors' duties would be to visit each district once a year, go with the highway engineer over the roads, audit the accounts of the board, and report to the State Legislature. These government inspectors to be paid by the State, and beyond this, except in special cases as below, the State assistance ceases.

An occasional demand for a loan from the State to some highway board may be made for the purpose of draining a large area or other heavy improvement upon its roads. These loans would be repayable by instalments within twenty years by the owners of the property so improved. The boards would also have the control of all new roads, subject to the right of appeal from the petitioners, and when refused by the board, should be definitely settled by the Supreme Court of the State. There is but little doubt that this form of control would quickly result in cheaper roads, with one great difference, that the taxpayer would have *good roads* for a less cost than what they are now under, viz.: Roads spasmodically attended to, and, as a general rule, not one mile in ten can be called *good*.

It may not be out of place here to give comparative examples of the old and new systems. Take ten townships whose mileage is about 400 miles, and the average appropriation, judging from one closely adjoining the city of Philadelphia, was, last year, nearly $45,000, or an average of $112.50 per mile. This is a low estimate, probably, as one or more townships are recorded as having appropriations of $6,000, or an average of $150 per mile, for their forty miles.

UNDER THE NEW SYSTEM.

Ten townships; with 400 miles, the Board consisting of twenty or twenty-five members, the expenditure would be about as follǒws :

Twenty-five members' mileage and all incidental expenses incurred by the Board during the year, about	$1,000
Highway Engineer's salary	2,000
Secretary	500
Treasurer	500
Four hundred miles of road, properly maintained, including main and cross-roads, at $75 per mile	30,000
Allowing to be expended on new roads	11,000
Total	$45,000

The ultimate result would be that the whole district would have really first-class highways, and all properties adjoining such would be greatly increased in value.

STATE ASSISTANCE.

The growth of civilization has irresistibly developed National progress, especially in the improved means of transportation—

First.—By turnpike roads.

Second.—By canals.

Third.—By railroads.

In the last two years much has been said about the national surplus. With such a plethora of money it would be of interest to expend some in the shape of loans, extending over thirty years at a low rate of interest, for the improvement of the various State highways and helping the weaker ones, so as to enable the same in time to assist their highway bureaus, and long before the time of repayment arrived the whole roads of the nation would have been put into good order, and thus materially add to the benefit of the people.   In the suggestions under the head of Highway Districts, boards by enactment would have vested in them, to hold in trust, all real and personal properties so far as the making of highways is concerned.   Under the provisions of the English Highway Act the powers of the board are limited in respect to expenditure by taking the amount of highway expenditure of each parish for the three years preceding the introduction of the act as a basis, and striking an average; beyond that, it would be necessary to obtain the consent of four-fifths of the ratepayers of such district; also in the obtaining of loans on mortgage of the highway rate, the terms of repayment are limited so as not to create an assessment of more than tenpence in the pound (4 cents on the $1) at any one time, and that the aggregate payment should not exceed in any one year more than two shillings and sixpence in the pound (12 cents on the $1). State assistance, with such form of protection, would be of inestimable benefit and of material use to both cities and country districts.

SUMMARY.

In conclusion, it is respectfully submitted that an endeavor has been made to comply with the spirit of the circular issued asking for essays, believing it requires more the *scientific and practical principles of the art of road-making and maintenance for the better education of the people to a necessity for State legislation for its highways,* and has treated more particularly the construction, economic and legislative features in such form, rather than giving any detailed method of construction, which would vary considerably with location, and necessitate plans and specifications for correct estimating, and concludes with the hope that the State of Pennsylvania may soon have *good roads, with equitable taxation for their maintenance.*

MARCH, 1890.

ROAD MAKING AND MAINTENANCE.

HONORABLE MENTION. PAPER No. 19.

BY

GEORGE B. FLEECE, C. E.,
Memphis, Tenn.

Modes of construction may be uniform only under like conditions. The ruling conditions are physical and financial—
which vary so widely that it becomes impracticable to compass
the whole problem in appropriate details—the nearest approach
being suggestions general in their application.

It may be assumed that good roads are a necessity anywhere
as ruling conditions of prosperity and progress, social and pecuniary, and become in this view appropriate subjects of legislation
and public support, with more or less relative importance as
special conditions may require.

In old, established and densely populated countries, the ruling
requirements are social and economic. In new territory they
become prominently developing agencies, and supplement other
less valuable speculative means of "booming" the country.

The value of good roads everywhere justifies their construction at any cost within reasonable bounds, varying according to
the nature of the object in view.

The following will apply as general, ruling conditions :

For country roads a general county tax on property and
polls should be levied, and this should apply to the whole county,
including municipalities.

This fund should be applied first to radial roads reaching
out from municipal centres so as to accommodate the bulk of
travel which is ordinarily in the line of largest trade and inter·
change.

Still, there are instances in which county highways are parts of long and important highways connecting cities or points of production with points of shipment or sale, and such roads may take precedence in order of importance over radial roads leading from county towns and large cities.

Provision should be made whereby individual contributions may influence the distribution of funds to any extent consistent with the accomplishment of the main end in view—to wit: the construction of county roads on lines of greatest general importance.

The limit of taxation for road construction would vary with the conditions, such, to wit: as relative demand, and existing financial conditions—such as taxable property, indebtedness, etc.

In some countries, notably new territory, owned and occupied by a vigorous and enterprising people, speculative considerations might justify expenditures on public roads far in excess of a normal and judicious rate in older established communities. Estimating for the latter, whether municipal or rural, it would be safe to fix the limit of total property taxation in cities at 2.5 per cent., and in country districts at 1.5 per cent. of taxable values, while the poll tax for roads upon every male inhabitant between the ages of 21 and 50 should be about $3. Within these limits, it would generally be a wise and remunerative scheme to approach a perfected and thorough system of roads and streets at such a rate of progress as would finish the work in twenty years, keeping pace meanwhile with increasing population. The average city and county cannot compass the work in a shorter time without a rate of taxation that would be seriously oppressive. But, of course, there are many localities where without serious or oppressive taxation the desired work may be accomplished in a shorter time.

All roads should be owned by the community and free to use as public roads. Roads built by individuals or corporations, and operated for individual or corporate benefit, place serious limitations upon trade and travel, and throw the burden of their maintenance generally upon a community of working men, who, while they are the most valuable element of ordinary communities, are at the same time least able to bear it. And further, when roads are paid for and owned by the community—each paying according to his pecuniary ability—the burden of taxation is uniform, equitable and seldom oppressive ; while the aggregated wealth of a community may accomplish with ease that which individual or corporate capital would never undertake without assurance of profit largely in excess of what the heaviest general tax should be.

The end in view being the construction and maintenance of country roads, upon the best modes possible within ordinary limitations as to means, which should be drawn mainly from taxation, I would suggest the following :

Not intending to attempt to formulate now in detail appropriate provisions for a general road law, I would suggest some ruling requirements of any road law intended to accomplish the end in view.

The proper administration of a public fund intended to be expended in the construction in detail of a comprehensive system of public roads, requires the simplest and most concentrated system of business management, as nearly like that of a private enterprise as may be safe and legally practicable.

The agents employed should have the required experience and intelligence for their respective duties, together with all necessary authority and clearly defined personal responsibility. Such an agency would be a board of road commissioners and an experienced civil engineer. This board should elect from their number a chairman and a secretary and treasurer, and it should appoint an engineer. This would complete the official road organization for the county.

Such a concentrated plan of organization will at once be recognized as a vast improvement upon the existing system, which devolves upon the county court—a cumbersome body generally of ordinary men, often fifty in number—the conduction of a business requiring special skill, personal attention in detail and large expenditure of money.

ENGINEERING—CONSTRUCTION.

We will suppose that an engineer of experience in road construction is employed with all necessary authority, to wit : to prepare forms of contracts, specifications and details applicable to the working execution of same—establish grades, alignment, and width of roadbeds, depth and width of ditches, both coincident with alignment of road and lateral so far as necessary for thorough drainage of roadway, together with such other powers as may become necessary or advisable to exercise, such as changes of alignment of established roads in cases in which important changes may be effected, and such police powers as may be necessary to prevent damage, etc.

Under such supervision the practical work of road construction should be conducted step by step as follows :

First, an instrumental preliminary survey should be made with a view to final location and construction. Such a survey with level and transit will afford data upon which to obtain all information properly preliminary to final location and construction, to wit : width of roadway at every point, maximum grade required, points in which it may be expedient to change or amend alignment of old road, number, length and capacity of required bridges and culverts, high water levels of streams, quantities of earth or stone excavation and embankment, average haul of each, etc.

Upon these data estimates of quantities and cost of construction should be made preparatory to letting the work of contract ; and contracts should refer to these estimates as being approximate preliminary estimates of work to be done, but subject to such alterations of grades, alignment, width, depth, etc., as the Board of Commissioners may choose to make, the *final* estimate only to determine the exact amount and value of work done by the contractor. Said estimate to be made by the engineer in charge, and his estimate under the contract to be final as between the contracting parties.

In awarding contracts, while it should be the rule to accept the lowest bid, yet it would be necessary to provide for the utmost liberty in making the award, the several elements of relative ability, experience and character of contractors to have due weight as considerations determinative of the proper award.

After said and such preliminary surveys, etc., and before letting to contract any part of the work, such a portion of the year's work as may be accomplished by the county or State workhouse force, also that of taxpayers who may be allowed to commute their poll tax with equivalent labor, should be reserved out of the section or sections to be put to contract, but under such arrangements as would provide for progress *pari passu,* so as to insure progressive completion in regular and not conflicting order.

So far as found practicable, it would be best to embrace in one contract all the work, earth, stone, bridges, culverts within a given section, so that conflicts and consequent loss may be avoided.

MODES OF CONSTRUCTION.

Beginning at city limits, the width of a graded roadbed should be twenty-four feet, with ditches through cuts five feet wide on each side, so that the top width would be uniform, while the side ditches should continue to connection with bridges and culverts, following the outer line of embankment in unbroken grade and alignment, at no point nearer the base of embankment than two feet. These ditches should slope in cuts from the edges of the graded roadbed to the outer line of ditch, at a depth of fifteen inches below the crown of earth roadway generally.

But if the line of drainage be long, the width and depth of side ditches should be accordingly increased, so as to afford assurance of capacity enough to carry without overflow the entire volume of water.

The outer slope of ditches should start from lowest point and take a slope outward from the roadbed to the top of the cut of from one-half to one and one-half to one, varying within these limits according to the character of the materials.

In embankments slopes should be one and one-half to one, this being the general angle of repose. But in rock cuttings the sides may be vertical.

In laying out the work, the engineer will find that in order to preserve the alignment, his main line of reference should be staked out seventeen feet from the centre, thus marking in cuts the outer line of ditches. With this line fixed by permanent stakes, the contractor may easily follow his plan if furnished with a profile on which the depths of cuts and fills should be written in plain figures at every station of 100 feet. It is impracticable on travelled roads to preserve the centre line.

In building embankments it is necessary to allow for more or less settlement as the manner of construction and character of material would indicate, the main modifying circumstance being the mode of construction.

Embankments built with scrapers are necessarily compact in the ordinary mode of using them, and such embankments may be generally accurately finished to grade, while embankments made with dump-carts should be raised above grade about one-half an inch to the vertical foot, and those built with the wheelbarrow or thrown up from the sides should be raised above grade about one and one-half inches to the vertical foot.

The width of roadway should diminish as the road is extended from city terminus, being generally twenty-four feet for the first mile ; twenty-two feet for the second ; twenty for the third ; eighteen for the fourth, the latter width being the minimum except in stone, in which a width of fourteen feet, as a matter of economy, would be admissable.

GRADES.

Generally, the maximum grade should not exceed three feet vertical to 100 feet lineal ; and while it is often necessary to raise the maximum to as much as ten feet in 100, such grades are very objectionable, increasing the hazards of travel in sleet and snow and imposing serious limitations on maximum loads.

It should be remembered, also, that the maximum grades, whatever the grade of other sections of the same road, rules and limits the pulling capacity of every team passing over it.

Inasmuch as travel increases as the city terminus is approached, maximum grades should be avoided near cities as far as practicable, while approaching the country terminus grades may be steeper.

Long grades, especially when steep, should, when practicable, be avoided, for two reasons. First, because they impose a protracted strain upon teams, often injurious, or requiring teams to stop, with the hazard of backing down grade or balking when required to start again. The second objection is the acceleration of currents of water in ditches, with the consequent violent abrasion of banks. So it would be advisable to break long grades with occasional stretches of level or descending grades. Again, level grades through cuts should be avoided, a slight descent being necessary to allow surface water to gravitate along side ditches, leaving the roadbed well drained after a rain.

The surface of a graded roadbed should be rounded up to a crown at the centre of about six inches above the level of the outer margin in all cases in which the road is to be finished as a dirt road, but when formed to receive a covering of stone or gravel, the finished crown of earth surface should have a rise of four inches in twelve feet.

In all cases, earth work should be done early in the Spring, so as to become compact before the rains and frosts of Fall and Winter ; and so far as may be convenient, this state of solidity should precede the spreading of stone or gravel.

Still, it must be considered that the spreading of stone or

gravel should also be early in the Spring or Summer, for it favors assurance of solidity to give it the time for settlement under travel before the rains and frosts of Fall and Winter.

But this would not be compatible with the best results in one season, and the best approach to this would be to push the grading to early completion and follow with the superstructure, beginning, say at the city limits and completing in the order of completion of the roadbed.

BRIDGES.

Bridges may be of iron, wood, or iron and wood combined, and these may be constructed upon a variety of plans. The engineer in charge may readily choose between them with little risk of error when he knows the relative price of iron and wood at the site or sites at which bridges are to be constructed.

Generally, iron bridges should be used for all spans exceeding fifty feet, and in many localities are the cheapest.

The engineer will find that in any locality near a railroad, bridges may be purchased and erected at a low rate per foot, which, being designed, often patented, and in every case fully tested as to strength and adaptation, may be relied on. So, also, may such wooden bridges be obtained in the same way. So that the engineer in charge may be fully competent for his position, even if his experience in bridge construction, or his scientific knowledge of the principles and details involved, may be limited.

Bridges of twenty feet span and under may be of the utmost simplicity, consisting only of stringers, flooring and stable points of bearing at the ends.

The simplest and best plan for such bridges would be to use only one size of timber, to wit: 2 by 12 plank. These, when used as stringers or floor beams, may be doubled and spiked together at intervals of four feet, with a strip of one-inch plank between, and spiked through. In all cases the required thickness of stringers should be obtained by using several thicknesses of plank all bound together, instead of one stringer of equivalent cross section—for the reason that the first will last longer, will require less labor or machinery in erection, may be obtained for less money and makes a more reliable beam.

Flooring in all cases should be secured at the exposed ends by a strip of like timber spiked down over the ends, thus preventing curling up under the influence of the sun.

Generally, the entire floor of bridges of fifteen feet span and under should be covered with gravel or broken stone, when such material is used in the road bed.

In my experience such a treatment results in great economy of maintenance—the flooring being thereby relieved of abrasion under the wheels, and lasts twice as long as when not so protected.

In alluvial soils, when timber is used in abutments, they may be of the very simplest form, consisting of caps, posts and a backing of two-inch plank. The posts, in such cases, should be sunk in post holes about five feet below the water bed, the posts, caps and stringers being securely fastened together.

For spans of twenty-five feet the stringer should be supported by braces abutting against a king post at the centre, or by suspension rods beneath. Spans of forty feet should have three panels, with queen posts and straining beams above, or suspension rods beneath—each upon plans in detail known to all engineers.

When spans exceed forty feet, the bridge should be a truss, with panels of about ten feet, the height and width being increased with length of span.

Often serious obstacles to the construction of cheap gravel roads are encountered in bottoms boggy and occasionally inundated. Means may not be available to pursue a permanent plan of construction embracing high embankments, etc. In such cases it may be sufficient to provide a practicable crossing after subsidence of floods.   This may be done cheaply by building at such point a

PLANK ROAD.

Such a road should be built flat on the earth's surface, and should consist of longitudinal stringers resting on cross sills, plank flooring spiked transversely on stringers, and all anchored and securely held in place by downright timbers spiked at the top and every outside joint to the stringers, and sunk into the ground vertically, like posts, about five feet deep, and well rammed for stability.   All the lumber may be 2 by 8 except mudsills.

Such a road will stand intact under a heavy overflow, and will be available for travel until it rots.

CULVERTS.

Culverts may be of wood, stone, brick, terra-cotta pipe and iron.   Of these, wooden culverts are the cheapest, but should be avoided when considerations of economy do not make their use compulsory.   When used, they apply to openings of five feet and under.   When the opening must be larger, it would be well to adopt the bridge form.   No culvert should be of less than twelve inches inside diameter.

For culverts of two feet opening rubble-stone masonry or terra-cotta may be used—the cheapest at the locality to be adopted.

In laying terra-cotta pipe, care should be taken to place the several joints well down upon the natural surface, in perfect alignment, with a slight fall, say three inches in thirty feet. Place the flange end downward, jam the ends well to close bearings, fill around with earth and tramp hard.

The lower end for two joints should rest on a firm foundation of stone or brick or timber, extended as an apron four feet below the end of pipe.   The common practice is to close the joints with cement, but this is an unnecessary and often troublesome expense. In laying hundreds of such pipes in the last six years I have never used cement, and have found no necessity for its use.

Arch culverts are very expensive, and the cases in which they are necessary or advisable are rare, except in cities.

SUPERSTRUCTURE.

The supposition is that the country road will be built of broken stone or gravel, these being the best, or certainly as good as country districts require and can afford.

As to the material, stone and gravel, the value of these relatively should be determined by the special peculiarities of each and their relative cost. Generally, broken stone is the best, yet there are varieties of gravel better than any quality of broken stone.

Taking limestone as the standard for macadam, any gravel of greater uniformity of size, hardness of substance and smaller dimensions is a better material for roads. When gravel is angular in shape, hard like flint and of uniform size, of, say the size of a pea to that of a pigeon egg, it will form a road bed hard, compact and durable, and almost absolutely water tight, and become, under the settling and compacting influence of travel and time, a homogeneous mass, solid, smooth of surface and capable of bearing without sinking or cutting the heaviest loads ; and this until it is worn down to a thickness of three inches or even less. But to insure this, it should be treated as follows :

The earth's surface should be smooth, dry and compact and settled to what may be called a final repose ; time, rain, travel and rolling will accelerate this, the most favorable condition for receiving gravel ; but in practice, it will not generally be found practicable to await such conditions.

However, avoiding a muddy and rough or uneven surface, it will generally answer every important requirement to begin gravelling on a smooth and dry surface, hard enough to hold up, without cutting, loaded gravel wagons of four inch tread on tire.

The earth's surface being slightly rounded up to a crown of about four inches, the gravel should be spread with a vertical depth of eight inches, loose at the centre, diminishing to three inches depth at the sides, the surface being left a flattened vertical curve, the width of gravel being twenty feet for a twenty-four foot earth grade and fourteen feet for an eighteen foot earth grade. This should be rolled with an iron roller six feet long of 8000 pounds weight, with three cylinders of four feet diameter, each working freely and independently on one axle, beginning on the sides and finishing in the centre, and repeating in sections as long as possible, as many times as may be necessary to secure a perfectly smooth surface of the utmost solidity attainable under such a process. A heavier roller will heave up a mass of loose gravel in front and will not answer.

After the rolling, travel may be admitted, but this should be followed by a regular system of surfacing, thus retaining the designed form of a road bed until the surface becomes smooth and fixed.

Generally this condition of superficial smoothness and solidity is attainable in a few days, the length of time being varied by the quality of gravel, amount and character of travel and the kind of weather.

Gravel with a slight admixture of coarse sand or iron deposits will settle promptly, and in some cases *concrete* to the solidity of stone.

But any species of gravel with the aid of dry sand or clay will, under travel, find final repose and become compact—almost water tight—and hard and stiff enough to resist abrasion or sinking under the heaviest wagon travel. This might be assumed theoretically, and is absolutely demonstrated on forty miles of gravel road built under my personal supervision in the last six years.

Such a road, whether constructed of broken stone of a size that will pass through a one and one-half inch ring or less, or of gravel, may be called the standard country road, and while it has not greater original stability than the Telford road, is never. theless better and much cheaper for the following reasons :

1st. The gravel or broken stone covering will not sink into the subjacent earth by its own weight, nor is it so liable to sink as it would be if the bottom or so-called foundation were rubble stone, as in the case of the Telford pavement, for the gravel bed, after becoming compact, arches the subjacent earth bed, making a natural homogeneous bond with it, and its weight, together with its load, is borne mainly by the arch crowning, and gravitation downward is arrested by the distribution of the weight over the entire under surface.

It is not true, as theoretically assumed, that the weight is " transmitted from the point of contact downward in the line of a cone, the base of which is to the apex as the square of the vertical depth," for while this is true of a weight or force all of which is extended on the bottom, it is not true in the case under consideration, for the weight or force is arrested by the bond of the mass through which the force must act ; so that the weight or force superimposed must crush through the compacted and interwoven integument of the mass before its direct influence is felt within the theoretical area of its natural spread. The weight that is transmitted through the gravel superstructure must first crush through the top crust. As long as the surface stands intact the bottom is unaffected. Therefore, if the superstructure of a compacted gravel or broken stone bed will not sink or break through and disrupt the bond, there is no need of a foundation of stone under it, except for drainage ; for it would but rest there, inert and useless, until such a superficial disruption should occur, and this will not occur as long as the gravel bed resting on an earth base shall be of more than three inches in thickness, as has been demonstrated to my perfect satisfaction, after knowing the results of travel on such roads for more than thirty years, and particularly on forty miles of such road bed built under my personal supervision.

I state it with perfect confidence that there is not a known instance of a wagon, loaded less than 8000 pounds weight, cutting through or disrupting the bed and bond of a properly constructed gravel or broken stone road of any compacted thickness exceeding three inches in depth, if properly drained.

Again, if such a roadbed will not sink or disrupt under heavy travel, it must be all that is necessary to meet the end of sufficient stability.

But it may be proposed to compound the structure, making the base or so-called foundation of rubble stone, with the fine material on top, as the Telford.

To this there are serious objections :

First, the surface section should be as deep as in the case of an earth base, for it is upon the integrity of the bond that we must rely for stability, and this bond cannot be effected in homogeneous and interwoven bed without a homogeneous mass. So that when there is a top gravel bed and a bottom rubble stone bed, the bond is broken at their line of contact. If the top be not strong and self-supporting, the natural and inevitable result will be a grinding force active along the line of contact, or line of change of material, the processes of grinding and wearing on the surface and at the gravel bottom, together with the disruptive effects of pounding between opposing forces, resulting in rapid ruin of the upper or gravel covering.

This result, naturally enough to be easily foreseen, has followed the Telford plan in sections of road built under my personal supervision, and the only remedy I have found has been to reconstruct, tearing up and removing the rubble, regrading and covering with broken stone or gravel.

But it is claimed that a substratum of rubble stone is necessary as a *foundation* for the gravel or broken stone superstructure. To this I reply that the graded earth surface is a suitable and sufficient foundation in all but an occasional, exceptional case, to wit : in soft material approaching the fluid state.

In such a case the remedy is to remove it down to a solid

bed, in which broken stone or gravel will *not* sink, and this point is obtained in a material in which rubble stone *will* sink. After the removal of mud in semi-fluid state, fill up to the surface with gravel, or if the material be very deep, drain it and build on the retained earth ; or, if this be impracticable, use plank for a bottom, or bridge over. In any case in which a coating of gravel will sink, rubble stone will sink also and much sooner, the one gravitating as a homogeneous mass distributed over the full width of the surface, the other as individual stones, each gravitating with its individual and unbonded weight.

Again, when a macadam road begins to wear, and at any stage of superficial wearing, it may be restored to grade by a fresh coating of the same material which, if the precaution be taken of loosening up the worn surface after the removal of mud or earth deposits, will adhere and combine with the mass, restoring in a short time the original, perfect and homogeneous bond—a bond which is impossible between two materials, the one in large masses and the other in the form of gravel or broken stone.

It will be observed (from the hypothetical, sectional diagram, not reproduced) that whatever be the cost of the section on top, which represents the macadam, the whole of the macadam is less than half of the Telford in quantity and cost of construction. In practice I have encountered a serious difficulty in constructing the Telford road, which does not occur in the macadam.

First.—A trench must be dug to receive the rubble stone, of say eight inches depth after the road earth bed has been formed. If in cuts, the earth excavated must be carted out of the way. And it is worth while to suggest that the trench itself is seriously objectionable for two important reasons ; the one that it is generally softer than the surface, liable to fill with water before the stone can be laid, and even then it becomes in its relation to its surroundings an artificial water basin.

Second.—If no trench is formed, and the rubble stone is

laid on the graded surface, it runs the roadbed so high above the original earth grade that fresh earth must be added to the slopes and sides, so as to afford a safe margin of earth at the level of travel, otherwise the metal bed will be sixteen inches higher than the earth bank, and wagons must keep a safe distance from the edge or run the risk of turning over.

So it must be accepted as true, theoretically and practically, that the generally received doctrine that a rubble stone bottom is necessary as a foundation is an error, and when it is admitted that it more than doubles the cost of a standard macadam road, and seriously accelerates the wear and disruption of it, there remains no apology for its adoption.

MAINTENANCE.

We suppose that the macadam road has been adopted and finished and worn to a smooth surface. Its maintenance is easy, simple and of trifling expense.

The best plan is to deposit, during construction, a twelve months' supply of gravel or broken stone at convenient points along the road, about 1000 feet apart. After every heavy rain send a gravel wagon with about five men, and have the sinks or ruts filled up and ditches reopened and culverts opened, if closed or gorged, and such other amendations made as circumstances may require.

I have found that on macadam roads properly constructed the cost of maintenance is less than 1 per cent. of the original cost per annum. All this is under the supposition that the system remains under the supervision of a competent engineer or road supervisor, who gives it proper attention.

It is important to protect earth embankments from washing. This may be done cheaply and permanently by sodding to quick growing, heavy sodding grass at the proper season for sowing. Effectual regulation by law of the tread or width of wagon tires in their relation to maximum loads is a measure second in importance to nothing for cheapening construction and reducing the cost of maintenance.

A rule may be safely adopted which would insure public roads against the main destroying agency to which they are subjected, to wit : heavy loads on narrow tires. The limit of loads should be 400 pounds to the inch width of tire, and when loads must be so exceptionally great, say over 10,000 pounds, they should be drawn on rollers of proper tread.

Wagons emerging from mud roads bring upon their wheels a large quantity of stiff mud, which, falling upon gravel roads, is again lifted upon wheels passing over it, and, being pressed on to the gravel surface, it brings with it, by degrees, coatings of fine gravel, making thus holes in the surface, and these, stripped of the hard, smooth surface, deepen rapidly by the repeated process.

A perfect system of roads would provide against direct wagon communication between mud and improved roads, either by throwing out lateral connections with them of, say 500 feet length, of rough rubble road, or by embracing in the system designed every road within it.

If mud roads could be abolished, the macadam road would meet every requirement of a first-class road for any purpose, save that alone of the heaviest city travel.

It is not necessary nor advisable to attempt to maintain by constant thin deposits of new material the original form and depth of road surface, for such thin deposits are soon ground into powder and blown away. But the plan of maintenance should be first to fill ruts and sinks as they appear, filling full and a little above the general surface—this to be kept up from year to year until the general surface has worn so thin as to show the thickness by occasional disruption of the bond. When this occurs, the original surface and depth should be restored fully by a new distribution of material over the whole road. How often this treatment will be required will depend upon the wearing quality of material and the amount and character

of travel.   On roads constructed six years ago, under my supervision, part of broken limestone and part of gravel, I cannot
observe any appreciable depth of wear or other indication of
failure.

All the foregoing applies to roads South of Latitude 38°,
where frost upheavals do not break up the superstructure.   In
colder regions provisions against disruption by frost should be
made as follows :

In advance of the work of spreading and forming the
superstructure, form sub-drains as follows :

At intervals of five feet cut trenches across the earth
grade, at right angles to its crown, eighteen inches wide at the
top, six inches wide at the bottom and eight inches deep.
Fill these full to the grade surface with coarse gravel or broken
stone ; then follow, before travel is resumed, with the gravel or
broken stone superstructure, as hereinbefore explained.

The gravel or broken-stone road, as above described, may
be considered standard for country roads, and the cost of these
should mark the limit of expenditure out of the general tax
fund for country roads.

But country roads often pass through populous suburbs of
large cities and form connections with municipal systems
embracing heavy traffic roads, pleasure drives, residence roads,
etc., in appropriate variety.   These often extend beyond the
city limits, and must be constructed in unbroken harmony,
system with system.

Reserving that the limit of expenditure of the county fund
would be the cost of the standard country road, larger expenditure may occur near cities from funds voluntarily contributed,
and thus it will often become necessary to vary modes of construction in such localities.

Municipal engineering, as applied especially to city pavements, is an interesting subject, but as I understand the circular of the University Committee, it is not embraced in the

subject they intend to discuss. Still, inasmuch as the suburban extensions of city roads are often parts of a county system, it would be proper to indicate in this discussion their relative adaptability to the variable requirements as such extensions.

It is supposed that these suburban extensions will embrace heavy traffic, light traffic, pleasure and neighborhood or residence roads.

I will be content to add some general suggestions and indicate in tabulated form their order of excellence for the respective objects, as follows :

Heavy Traffic Road :

1. Block Granite on Concrete Foundation.
2. Block Granite on Gravel Foundation.
3. Vitrified Brick on Concrete Foundation.
4. Rubble Stone on Gravel Foundation.

Light Traffic :

1. Vitrified Brick on Concrete.
2, Block Limestone on Concrete or Gravel.
3. Block Wood on Plank.
4. Gravel or Fine Broken Stone on Natural Surface.

Pleasure Roads :

1. Asphalt on Concrete Foundation.
2. Vitrified Brick on Concrete Foundation.
3. Block Wood on Plank.
4. Gravel or Fine Broken Stone on Natural Surface.

Neighborhood or Residence :

1. Gravel or Fine Broken Stone on Natural Earth Surface.

When I use the term *Gravel* it applies also to fine broken stone, except in cases in which a distinction is otherwise indicated.

GENERAL SUGGESTIONS.

The main desiderata in road or pavement construction are :

First.—A smooth surface, forming a safe footing for teams and an unyielding bearing for heavily loaded wheels.

Second.—An enduring material, both superficial and funda
mental. The main problem is how to construct and maintain a
smooth surface.

The forces that conspire to wear and disrupt the surface
are compound—that is, dynamic and static—being mainly the
impact of wheels running under heavy loads.

These two elements, weight and impact, or weight impelled,
to be specifically provided against by appropriate provisions.

The prevailing theory with regard to foundations for street
pavements is precisely that which applies to foundations for
ponderous buildings, and herein may be found the source of
much error and enormous waste of money.

This theory rests upon the idea that the important element
in every foundation is to resist and arrest gravitation downward
in heavy structures of stone, brick or iron, whereas the simple
requirement as applied to pavements is a foundation which shall
have sufficient stability to bear so much of the superimposed
weight as the superstructure itself cannot bear, and shall be of
such material or hardness that the blocks or other form of material comprising the superstructure shall not cut into or penetrate it.

Theoretically, any properly constructed pavement forms,
independently of the material under it, an immovable arch which
cannot sink unless disrupted by forces so violent as to crush its
component parts by force of impact or gravity, so that when we
observe disruption or sinking we will find that the arch is defective at that point, and the footing on which the sunken blocks
rest is a material soft and easily penetrated. These are the
defects or weaknesses principally to be provided for.

But these defects in the arch cannot be prevented within
any reasonable limits as to cost, for to construct a perfect arch
of stone requires perfect blocks, absolutely true and compact,
cut to the line of radii from a centre.

So the next device is to provide against a defective arch.
Now, obviously this device would not be to construct a deep

foundation of absolute statical immobility, but only to provide a material to receive the thrust of a single block driven by force below its original surface level, and penetrating into a substratum not hard and strong enough to arrest it. No *depth* of foundation can avail to keep the superstructure immovable if any block comprising it can be forced into the surface of the foundation, nor, indeed, will any depth of foundation lessen the force of gravitation, but rather will increase it by the measure of its own weight down to the point of absolute stability.

Practically, the point of best stability is generally very near the surface, just below the alluvial deposit.

Grave errors prevail as to the force and weight upon foundations of superimposed pavements with their loads added.

Supposing that the superstructure be in simplest form, to wit, a bed of gravel, worn to a smooth surface and compacted through and through in a state of final repose, even such a structure would bear the weight of wagons of 5000 lbs. weight on-four-inch tires, and no greater proportion of this load will reach the foundation than would if the road bed were a solid iron bridge over it, for in practice the surface does not sink to any visible or measurable extent, and therefore is lost in the mass and practically only increases the weight of the mass, itself self-sustaining.

As stated hereinbefore, it is not true that a superimposed weight is transmitted in the line of a cone to the foundation, if the mediums through which it is transmitted have any resistive power, and in all cases in which the weight is not sufficient to break through the intermediate medium, it reaches the foundation only as a weight acting upon a solid surface, and is distributed over a foundation as hard as the immovable surface may be. So the problem largely involves two things :

1st. A superstructure that will stand under pressure and impact of passing loads.

2d. A foundation that will arrest the downward thrust of

defective parts of the superstructure, the force to be arrested being, not gravitation, but the impact and resultant of passing loads like that of a pile driven by a pile hammer.

The principle involved is illustrated in the ordinary mode of securing superficial stability of block wood pavement, which is often laid upon a subsurface of plank—two inches in thickness —and laid evenly upon a smooth earth surface below.

In this case and in that of block stone, the vertical weight is the same, while the impact is less on the wooden block, for the reason that the wood surface is generally more nearly perfect.

Since it is demonstrated that a double layer of inch plank well laid on an earth surface will, while it remains sound, arrest the downward thrust on the surface of block wooden pavement of the heaviest wagon loads; and while it is also demonstrated that a simple compacted bed of gravel of four inches thickness will not sink or disrupt under similar loads, it must be admitted that a layer of either material, plank or gravel, of the thickness and consistency of each will form a reliable foundation for block granite or limestone with a large margin of safety, for in the case of granite used as a foundation bed for block stone, the weight or force that will not break its surface even when transmitted from a mere line tangent to the tire of a wheel, cannot impose upon it so severe a strain when transmitted through a block wedged into a continuous structure, and having at its surface contact with the foundation bed a distributing area largely in excess of the tangential line of the wheel.

Brick and asphalt make the smoothest surface and best footing for teams, but what is the value of these elements?

It must be admitted that they are of very great value.

The wearing and disruption of surfaces are largely due to violent impact of moving wheels, moving rapidly under heavy loads.

So when a wagon passes over a rough surface the dynamic force, i. e., the impact of wheels, is at its maximum, but when passing over a smooth surface it is at its minimum, and so greatly is this most destructive agency—the impact force—reduced, that there remains but the force of gravitation, the statical, which of itself cannot abrade the surface, and if properly distributed passes into the foundation with no effect whatever on the surface.

This theory has been verified in my city, in which there are two model pavements both founded on concrete of same composition and depth. Upon one is laid a crown of block granite; upon the other, one course of vitrified brick, both in use the same time and under about equal travel. The result is that the brick keeps a perfect surface and no sign of abrasion can be found, while granite has lost original surface at many points and never did compare with the brick in superficial smoothness.

Applying these principles, a natural and effective mode of construction within such limitations as are general in matters of material, location and cost, would be about the following— in which it is assumed that the true structure is that underlying natural material upon which the whole construction rests, and that this will be earth or clay.

Building then necessarily upon a foundation of earth or clay and starting at its depth of greatest solidity, which is generally near the surface, the foundation dependence for statical immovability is an earth base, whatever the superstructure may be. Resting upon this earth surface there should be a firmer material of greater hardness and stronger coherence, which will serve to distribute superimposed weight and resist dynamic force from above. This is usually called the foundation. This would be accomplished effectually and very simply by a layer of plank two inches in thickness, as when used as a bearing for block wooden pavement.

But perishable material, such as wooden plank, is not to be considered in this problem, but the illustration indicates that any material and construction that will act in the same way, to wit: distributing and arresting weight and impact, is the desideratum as a foundation resting on earth or clay.

Any compacted and homogeneous mass strong enough to receive and distribute the superimposed weight without crush-ing and breaking its bond, and hard enough to resist the impact or cutting force from above, will, just as plank will, form an immovable surface for the structure built upon it.

While it is practicable to strengthen an earth foundation by piling driven vertically, it is not necessary to consider any such device, save in exceptional cases, such as occur in swampy material—soft or approaching the fluid state. Generally, the natural earth surface is to be adopted as the bed of the super-structure.

Proceeding, then, to construction upon a base of such material, I would suggest the following:

First.—Grade the earth bed to a smooth surface, with a crown at the centre corresponding exactly with that intended for the upper surface of the finished pavement. This sub-crown is important as forming a natural line of drainage out-wardly from the centre toward the ditches.

Second.—Exclude from the earth foundation all foreign substances, such as old brick, wood, etc., to the end that the material relied on for foundation may be absolutely homoge-neous, so that if there be any settling under superimposed weight, it shall be uniform and not affect the integrity of the upper plane.

Third.—After rolling the earth's surface with a light roller of about four thousand pounds weight, until it shall have a uniformly compacted crust, spread upon it, when dry, a layer of coarse gravel, and roll to two inches in depth, this being intended for subdrainage.

Fourth.—Spread over this, in sections of one square in length at one spreading, a layer of gravel containing a slight admixture of sand or fine clay, which, after being rolled with a roller of eight thousand pounds weight, shall have a compacted depth over the sub-layer of coarse gravel of four inches.

Fifth.—Or if considerations of relative cost are ignored, a monolithic course of concrete of four inches depth on the sub-course of coarse gravel would be better, as being a better medium for distribution of superincumbent weight, and more nearly water tight than compacted gravel. This also should be laid in large sections and covered over with a thin layer of sharp sand as a cushion-bearing for hard blocks. The concrete course should not be rolled.

Sixth.—Upon this foundation build the surface course as follows :

Supposing it to be block stone, it should be of uniform dimensions in width and depth, and with a depth not less than six inches. The width and length should be largely in excess of what is ordinary, but should not exceed 12 by 20 inches. If there be irregularities in the dimensions, this is only allowable in widths and lengths, but never in vertical depth.

In case of irregularities in dimension, care should be taken to assort the blocks by respective dimensions, laying them in sections to themselves, so that the general surface shall be pre-served, and not broken here and there, as often occurs when a single block is driven below the level of its broader neighbors.

Seventh.—When a section has been laid, every single block should be driven to a bearing with the heaviest hand mauls available.

Eighth.—This should be followed with a coating of sharp sand, swept into joints and sifted down, filling up interstices.

Ninth.—The entire surface should be rolled, alternating from gutters to centre and from centre to gutters, beginning at slow speed, and, by slow degrees, increasing to the highest speed attainable, until the entire surface has attained the utmost stability possible under such treatment.

Tenth.—After rolling, the whole surface should be treated with a coating of coal tar or pine pitch heated to boiling point and poured in liquid state, filling joints even up to the surface. It would be an improvement upon the existing plan to lay the blocks to an angle of forty-five degrees to the curbing, and increase their surface dimension, while a matter of utmost importance is to have them of uniform depth, the bottom and top planes being parallel, so as to avoid tilting and consequent break of bond, etc.

While I recommend a roller not exceeding 8000 pounds weight on the gravel surface, a heavier one of different form should be used in rolling the stone pavement resting on a gravel bed. For this purpose the roller should be limited to 15,000 pounds weight. This being so much under the usual weight of steam rollers requires explanation or defence.

The usual form of rollers is a cylinder of four to six feet in length, and is required to have a weight largely in excess of the greatest weight that the heaviest wagon load can be expected to impose. Such being the basis, the estimate may be that wagons, loaded to 12,000 pounds on four wheels of three-inch tires, will touch the line of contact with a weight of 3000 pounds to a length of three inches of tire, the equivalent of which as applied to a roller five feet in length would be 60,000 pounds, total weight of roller.

But it should be considered that

1st. Such a weight imposed upon a freshly laid surface not compacted to final and ultimate stability, will depress the surface immediately under it, forming a wave in front which may break the bond, disturb the homogeneity of the mass and disrupt the surface so that its application at that stage is hazardous.

2d. A roller of much less weight may be so constructed and so applied as to assure the end in view, to wit, the solidification of the road bed to the degree of immovability required, in the mode following :

Let the roller be a wagon on four wheels, each with a twelve-inch tire.

Load the wagon to an aggregate of 15,000 pounds weight, so distributed that the forward wheels shall carry a weight of 6000 pounds, the rear to carry a weight of 9000 pounds. The lighter weight being in front prepares the way for the heavier in the rear, and thus no violent change of surface or disruption will occur, while the rear will follow in the same track, gradually compacting the surface.

Beginning at the gutters and finishing at the centre, then reversing, ending at the gutter; continue rolling at low speed as long as the wheels make any perceptible impression on the surface; then increase the speed gradually and regularly, reaching before finishing the highest speed attainable.

Thus, within a few hours the pavement, by a gradual, safe and effective process, having withstood all the forces statical and dynamic to which it will ever be subjected, may be relied on as having attained the required compactness, smoothness of surface and stability, and may be safely opened to travel, after being treated with a coating of coal tar or pitch, as explained herein.

LEGISLATION APPLICABLE TO COUNTY ROADS.

To render effectual any system of construction and maintenance of public roads, provision should be made by appropriate legislation for concentrated administration, intelligent personal supervision, fixed personal responsibility, and the broadest authority to locate, construct, maintain and protect the communal property in such roads.

These ends require about the following :

A board of road commissioners, three in number, in every county. They should meet within ten days after their election or appointment and proceed methodically as follows :

First.—Elect a competent engineer of county roads and bridges, who may be one of the board, also a chairman and secretary and treasurer, the latter to be combined.

Second.—The engineer should be required to proceed without delay to prepare an estimate of the cost per mile of grading, bridging and graveling county roads, also the cost of repairing other county roads not to be graveled. This report should be rendered to an adjourned meeting not longer than thirty days later.

14

Third.—Upon the data furnished by the engineer's report the rate of road tax should be fixed and the work of the year determined.

Authority to levy such tax might be conferred on the county court, or in some States on the board of road commissioners.

The salaries of commissioners may be fixed by the county court, and that of the engineer by the commissioners.

Each commissioner should be required to give proper bond and to subscribe to an oath of office, embracing prominently that he has not influenced or attempted to influence his own election by any promise to do or not to do anything for any person whatever or any section, entering upon his term perfectly free and untrammeled to do his duty to the public without fear or favor.

The engineer of roads and bridges should have authority to amend or change locations, establish grades, alignment of roads, condemn material for construction, such as earth, timber, stone or gravel, under proper restrictions and provisions for compensation to owners. He should have police powers to arrest and report violators of road laws, to appoint deputies, and exercise all other legal powers conferred on him by the board.

The width of wagon tire should be regulated by law so that there shall be a width of one inch to every 400 pounds on a single wheel, and this proportionally to maximum loads.

Road commissioners should, when they demand, have the free use of county convicts in any work undertaken by them.

State convicts should be apportioned for road building to the several counties, upon demand, under such regulations as may be necessary to insure safe custody and proper treatment.

These important features should be a part of the general road law of every State in which they apply.

ROAD MAKING AND MAINTENANCE.

HONORABLE MENTION.   PAPER No. 42.

BY

FRANK CAWLEY, B. S.,

Instructor in Civil Engineering, Swarthmore College,
Swarthmore, Pa.

THE object of this essay is not to deal with those streets or roads which lie within the limits of incorporated cities or towns, but rather with those through less densely populated districts, where the principal industries are agricultural and the principal taxpayers farmers.   Neither is it my purpose to go into an elaborate discussion of how special roads should be constructed; such matters are amply provided for by writers like Messrs. Gillmore, Gillespie, Parnell, Morris and a host of others whose conclusions are open to the public.   What I do propose to show, however, is that a system of road management may be devised by which, in a limited number of years, at the same annual cost for road purposes which we now expend, perfect traveling facilities may be enjoyed all over any country which will adopt such system.   This, and more, I think, I can establish as true and practicable beyond the slightest doubt, and should the ideas here brought forth prove of value, the writer will feel amply repaid for his labors in perfecting them.   With these few introductory remarks, the writer submits the following essay to the Board of Adjudicators, and, if it should be so successful, to the public at large.

In the rural and suburban districts our roads are usually in various states of impassability from December to April inclusive.   In order to remedy this condition we must first inquire into the working of township affairs in these districts

TOWNSHIP ORGANIZATION.

We find that each year a supervisor, overseer or road-,
master, as he is variously termed, is elected by township vote,
to superintend all work on the roads of his township. He is paid
for his services, under the Pennsylvania law, at the rate of one
and a-half dollars per day, and to raise the money for him,
and to pay for the labor and material used by him, he is allowed
to levy a tax on all property within the township limits at its
assessed value, the rate of the tax being fixed by him and usually running from two to ten mills per dollar. This tax is called
the road tax, and in Pennsylvania is collected by the supervisor
himself.

After the supervisor has been duly elected and sworn in,
he is free to spend the appropriation as he deems to the best
advantage of the community, theoretically; to himself and
friends, practically.

When he decides upon improving any special piece of road,
he calls his friends and neighbors to assist him, and pays them,
by remissions of tax, at the rate of one and a half dollars per
day of labor and three dollars per day for a team.[1]

These rates are uniform, or nearly so, throughout Eastern
Pennsylvania and New Jersey.

In this way of selecting laborers very many hands are employed at the above rate who cannot move as much earth in a
whole day as an average laborer on a railroad or other contract
work will move in two or three hours, and the latter class of
laborers do not, as a rule, receive above one and a quarter dollars per day for their work.

Within the past two weeks, in a township not very far outside the limits of Philadelphia County, three hands were observed mending the road. One was an old man of perhaps 75,
another a man with one hand only, while the third was a boy.

My informant does not state whether or not the supervisor

---

[1] Two horses, driver and wagon, carts, plows, etc.

was sitting on a rock directing the work at a rate of a dollar and a half a day; but it is assumed that the three workers seen each received that amount, while the supervisor is pretty certain not to be left in the lurch.

METHODS IN VOGUE.

I find that the repairs usually made upon the road consist in plowing up the sides or gutters and throwing the earth or material thus loosened into the centre of the road, in order to give the road the necessary pitch or camber.

Of this method Gillmore writes as follows : "A pernicious custom prevails throughout a large portion of the United States, of repairing country roads only at certain seasons of the year. The cost of maintenance would be greatly reduced by frequent repairs, and especially by keeping the side ditches open to their full width and·depth, by promptly filling the ruts and ¡by maintaining the required slopes from the centre to the sides. It will seldom be found that the material obtained by cleaning out side ditches is fit to put upon the roadway."

The material thus obtained is usually composed of soil, sand and decaying animal and vegetable matter, and, as above stated, is utterly unfit for road purposes.

Another favorite recipe for road cure is to cart stones and dump them into a mud hole, with a view toward filling it. No effort is made, however, to drain the place, and the stones are soon buried beneath the mud and lost. To add to the confusion thus formed in the road management, there appears to be no unanimity of action on the part of supervisors. One year the supervisor for that term will plan out some perhaps valuable work, which he will start in a creditable manner. The next supervisor, deeming the expenditure of the taxes more desirable near his own home, does not continue on the foundation formed by the previous man, but leaves it to accomplish its own destruction, or aids said destruction by throwing gutter mud on it.

These are the customary methods of carrying on the road
affairs in our townships, and they are as old as any others of
our time-honored customs. In their youth, perhaps, they were
all that could be desired, but one thing is certain, they fail
utterly to fulfill their object to-day. To entrust the average
supervisor with the superintendence of road repair is a gross
mistake, and the custom of empowering him to expend as he
sees fit moneys which he raises from the taxpayers in amounts
to suit his purposes is a crying evil. What supervisor is competent, with his limited knowledge of the scientific treatment
of road business, to expend judiciously the large amount of
$16,000 annually on the roads of his township, yet an instance
in which a supervisor does spend that amount, not five miles
from the city of Philadelphia, exists.

SUGGESTED REMEDIES.

Methods have already been suggested by which it is claimed
that the above evils may be remedied. Some suggest legislation by which State aid may be obtained, such measures usually
arranging for the State to pay from one-third to two-thirds the
expense of all permanent improvements. Some suggest bonding the township to as high as 7 per cent. of its assessed valuation, if necessary, and, with the money thus raised, to place the
roads in first-class condition—their claim being that this can be
done without increasing the tax rate, the present rate being
sufficient to provide for the interest on bonded debt, road repair
and sinking fund maintenance. Some suggest raising the tax
enough to put and keep the roads in good condition, while still
others clamor for a board of six supervisors instead of one,
similar, in most respects, to our school boards.

These suggestions are all wrong, inasmuch as they leave
the expenditure of the money raised in the hands of the same
incompetent persons who at present handle it. Would we be
willing to entrust the medical work of our townships to farmers
elected each year? Or would we be willing to entrust the agri-

culture of our county farm to a physician or a preacher elected in the same manner? Either would be equally capable of doing the work for which he was elected as is the average supervisor.

In order to spend money to advantage, a man must be thoroughly educated in the work or interests in which he is spending it, and he must be able to do things from a scientific basis. Who of us who owns a manufacturing interest would be willing to appoint a farmer as superintendent of our works until he had thoroughly mastered the business? The supervisor is not so much at fault as he is generally accused of being. He does the best he can ; he has a hard task to perform, and knows but poorly how to set about it in the right manner.

In regard to the suggestions above mentioned, aside from the objections of the supervisor rule, which still exists under them, each is subject to objections which, to my mind, bars it out from practical use.

State aid, after it is obtained, is nothing more nor less than taxation, and is paid by the people, and unless the said aid is distributed to all townships of the State in proportion to their taxable value, some will have to pay for improvements which are many miles distant from them. When, in a township, a man has to pay for improvements to a remote road, while his own goes unimproved, he always finds fault. Yet just such men advocate State aid, which is the same thing.

Bonding the townships seems to me to have three serious objections. The money spent as interest does the road no good. The money raised, if spent by the average supervisor, will do it no more good. And, lastly, the non-necessity of such a measure. Why should a township become debtor to anyone when it has the means to do its work itself, and that it has the means I will show in a succeeding paragraph.

Increasing the taxes can only enable the supervisors to do more work of no moment, and will practically drive such farmers as have to pay rent or interest on mortages out of the business and into a poorhouse. A farmer cannot afford to pay any

higher tax than he at present pays. Not one farm in twenty
pays the man who tills it half as much as it pays the man
who holds the 6 per cent. mortgage on it. No business of which
I know is so poorly remunerative as farming. A bad year, heavy
taxes, mortgage—and the farmer's doom is sealed. The majority
of farmers would prefer to work on the road at seventy-five
cents a day rather than hire a man ·at double the amount to do
it. And if the rate was lowered from one dollar and a half to
seventy-five cents, there would still be enough help to spend the
yearly appropriations, and double the work now done could be
accomplished—the only change necessary being the proper
application of the energy thus made available.

The matter of having the responsibility of supervisorship
vested in six men instead of one is but little better than the
present method. No two of the six could be made to think
alike, as is too often the case in school boards. And no one of
them bids fair to know more about scientific road making than
does the present supervisor.

We do not want State aid, nor borrowed money, nor increased taxation; neither do we want six supervisors in place of
one. What we do want, however, is an experienced man in
every county of the State to take the office of county engineer.
And that such an office may be constituted, and the incumbent
be enabled to perform his duties to the best advantage, a law
should be enacted permitting any county, through its courts or
otherwise, to appoint at its own option an engineer, and do
away entirely with the supervisor.

This is better than requiring the present supervisor to
be an experienced engineer, for that would be an expensive proceeding; there not being sufficient work in one township to pay
a professional man's salary is readily admitted. By this method
of making it optional with the counties, we would have one or
two counties to start the matter. In a few years, as I propose
to make clear, the roads of those counties will be greatly improved, and will show that in a very short time perfection may

be expected, and, what is of as great interest, property value *raised* and- taxation *lowered.* And neighboring counties, perceiving this change, will be quick in doing the same. After a sufficient number of county engineers are appointed, then we might have a State engineer, to whom the county engineers could make reports and from whom they could receive directions to so connect their labors that we might have State roads. Other States would soon follow the same plans, and when a sufficient number of States had thus joined in the great work, a National Bureau of Roads could be established, and the whole work systematized and consolidated. So much for the scheme of county engineers in general.

SKETCH OF THE ENGINEER'S DUTIES.

He should be as much the authority on all matters of an engineering nature in the county as is the chief engineer of a railroad on his line, and should either do or direct all work of this kind which is to be done at public expense.

Thus, he should be the engineer of all new roads, both as regards their location and construction, in the former acting in connection with the road jury.

He should, at specified intervals, inspect all roads and bridges in the county, and give directions for any repairs which may be needed.

In each township he should be empowered to fix the rate of road tax and should spend money thus raised in the township in which it is thus levied, both as regards labor and work, such rate being subject to an appeal by the citizen's of the township— the appeal to be decided by a jury of disinterested parties, as should be all other appeals which may arise.

In each township he should divide the road mileage into sections of from three to seven miles each, and appoint over each section a man who lives on and travels over that section, as a section boss, as he would be called in railroad work—such section bosses to work under the orders of the engineer and to report all emergencies to him.

. To make opportunity for all to work out their road tax, and *only* the road tax, and to give orders for the same when worked out.

He should keep accurate accounts of all work done either by him or by his order. Such accounts, where public moneys are involved, to be open to public inspection at any and all times.

And such other requirements as might at the time become necessary should be made, it being difficult to lay down an unswerving rule for the guidance of these engineers throughout the State. For in the different localities the needs and requirements are of different natures. Therefore, it would be wise to lay down a general plan as above, and allow each county to expand upon that plan as they found expansion necessary. When we come to reorganize and appoint a State engineer we can gather information from all quarters and lay down more definite rules which may better suit all cases.

In regard to the first of the above requirements—being thus made a very high officer in the county—he supplies the need for a leader to direct the action of all subordinates. Instead of every fellow for himself, as it now stands, all would follow the plan of one thoroughly capable brain. All work of any magnitude must have brains at the head of it; there must be a good reason for doing everything, and all work must be advanced from a scientific basis. An engineer can do this.

He should act in conjunction with the road jury, and it might be of advantage that he be one of their number, though I can see objections—in case of an exception being taken, for instance, in which case the engineer would be thrown out of the case entirely when a new jury was appointed. Another objection being that he should have the power to make an appeal from the decision of the jury, should they, in his opinion, make a wrong one.

A very necessary part of his duties are the inspection trips over all roads and bridges. These will be of great value, in that on these trips he will naturally visit the section bosses to give them his orders and to confer with them in regard to their sections.

It is best that he fix the amount of the appropriation in each township, but it is also necessary that some easy means of appeal be furnished. Justice demands that the money raised in one township be worked out in that township, and also that the residents of that township receive it for labor done by them.

In regard to the section bosses, it seems to have proved successful to the railroad companies to employ such hands, and from an instance in which something of a similar nature has been tried on road work, the writer has reached the conclusion that the section bosses will make a valuable part of the new system. They should be appointed by the engineer, for they will then be more apt to work in conjunction with him, and being situated on the roads over which they are in charge, they will be working in their own interest when they do any work upon the road. They should be the only parties who are entitled to receive more than their road tax assessment, and their duties should be to patch the road as often as a hole or rut forms, and in case of an earth or gravel road scrape it as often as necessary, always under the instruction of the engineer. If rain or any other agency makes a flaw in a road or bridge, the section boss should immediately report the same to the engineer, that he may take measures for its immediate repair.

· To afford all an opportunity to work out road tax is a question which cannot be definitely settled until, under the new system, all of the permanent improvements have been made. At present, by a State law, it is necessary that such opportunity be offered, and the writer thinks rightly so, but in some localities there seems to be no necessity for it. Wherever it is done the work has a tendency to run into a school-boy style of doing it. There will be a good deal of bluster and fun, but the work has always lacked thoroughness. For the first few years of the new *régime*, however, there will be plenty of work at which the public can be advantageously employed, and after that the question can be finally settled.   That it is right that the taxpayer should have the opportunity to work out his road tax, where possible, on the road seems to be without a doubt, for if we will agree, as we all must, that in a community in which there is some public work requiring a certain number of days' labor during the year to keep it in repair, each member of the community owes the work his share of those days' labor.   If he fails to perform this labor, or sends a substitute, then he should pay a fine or tax sufficient to pay someone else to do the work for him.   Now, if we say instead of days' labor, their money equivalent, we have the road tax.

The objection to such labor in the past has already been mentioned, but this objection can, I think, be overruled by the proper direction of the work by the engineer and his section bosses.

When the engineer contemplates any extensive work in the township, he should advertise for labor a sufficient time beforehand, and arrange a time by which that labor shall report, that it may be ready for work when the time for the work arrives.   In the advertisement he should state the nature of the work, the number of days which he proposes to be at it, and the number of men and teams that he wants.   No person should be allowed to draw an order for more than the amount of his road tax bill until all that wish have either worked out their tax themselves or have had it worked out by substitutes.   In regard to the work of patching, all patching should be done in small portions, as flaws occur in the road's surface, the object being not to allow the flaw to grow to any considerable size.   This requires the work of one man, who should have an interest in the section of road, as does the section boss.   To do this work to the best advantage, the boss should have the material at hand and mixed ready for use, if any mixing is necessary, and let it only be needful for him to take a horse and cart and patch half his section with one cartload.   This method, I believe, is employed upon

the roads in France in some such manner as I have described
above.

MAINTBNANCE.

The requisites for the proper maintenance of a broken-
stone road are given by Gillmore in his " Roads, Streets and .
Pavements," to be as follows :

First.—That it should be kept thoroughly clear of dust, and
therefore clear of mud.

Second.—That thorough drainage should be maintained.

Third.—That minute repairs to the surface should be made
systematically in small patches as often as, and as soon as, ruts
or depressions begin to show themselves.

It is just as necessary that these three rules be enforced
upon a cheap earth road or a gravel road as it is upon the best
Telford or macadam surface.

In regard to the sweeping of the dust from the road surface,
it will seem to be unnecessary to the average rural taxpayer, but
experience on the French and English roads has proven that it
is necessary for the preservation of the surface, the lessening of
the draught, and the provision for the absence of mud and dust.
The sweeping may be done by a machine, which need not cost
more than a few hundred dollars, and one such sweeper might
be made to answer for a whole township.   The sweepings
should be deposited in the gutter by the machine, to be afterward gathered up and used with the other gutter dirt in banking
off the water from neighboring fields.

Thorough drainage must be insisted upon, for on this
depends the life of any road.   The bed must not be allowed to
become a pasty mass, or the surface materials will inevitably
sink, while the mass will rise.   And the systematic addition of
material in small quantities has proven itself to be the best
small way of mending a road.   Where this is insufficient, the
road should be carefully swept and the materials spread on to
the thickness of from two to four inches, as occasion requires,
and if they are not compacted with a roller, they should be care-

fully watched and the ruts all raked in until the new material is thoroughly compacted. This method is only to be used when the other method fails to keep up the requisite depth of roadbed, and this method should be adopted in conjunction with the other.

I have described at sufficient length, to make my meaning clear, the manner in which I think the management should be carried on, and, at the same time, said all that seems to be necessary in regard to repair and maintenance. I must, however, before closing, fulfill my promise to make clear the possibility of making our roads perfect in a very few years with a tax rate no greater than that of the present. I have obtained figures from the commissioner's clerk of Delaware County, which county may be taken as an example of the more wealthy and pushing counties of the State, and as one in which many interests are represented. It is also, perhaps, one of the worst supplied with good roads. I find that during 1889 the assessed value of the property on which road tax was levied was $38,479,437. The townships have fixed their rates at from two to ten mills and will probably average about four mills. This will certainly be on the safe side, for the most wealthy townships are the ones that raise the highest rates, as, for instance; Upper Darby Township, which is assessed at $2,619,586. for a county tax, from which the salaries and emoluments must be deducted before reckoning the road tax, raises a road tax of $16,000. We may therefore be pretty safe in saying that four mills per dollar is under the average assessment for road purposes in that county. At this rate, nearly $154,000 must have been raised last year, and, as yet, no improvements of a permanent nature have been made. Telford and macadam roads have been laid, but by subscription, and not from township funds. This large amount of money has been expended entirely on township roads, and in no case in corporate limits, and we have nothing but almost impassable roads to show for it.

$154,000 will build from fifteen to twenty miles of Telford road, or from twenty to thirty miles of macadam, and it will drain, ridge and surface between seventy-five and a hundred miles of common road in what is called piking.

From an atlas published in 1870, I find that there were then about five hundred and fifty-three and a half miles of road in the county. This number has probably been considerably increased during the past twenty years. Of this amount perhaps one hundred miles would be best made substantial by what is known as Telfording it, perhaps two hundred miles more should be macadamized, and the remaining distance, probably three hundred miles, should be piked with either broken stone or good gravel. These figures are, of course, merely conjectural, being only ascertainable by careful surveying and the use of sound judgment. The one hundred miles to be Telforded will require the first attention, for they are, necessarily, the worst in the county at present. If five miles, then, are Telforded each year, and done with some system, extending in each instance from some place to some other place, in twenty years we will have our Telford all down. Next the macadam claims attention. The ten miles of Telford will require about one-fourth the appropriation, or perhaps a little more, thus leaving us about a hundred thousand dollars for macadam and other systems. At the rate of ten miles per year, we would, in twenty years, have all roads macadamized which would require such treatment. The ten miles costing about $75,000 in round figures for all expenses, we still have $25,000 or $30,000 left for piking and current expenses, and we may, out of this, pike ten miles yearly, or in twenty years have two hundred of the three hundred miles that are left after the Telford and macadam are taken out, in an excellent condition. The first expense now on the two last-named roads ceases, and if, say, five years are allowed at the same rates of taxation, or, in all, twenty-five years, we can add to all our roads neat footpaths, thorough drainage and nicely-graded slopes, besides completing the piking.

By the end of this twenty-five years all property will have increased in value, the average increase being perhaps safely estimated at 25 per cent., thus making the taxable value of property for road purposes nearly $50,000,000. After the roads are in condition, or at the end of our twenty-five years, $100 per mile should be an ample average allowance for the cost of maintenance, or less than $60,000 for the county. At an assessed value of $50,000,000, an average tax of one and one-fifth mills will raise this amount.

Necessarily, much of this is theoretical, but I have been very careful to keep on the safe side in all instances. When this measure is proposed, the objection that it is impossible to take the entire, or any portion of the present appropriation from our roads, or they will become impassable, is offered. This, however, is not the case. A very small amount of money in the hands of a competent engineer will so drain the roads that they will be in a better condition than they now are under the expenditure of $160,000 per year.   .

As I have already intimated, much of this money is worse 'than wasted. We are literally building roads with paper dollars, as I heard a taxpayer remark a few evenings since. Besides, to guard against this contingency, we have the margin of increasing valuation, of which I have not made any account, until after the expiration of the twenty-five years.

This applies particularly to Delaware County. Of course, to the less wealthy counties a longer time would necessarily elapse before all roads could be placed in the above-described condition ; but everywhere the roads can, at least, be piked with stone or gravel. In any locality there is no excuse for not having good roads, even if they are necessarily restricted to earth roads entirely. An earth road can be successfully constructed over a morass, by ditching on each side the roadway, and throwing the earth thus excavated upon a brush foundation for the roadway itself. Where necessary, sheet piling may be employed at no great expense, and on the top of the road thus formed carefully spread and compact a surface cover—anything, from clay and sharp sand to the Telford, as fortune places it at the command of the engineer. If this can be successfully done, as it is all along both sides of the lower Delaware and in places all over New Jersey, why can we not have a good earth road anywhere in our State ?

It is not necessary in an article of this kind for me to lay down any rules or directions by which roads of any particular class must be constructed. How heavy the macadam stone must be, or how thick the Telford bed should be constructed, are things supposed to be known by the county engineer. At best, I could only repeat what is laid down as the practice and experience of road builders, which has been done by writers on the subject so often that the public must now know all about the distinctions between the different roads. It is not necessary for me to go into a detailed description of how much grade is permissible for loads of certain tonnage, nor is it pertinent that I should discuss the relative value of the different systems, further than to say that the Telford affords a little better facility for drainage than does the macadam, and is less likely to sink in a soft sub-grade. All other systems, as a rule, give place to the three systems named for work outside of paved towns. It will be noticed that I have insisted on thorough drainage throughout my essay. In providing for good drainage many seem to think that water soaking through the roadbed must be provided for. If, however, the roadbed be of the proper construction, no matter what its constituents are—whether gravel or sheet asphalt—very little, if any, water will permeate through it. It is only in cases of not being able to get off in any other manner that the water takes this method of seeking its natural courses. In order to keep the sub-grade solid, it must be above the standing water on either side, and, where necessary, tiled to convey its moisture to the side drains. This, I think, covers all that it is necessary to say in the description of the system herein proposed. And with the adoption of some such system by which our roads may be made passable, a long-existing want will be supplied.

15

ROAD MAKING AND MAINTENANCE.

HONORABLE MENTION. PAPER No. 44.

BY

FRANCIS FULLER McKENZIE, C. E.,

Landscape Gardener and Civil Engineer,
5774 Germantown Avenue, Philadelphia.

BEING much struck with the very unsatisfactory condition of most of the roads in this important and flourishing State of Pennsylvania, notwithstanding the enormous annual cost of maintaining them, even in their present state, and being myself a practical road engineer, and my father before me, in whose office and upon whose works I spent many years of my youth, I gladly avail myself of the opportunity now afforded me of placing my views of road construction and maintenance before your learned body.

Although it will be necessary to somewhat elaborate this paper on road making, that I may the more readily convey my views on the subject, yet I venture to say that the true principles of economic road making might be summed up in the following few lines : A firm, dry foundation, sound materials laid on scientific principles, proper and ample drainage of both roadbed and surface, easy gradients, easy and natural curves, a hard and compact surface, free from all ruts and depressions, with a surface neither too flat to prevent the flow of surface water nor too convex to be inconvenient to traffic.

Roads being preparatory to railways, and I may say even of more importance, for it must be remembered that every ton of goods conveyed by rail has, firstly, to traverse the roads leading to the depots, it seems strange that in the construction of the latter the highest available engineering skill is employed, whilst the construction of the former is generally, if not always, left in the hands of unskilful and incapable men, ignorant alike of either the theory or practice of good road making. A lasting legacy is thus left to posterity in expensive maintenance, instead of good roads that, while saving animal labor, facilitate commercial intercourse, render traveling easy and expeditious, and at the same time are vastly cheaper to maintain.

It will, I think, readily be conceded, that on the state of the roads, even more than that of the railways, the material prosperity of the country depends, for unless the utmost care is taken in selecting the best lines to follow, the development of the country is much retarded. It will therefore be admitted that the roads should be laid out with the greatest possible care, so as to develop to the fullest extent the best features of the country, both for building, agriculture and commercial purposes. More especially imperative is this in the neighborhood of large cities and towns, where every available site is eagerly bought up at a very high rate for residential purposes.

I fear carrying into effect the suggestions which it will be my duty to make, will entail a very heavy outlay of capital, but to a State of such vast importance as Pennsylvania, and to a people of so much intelligence, enterprise and wealth, a way will be found to overcome this difficulty, and in such a manner that posterity shall contribute its share to the advantages received in having a country traversed by such roads as will be a credit to the State and a model for others to imitate.

I will, with your kind permission, divide my essay into two parts, namely, Construction and Maintenance.

CONSTRUCTION.

The line of the proposed road being decided upon, a careful survey should be made to enable the engineer to fix upon the best and easiest grades, and in such a manner as will admit of the road being made with the least possible removal of soil, and so that all cuttings and embankments shall balance, that there may be no surplus soil to dispose of. Steep gradients and sharp curves should, if possible, be avoided. No grade, except in very hilly countries, should exceed one in thirty-three. And here I must say a word against the formation of dead straight and level roads, often necessitating as much cutting and filling as a railway. Of course, it is well known that so far as traffic is concerned, the straight and level road is the best possible, and for cities and towns probably nothing can equal it, for in this case the adjoining land is quickly graded down or filled in to the street level. In the suburbs and country, however, this is very different, and, with the exception of very flat countries, I am of opinion that this road is the worst possible, because, in the first place, it is generally the most costly, as the cuts and fillings are often very heavy, and in the next, the frequent cuttings and embankments effectually mar the beauty of the country, thus driving away would-be residents. Perhaps the greatest evil arises from the destruction of a great number of otherwise excellent building sites, often leaving one property ten or fifteen feet, and often more, above the road level, whilst the adjoining property is as many feet below, thus reducing the value of the land considerably. Had the engineer given way a little in the gradients and followed more the contour of the country, he might have saved a considerable sum in the construction, although making a slightly longer road; have heightened the natural beauties of the country, thereby drawing residents, and, at the same time, have enormously increased the value of adjacent properties. I must also enter a protest against changing abruptly from one gradient to another. On certain roads that I could name, one can actually feel, while driving over them, immediately one passes from one grade to another, whereas, had the road been made with a flowing grade, it would have been very much pleasanter for traffic, and, at the same time, more beautiful. Whoever saw in nature contours made up of straight lines?

Having now the line carefully surveyed and set out, all necessary cuttings and embankments formed, the next work of importance is :

THE FORMATION AND DRAINAGE OF THE ROADBED.

Above all, the roadbed should be perfectly drained; the want of special attention to this necessity is the chief cause of the heavy annual expense in maintenance. A road badly designed and made can seldom be rendered satisfactory, and may as well be abandoned at once, and a new line of road adopted, this being in most cases the cheapest in the end, and in every case the most satisfactory.

DRAINAGE.

Great care must be taken not only with the drainage of the road surface, but also with that of the roadbed and adjoining land, and where the road is to be constructed on a wet, retentive soil, a system of under-drainage must be provided by cutting trenches across the roadbed, and discharging into the side ditches. These trenches should be from twelve to eighteen inches deep and about one foot wide at the bottom, having the sides sloping outward ; in these should be constructed porous drains, composed of old bricks, flat stones, or whatever suitable material is at hand, and the trenches filled up again to the level of the roadbed with rough stones. The number of these cross drains must be regulated by the nature of the soil ; in stiff, heavy clay they ought to be every thirty or forty feet. On each side of the roadbed, at a distance of from twelve to sixteen feet, should be cut open ditches of a sufficient size and declivity to readily conduct away all water that can possibly fall on the road. Where footpaths are to be constructed, they will be formed on the strips of ground between the road and open ditch, with a curbstone six inches above the level of the edge of the road ; surface water will be collected thereby and conveyed by pipe drains, fifty or sixty feet apart, under the footways into the side ditches. Where no footpaths are to be constructed these strips should remain in sod, with a neatly-cut edge defining the metaled road, which will serve the same purpose as the curb edge, and will be connected with side ditches by open grips running across the road.

These grass strips will be found in every way preferable to the general plan of removing the surface to the same slope as the road, as so many roadmakers do, with the mistaken idea that it facilitates drainage, firstly, because the cut edge helps to collect the surface water, and readily discharges it into the proper channels ; and, secondly, because they will always be clean and prevent the sides of the road from becoming poached by cattle, and the consequent carrying of mud on to the road surface—not to mention the neat and tidy appearance they give to the road when nicely trimmed, at the same time saving the cost of removal.   These edges should never be so high as to prevent the passage of wheels in the case of emergency.   Where sewer, gas, or water pipes are to be laid, they should be placed under these strips or footways, immediately off the metaled road, and thus save the road from being constantly torn up for repairs.

WIDTH AND CROSS SECTION.

All roads should be made wide.   It is a mistake to suppose narrow roads are the cheapest.   Of course, when constructing a new road the cost is in proportion to its width, but a narrow road is always the more expensive to maintain, owing to the vehicles being compelled to keep more or less to one track in the centre, nothing being more destructive than the constant wear in one track.   A wide road is always more evenly worn all over, provided, of course, that it is constructed according to scientific principles and kept in good repair.   But there is yet another, and a very important, advantage that wide have over narrow roads ; this is, the greater amount of light and air obtained, and it will be found that a wide and open road will always be dry long before a narrow and confined one.   When roads, especially main roads, are laid out, care should be taken to secure plenty of land for the eventual full width of the road, as it can then be obtained at a very slight additional cost, otherwise the widening of an old road is always a most expensive work for all concerned, not to mention the number of fine trees, plants, and often buildings, destroyed thereby.

THE CROSS SECTION

of a road is a very important point, and one over which there have been great differences of opinion.   It should neither be too flat nor too rounded.   In the former case the surface water remains on the road instead of draining off into the side ditches, whereas, in the latter, owing to its great convexity, vehicles can only travel with comfort. or, indeed, with safety, in the centre of the road, thereby soon making three tracks there, and, as has been before remarked, nothing destroys a road sooner.   But there is yet another disadvantage, and that is, that as soon as the traffic is driven off the centre of the road a double wear takes place, owing to the tendency of the vehicle to slide down the inclined plane by force of gravity, and as this tendency is perpendicular to the line of draft, the labor of the horse, and the wear and tear of both wheels and road surface, is much increased.   The sole object in rounding the surface is to allow the water to run off freely, and I think that it is now agreed that a slope of one inch to every six feet width of metaled road, or a slope of one in seventy-two, is sufficient for all roads constructed of good hard material : provided, of course, that they are kept in good repair.   Macadam says : " I consider a road should be as flat as possible with regard to allowing the water to run off it at all, because a carriage ought to stand upright in traveling as much as possible.   I have generally made roads three inches higher in the centre than I have at the sides when they are eighteen feet wide ; if the road be smooth and well made the water will run off very easily in such a slope."   The drainage of surface water is much more effectually obtained by selecting a course for the road that is not horizontally level, because then the slightest wheel track becomes a channel to carry off the water, whereas, in the case of a level road it must be apparent to every one that no matter how rounded the surface may be, every track mark becomes a basin to hold it. The roadbed must now be excavated to the same contour as the finished road is to be, not with any idea of drainage—because it must be remembered that as soon as the road becomes subject to rolling or the pressure of heavy vehicles, the road material becomes so forced down into the roadbed, and the soil, in its turn, worked up into the stone, that the whole becomes amalgamated— but because by so forming the roadbed there will be an equal thickness of material over the whole surface, and if a road is made and maintained according to scientific principles, there is no reason why any one part should have a greater thickness than another. The bed being now formed, if on clay or stiff soil, should be well rolled with a horse roller from two to three tons in weight, when it will then be ready for the

MATERIAL.

This, of course, very much depends upon what is found in the neighborhood. Where good stone is found, this is undoubtedly the best material for country roads, but where no stone is found, either gravel must be used or stone must be brought from a distance, in which case it is merely a question of cost. But here in Pennsylvania, where good stone is so plentiful, we need not bother about anything else. But I may say that most excellent roads can be made with gravel, if care is taken in the selection of the same, and they are well rolled and grouted with a good binding material.

The most important quality in stone for road making is its *toughness* to withstand the crushing strain of heavy loads. The best stones are, therefore, the granites and trap rocks; good roads may be made with beach pebbles, but being round, they must be well grouted with a good binding material. The harder limestones also are suitable, but owing to their property of absorbing moisture, they are too liable to be injured by frosts.

FOUNDATION.

The great desideratum in road making is to so construct the road surface that no moisture shall penetrate to the foundation, so preventing the mud from working up into the stone. To insure this there must be a compact and solid foundation. Macadam's idea of having an elastic road bed is, I think, quite exploded by this time. In theory it is quite correct, and if a truly elastic road could be made it would doubtless be the best for ease of draft ; but no elasticity, except it be on the surface of the road, should be allowed, and with the material used at present this is an impossibility. Wood pavement, set on a solid concrete foundation, is the nearest approach to an elastic road yet discovered. But in the case of a stone road the foundation cannot be too solid. It has been proved by actual experiment that in the case of a stone road built on a yielding or loose foundation great wear takes place toward the bottom, whereas, when constructed upon a solid or rigid foundation the wear of the base is almost imperceptible, all the wear taking place upon the surface. And I think I am correct in saying that all the best authorities now recommend what is called the Telford road, which is contructed upon a roughly-paved foundation composed of good tough stones from nine to twelve inches deep carefully laid by hand across the road, with the thinnest edges upward ; this is then gone over with hammers, all projections knocked off, and the interstices filled up, the whole surface then shaped up to the proper contour and thoroughly rolled and consolidated. At all places where a great wash of water may be expected, rough stone gutters should be constructed of the same material as the road foundation. Where stone is scarce, a good foundation may be made with well-burnt clay, old bricks, etc., but anything likely to rot or decay should by all means be avoided. If the line of the road passes through a bog or spongy ground, preparation must first be made for the foundation by laying two alternate layers of fagots, crosswise and lengthwise. Macadam was exceptionally successful in constructing roads over such ground, and, in fact, said he would rather lay a road over a bog than over solid soil. This is how he became so favorably impressed with the idea of elastic roads.

Having now obtained a perfectly solid and rigid foundation, the road is all ready for the reception of the finer stone, and a three-inch layer of the toughest stone, broken to pass through a two-inch ring, must now be laid and thoroughly rolled, when a second three-inch layer of the same stone, broken to pass through a one-and-a-half-inch ring, must likewise be spread and consolidated, great care being taken with this layer to properly shape the road surface to desired contour. The road is now ready for its final dressing, and this should be a layer of the best trap-rock screenings, only sufficient being spread to fill up all interstices so as to present a firm, smooth surface for traffic ; any beyond this will merely be wasted, as it will be turned into mud in the Winter or dust in the Summer. This last layer should be well watered while rolling, so as to wash the fine material into all spaces, and so form a compact, impenetrable crust to the road. It is most important that this last layer shall be perfectly clean and free from any soil or mould. Otherwise, in wet weather it will soon turn to mud and stick to every wheel that passes over the road. The foregoing measurements and quantities apply to main roads subject to much traffic. In the case of accommo-dation roads less material will be found sufficient. A very good road may be made with a six-inch foundation of rough stones, one three-inch layer of one-and-a-half inch stone, with necessary layer of screenings on the top.

SIZE OF MATERIAL.

With regard to the size the stone should be broken, much difference of opinion exists, but I am of opinion that no stone, except for the foundation pavement, should be too large to pass through a two-inch ring nor smaller than that passed through a one-inch ring. That stone will be found best for road making that breaks into pieces as nearly cubical as possible ; that which splits into long, thin pieces should be avoided. Stone broken by machinery can be used of a much larger size than that broken by hand, because the action of the crusher is to splinter some stones without breaking them, when the first heavy weight passing over them completes the fracture.

ROLLING.

I must here say a word on the utmost importance and economy of thorough rolling and consolidation of all newly-made or repaired roads before allowing traffic thereon. The old custom of laying a thick layer of stone on either new or old roads, and leaving it for the traffic to grind down level, is little short of barbarous to the horses, destructive to vehicles and wasteful material, at the same time costing a considerable sum in watching and maintenance. It is true that in time the desired end may be obtained, but not without great waste of material, owing to the grinding down of the stones, in which process the angles are rubbed off until their surfaces become rounded, thus rendering them liable to be constantly loosened. Mr. Burt, the well-known London contractor, says : " That quite one-third of the loose road material used in London is literally wasted by being ground up under the traffic before the consolidation of the surface is effected."

The advantages of rolling may be summed up as follows : Economy, facility of perfect construction, comfort to persons and horses using the roads, improved surface, diminishing the wear and tear of vehicles, and a saving of material amounting to as much as 25 per cent. to 50 per cent.

The advantages of steam rolling over horse power are, firstly, economy ; secondly, ease of manipulation, and thirdly, obviating the destruction caused to the roads by the horses' hoofs while drawing the heavy roller, at the same time in every way doing the work better. The steam roller may also be used for tearing up the old stone roads for repairs. Road rollers should not be heavier than ten tons nor lighter than five.

The road will now be found quite ready to open for public traffic, and the only thing further to consider will be its

MAINTENANCE.

It matters not how well a road may be made, if it be not well looked after, and all mud and dust removed as soon as made, it will soon get into bad condition, the mud acting as a wet blanket to the road, continually rotting and softening the material. For economical and convenient traffic all roads should be maintained in thoroughly good order, but how seldom is this the case. This is the more inexcusable, as it has been proved over and over again that roads well kept and maintained actually cost considerably less in the end than neglected roads. But beside actual cost, we must also take into consideration the saving in animal labor, extra wear and tear of vehicles, and not to mention tempers, effected by good roads. Mr. Edwin Chadwick, C.B. (England), speaking on this subject, remarks : " In the present condition of the country it is of vast importance to reduce the cost of transit to the uttermost. If by the improvement of the rural roads, four horses could be enabled to do the work of five, the saving to the country in agricultural horses would not be less than seven million (pounds) a year. If the urban traffic is taken into consideration, we believe the cost of transit to be saved by improvement in roads would not be less than from seventeen to twenty millions a year."

The formation of small local associations for the construction, repair and improvement of the local roads is an unwise, although highly laudable, work. All public roads and footways should be under the direct control of the county, and each county under the control of the State legislatures. City streets and pavements will, of course, be under the control of the city authorities. When one county is too small or too poor to work alone, two or more adjoining counties should amalgamate, so as to enable them, in the first place, to appoint a capable road surveyor and engineer, to pay him a salary fully equal to his worth, and, secondly, to own all necessary plant, especially a steam roller, water carts, horses, etc. This will be found to be true economy, nothing being so expensive and wasteful as leaving the construction and repairs of roads in the hands of incapable and ignorant men.

Then comes the question, How is the money to be raised for this work? And this is a serious question. But I am of the opinion that the best way will be to impose a small tax on the assessed value of all lands in the county, of course rating building lands very much higher than farm lands, for the advantages of having the county traversed by good roads ; and also, further, to tax all wheels in the county, thus making those who use the roads most bear the greater share of the cost of repairs and construction. The only other way would be to establish turnpikes all over the State, and, although this was found to be very successful in England, so far as the condition of the roads was concerned, yet it was found to cause so much annoyance and delay that they have now all been done away with. Another serious drawback to this system is, that foot passengers, although deriving great benefit from good roads, pay nothing toward their cost. Where new roads are to be constructed, the money should be borrowed to pay the actual cost of construction, and repaid over a period of not less than ten years.

I must here say a word on the advisability of the county owning all the public sidewalks. There seems no good reason why a man should be compelled to construct and keep in repair a public footpath in front of his property any more than that he should construct and repair the public highway. But the great benefit will be derived from the uniform condition and appearance of all sidewalks. And where the line of the road is to be planted, this also should be carried out by the county, so doing away with the bad effects too often seen, where one plants a line of maples in front of his property, while his neighbor on the right plants a row of elms, and the neighbor on his left plants, perhaps, Lombardy poplars, the chances being that each one chooses a line for himself, while the trees are all different sizes and ages.

For the better maintenance of roads, they should be divided up into lengths, and each length given to the charge of an intelligent and reliable laborer, who should never be changed from one length to another, but always remain on his own road. This man must be thoroughly reliable and must be out wet or fine ; in fact, it is more important that he should be out in wet weather than fine, because he can then readily see where the wet stands on the road and where it needs draining. He should never be allowed to let his road get out of order, as in no case does the old proverb, "A stitch in time saves nine," apply more forcibly than to road mending. He should be instructed to remove all mud as soon as formed, sweep quite clean of dust in Summer —for it must be remembered that Summer dust makes Winter mud—and it will be found easier to remove the dust than the mud, while doing less damage to the road ; to fill in at once, with nicely-broken stone, any rut that may show itself, and in Summer to remove every loose stone from the road.

This man should have the power of obtaining extra help on emergency, as great injury may be done to a road at the breaking-up of a frost if proper help is not at hand. An active man on a good main road can keep from three to four miles in good condition. In Summer he will be fully employed cleaning the water-tables, cutting weeds, removing loose stones and cleaning off all dust, horse droppings and dirt.

Nothing is so destructive to a road as a visible wheel track ; when once formed it not only prevents the proper drainage of the road surface, but every subsequent vehicle will be sure to follow in the same track, thereby aggravating the evil. The effect of this may be seen by any one by examining any road showing wear. No matter how bad the ruts are in the straight parts of the road, the road will be found in good condition at all the turnings, because here every vehicle goes its own direction, and so keeps the surface compact and even.

Where, from unavoidable causes, three ruts or tracks have been allowed to form in a road, only one should be filled in at a time, and it will be found best to fill in first that caused by the horse, as by so doing it will have the effect of driving the traffic off the centre of the road, some to one side and some to the other, while three times the amount of road will be got over in the time. By judiciously putting the stones on in small quantities the traffic is dispersed and the road kept level and hard. Only the smallest stone chips should be used for the repairs during Summer, and, as far as possible, all repairs should be done as soon as the roads get soft in Autumn and early Winter. When it is found necessary to redress the road, and the surface is very hard and compact, it should first be loosened with picks, or it can be done well and quickly with the steam roller by fixing spikes in the periphery of the roller. The road should then be shaped up to proper contour, and a layer not more than three inches thick of well-broken one-and-a-half-inch stone spread over the whole surface, well rolled and consolidated, and then faced up with the screening, as in the construction of new roads.

CARTING.

All carting, as far as possible, should be done during the Summer, when the roads are hard and dry, and the broken stone should be placed in heaps at regular intervals along the sides of the road, because not only does the carting then do less injury, but the stones improve, as all stone hardens when exposed to the weather.

WATERING.

It is most important that the roads should be well watered, not only in Summer, but also occasionally in Winter. In Summer, during the dry, hot weather, the road surface becomes extremely brittle, and should then be well watered, having first removed all dust and refuse. Sometimes in Winter, especially after frost, the road gets very sticky and picks up freely on the passing wheels. It should then also be watered and all slush

and mud removed.   The watering should always, as near as possible, resemble a light shower of rain.

WIDTH OF WHEELS.

Great destruction is caused to roads by the growing practice of using vehicles carrying heavy loads with wheels insuffi-
ciently wide to bear the weight imposed upon them.   Telford's
rule was one-inch tire for every five hundred-weight on the
wheel, and it has been proved over and over again that a two-
and-a-half-inch tire causes double the wear of a four-inch.
Small wheels also do more injury to a road than large ones, as
the action of the former is rather to push and move the stones
out of their places, while the latter passes over them, helping, in
fact, to consolidate the road.   Large and broad wheels, while
doing less damage to the road, cause less draught on the horses.

TREES AND HEDGES.

There can be no doubt that, as far as the road is concerned,
both trees and hedges do a great deal of injury, especially the
former, for not only do they, to a great extent, deprive the road
of the drying action of both sun and air, but in wet weather they
are continually dripping on the road surface, thus keeping it in
a constant state of wet and mud.

However, a country road without trees is a dreary object
indeed, and where it is decided to plant the line of a road, the
trees should be placed as far off the metaled roadway as space
will admit.   The same applies, although in a less degree, to
hedges.   So far as the road is concerned, nothing can be better
than the post-and-rail fence, on account of the extra light and
air thereby admitted, but a hedge is infinitely more beautiful.
Where the adjoining country is well wooded and planted, I
would advise that no trees be planted along the line of the road.

I understand that this essay competition is for country
roads only, so I have confined myself to them, but before
closing I should like to say just a few words on

STREETS.

In the first place, I would advise that all main streets and thoroughfares where the traffic is excessive should be paved with the best asphalt pavement.   Secondly, that the residential and less busy parts be paved with wood pavement.   And thirdly, that side streets and less frequented parts be paved with granite blocks.

ASPHALT.

In London, after severe and lengthy experiments, the Val de Travers asphalt laid on a solid foundation of at least eighteen inches of concrete has been found to be the best and most lasting.

WOOD PAVEMENT.

This should be laid on a foundation similar to the asphalt, carefully shaped up to the desired contour.   The wood blocks should be of the best creosoted yellow pine, three by nine inches and six inches deep, laid lengthwise across the street, with the fibre of the wood in a vertical position, and with a water-tight joint of not more than one-half inch between each block.   The great point in laying wood pavement is to make the surface so water-tight that no moisture shall reach the foundation.   One of the best wood pavements is that known as the Henson.   The great advantage of wood pavement is that it is almost noiseless and at the same time affording a good foothold for the horses.

GRANITE PAVEMENT.

This is perhaps the cheapest and most lasting pavement in existence, but it has one serious drawback, and that is the excessive noise made by traffic thereon, and this is serious enough to banish it from all the most crowded and principal thoroughfares. The granite blocks should be dressed about 3″ x 9″ and from 6 to 9 inches deep.   The foundation is prepared similar to that for the Telford road, with a layer of clean, sharp sand on the top, in which the blocks are bedded ; these are then well rammed and filled in with a grouting of cement and sand.

16

SEWERS, GAS PIPES, ETC.

In all the principal thoroughfares it is most important that sub-ways at least six by four feet should be constructed under the centre of the pavement, in which all water and gas pipes, telegraph, telephone, and other electric wires must be laid. And under this sub-way should be constructed the main sewer.

This may at first sight seem to be a very expensive and perhaps needless work, but if the water, gas, and electric companies be charged rentals for the privilege of laying their pipes and wires therein, it can soon be made to pay for itself, and at the same time saving the pavement from the continual and inconvenient tearing-up for repairs so frequently seen.

In conclusion, there is nothing recommended in the foregoing essay at all inclined to be experimental or fanciful, but everything is the result of thorough and severe tests carried out during the last century in England. And I think every one will admit that England is as much and as justly celebrated for her beautiful roads as London is for its pavements.

DIGEST OF THE CONTENTS OF THE REMAINING CONTRIBUTIONS TO THE ROAD PRIZES.[1]

INTRODUCTORY.

NUMEROUS other papers were submitted containing valuable suggestions intended for the use of the public, and the committee have thought it expedient, therefore, to cause a synopsis of these several contributions to be prepared, so as to give a concensus of the views of the writers as a guide to the formulation of better laws and regulations on this important subject.

The contributions not already published in full were placed in the hands of the secretary of the Committee on Better Roads, with the request that he should review them, making such extracts as might be of service to the general public, and giving in substance the opinions of the authors.

In compliance with this reqest the following synopsis is submitted, exhibiting the views of the numerous and widely diversified interests represented by these papers.

For greater facility of reference, an attempt will be made to classify these opinions under various sub-divisions, as economics, construction, cost, suggestions, criticisms, and benefits, followed by a summation, stating the general conclusions and recommendations of the writers.

The first step in all reformations, whether material or moral, requires that a careful diagnosis be made of existing evils, and that measures be taken as speedily as possible to ameliorate them. Following this order, we will proceed to examine first, the several defects of existing roads and the laws relating thereto, as set forth in the contributions before us.

---

[1] The numbers affixed to the extracts are those attached to the papers submitted for competition.

(243)

GENERAL DEFECTS AND ECONOMICS.

Thus we find it stated that the condition of our roads is a disgrace to our civilization, and in support of this generally accepted opinion, some statistics are given which will serve to measure the great waste caused by the neglect and mismanagement of our highways.

A contractor who could have hauled thirty-five tons of hay seven miles in three days, at a cost of $50, on a macadam road, found that on the mud roads of Philadelphia County, it actually took him two weeks, cost $200, and nearly killed his horses. Instead, therefore, of costing him twenty cents per ton-mile, the actual cost was eighty-two cents, being a tax of sixty-two cents per ton per mile, to say nothing of the injury to the road, wagon, harness and team.

The writer remarks that the cost of movement for this short distance "was more than the product was worth, and put a stop to the business." This instance exemplifies a general law in regard to increasing facilities of transportation by reducing the resistance and cost.

15. Another writer estimates the economy of good roads as follows : In Pennsylvania, the estimated number of horses January, 1888, was 94,297, and the average price was $105.46. The average life was twelve years, and if, by better roads, but one more year were added to his life, it would effect a saving of $49,776.87 ; or, otherwise, the value of the horses being $9,955,-374, the legal interest on this sum for one year is $597,322.44, and one-twelfth of this principal, or $829,614.63, is the annual loss. Prolonging his life one year would save the interest on this amount, or $49,776.87. A similar computation for the saving upon mules, putting their life at 20 years, gives $3,391.44. The interest on this total, amounts to $3,190.09, which, added to the principal, gives a total of $56,358.40.

The census of 1880 gave the farm products of Pennsylvania as 6,500,000 tons, half of which is consumed on the farms, the balance is hauled an average of five miles to market. Assuming

that a two-horse team makes two trips per diem, at a cost of
$2.50 per day, the cost of movement on clay and macadam will
vary as follows:

	CLAY.	MACADAM.
Load for two horses, . . .	1400 lbs.	2180 lbs.
No. of loads for the 3,250,000 tons, .	4,643,000 "	2,981,000 "
Cost at $1.25 per load, . . .	$5,703,750	$3,726,250
Saving by reducing surface resistance, . .		$1,977,500

This is the waste entailed upon the farm products by clay
roads. It is enough to keep in repair 30,000 miles of turnpike
at an annual cost of $66 per mile. Or it represents 831,000
days' labor, which might be employed in other wealth-producing
industries.

Other freights would swell the waste to $4,000,000. In
England the saving between well-kept and neglected turnpikes
is estimated to be $100,000,000, which represents the difference
between three and four horses for a load.

The estimated loss on the marketing of the hay crop of
940,000 tons was $1,560,000, due to bad roads, while the total
annual losses are not less than $6,000,000, or the interest on
$100,000,000.

The road tax of Allegheny County amounts to about $140,-
000 annually, while for the entire State it is, according to the
best estimate obtainable, about $4,000,000. What have we to
show for it?

————

6. To get rid of the abominable libels dubbed roads, and
reach something near perfection, ought to be the object of all
true legislation on the subject.

The result of the existing mode of working out taxes is "a
lot of muddy, treacherous paths denominated roads, dangerous
to life and limb, and causing, directly or indirectly, by wear and
tear of vehicles, and extra exertion to draught animals, the loss
of thousands of dollars more than would make and maintain a
system of roads equal to those of any country in the world."

7. Our present system of road making is an extravagant waste of money. Almost all of the supervisors of our public roads . . . are the offspring of corrupt political rings, and but few of them know anything of making or putting in shape a good road, nor do they care or know how to economize, nor get a fair return in labor for the money paid those they employ.

---

11. The cost of any kind of hard surface will be large, and if the expense has to be borne by the rural population, without aid from State or National Government, it will be long before a general improvement is effected.

---

12. Much has been said about the inability of our supervisors ; that they are lacking in qualifications and experience, and for these reasons it is necessary they should be placed under some competent authority that would instruct and direct them in the proper fulfillment of their duties. Such an arrangement might be well were it not that taxes for road purposes have about reached their highest point, and any increased expenditure during the present depression of farming industry would not only be burdensome but oppressive. California assesses a road tax of two dollars against every male inhabitant, and this tax is collected from every employer, who is given a tax receipt for every male employé.

---

17. It is estimated that every half hour lost in consequence of bad roads is worth $72 per year for a single one-horse team.

---

18. The greatest enemy of all roads is water. Frost is an enemy, but only as it acts on the water in the roadbed. Heat is an enemy by expanding the particles, admitting the entrance of water. Collision and friction are the remaining enemies. . . Thousands of dollars are wasted every year in throwing broken stone into wet roadways. The mechanical strength of the roadway has rarely been considered, though it is an important factor in many cases. . . . . .

There is no person but in some direct or indirect manner is pecuniarily interested in the maintenance of a good road. It is important that this fact should not be lost sight of, as the practice that has led to turnpikes and toll gates, placing the cost wholly on those with vehicles passing through the gates, is manifestly unfair. In some way improved roads should be made a charge on the whole community. . . . The proper method should be that the township or county should be authorized to contract highway loans, and abutting property should be assessed just sufficient as a highway tax to pay interest and the sinking fund for the final extinction of the loan. The increased income from taxation, due to appreciation, will cover the cost of maintenance. . . . For construction and care of roads the contract system is the best, provided it be not by the square yard, nor by day's labor.

22. Macadam or "turnpike" makes the best and most durable road that can be obtained, but rather expensive in some localities, owing to the dearth of the kind of stone suitable for the purpose; but where limestone is plentiful, or any kind of stone that is not too hard to pulverize and cement together, will do for the first coating or bed of the road. Many persons favor raising money by county bonds at a low rate of interest, but we believe the work can be done more economically by stock companies. If the county were to build the roads at $2000 per mile on money at 4 per cent., the interest would be $80 per mile, which, with the $60 required to keep it in repair, would cost annually $140. This would embarrass farmers, and depreciate the value of their farms. Neither would it be desirable for the counties to collect tolls, as it would lead to political corruption. The best way would be to authorize private stock companies, in which the counties should take from two-fifths to nine-twentieths of the shares. Residents can work out their shares of stock very cheaply, and if the road only paid 2 per cent. dividends, the increased facilities and value of property

would amply repay the investors. They would take more interest in the roads, select officers for their fitness and integrity, and no one would suffer. Such improvements would save at least one horse annually, equivalent to a 4 per cent. investment on $600 or $1000. As to the county, if the road paid dividends equal to her interest, the road would cost her nothing.

---

23. Repairs should be contracted for on terms of from five to ten years, to give the contractor an opportunity to provide suitable machinery.

---

28. There are places where it would be cheaper to change the road so as to go around the hill instead of over it. . . . . Many miles are so low in the middle as to serve as gutters. The only remedy on side hills is to fill with solid material. . . . . Large stones dumped into a road are always a nuisance. It is always within reach of each of the supervisors to make thoroughly good roads with stone or gravel, at least half a mile, each year. In soft places twelve inches of metaling would be barely sufficient, while on solid ground, such as our red shale, six to eight inches would be enough. . . . . It would be true economy to abandon wood for bridging as rapidly as possible. . . . . To borrow money for roads is not good policy. Supposing a pike of reduced width could be built for $1500 per mile, and that fifty miles should be made, at that rate, costing $75,000. The interest on that, at 4 per cent., would be $3000. The repairing on that at $40 as a minimum would be $2000. There would still be left fifty miles of this township to be repaired at the present rate of $35 per mile, $1750, which would make a yearly expense of $6750, without allowing for sinking fund, or over six and one-half mills per dollar, with a local debt of $75,000. With such a burden of tax the roads would be neglected, and a poor turnpike is a bad road all the year round, while a good dirt road is preferable to almost any pike nine months of the year.

Road officers should be elected for three years instead of two, as now. Road districts should be allowed to buy land containing suitable material for road purposes.

---

30. It is evident to all who honestly desire better roads that the old methods are entirely inadequate to construct good highways. It has become a system of deceit and fraud. No one can believe that the supervisors return any just equivalent for money and time expended. It was stated at the recent agricultural convention "That in the last fifty years $200,000,000 had been spent on the roads of Pennsylvania, and that $7,000,000 are now spent annually. At the high rate of $10,000 per mile, this would build 700 miles in the State, or about ten miles in each county. The time and labor put in by the taxpayer on roads is generally a double loss to him. From $5000 to $10,000 are levied in many townships, and not one rod of road is permanently built. This sum is lost each year in throwing clay into the road, which works back to clog up the ditches. A low and corrupt state of moral and political principle is created. . . . On an average, there are sixty supervisors to each county, most of whom seek the office for the money to be made, very few with the higher motive of improving the roads. . . . . The utter failure, after 200 years, to build good roads under the present system, the waste of so many millions in that time—sufficient, if honestly used, to have built and macadamized every mile of road in the State—ought to convince all who have used the roads that they have not been properly made, and never will be, under this system. Under the present law, supervisors superintend the work, levy the tax, allow the accounts, even their own—there being, within some limits, no check, practically, as to how the road tax may be expended. . . . . Roads should be built consecutively, and not by patchwork. . . . . If properly and honestly managed, the reconstruction of the roads of the State would not greatly

increase the burden of the property holders, and would, in many respects, improve their property.

———

33. A permanent road may increase the value of a farm, yet it cannot increase its productiveness; so that the only immediate benefit will be from less cost of transportation. Farmers say: "We want no country pikes," having in mind the illy-constructed, illy-repaired pieces of pike to be found at this time in all rural districts. The piking of roads needs State aid and supervision. They should be revised, both as to grade and alignment, by juries taken from adjacent counties.

———

36. The intelligence displayed in the construction and maintenance of our public thoroughfares is of no great credit to us as a nation. Of all civilized countries, America can lay claim to the poorest roads. . . . . Some of our richest mines are comparatively valueless because the roads are either entirely wanting or so poor that the cost of transportation would exceed the value of the metal. Many luxuriant crops of perishable fruits and vegetables perish because there is no facility of rapid transportation. Until within a few years, the cattle of the Pampas were slaughtered for their hides and horns, and in Spain thousands of sheep were killed annually for their fleece only; but this waste has been largely stopped by the construction of highways and railroads.

Good roads affect the farmer directly by carrying his products and merchandise at a cost which decreases directly in proportion as the road becomes better.

Dense population and manufacturing industry always make a good market for farm products, and by roads alone these cities and towns may extend themselves indefinitely.

A report of a committee of the House of Commons says: "By the improvement of our roads every branch of our agricultural, commercial and manufacturing industries would be materially benefited. Every article brought to market would be diminished in price, and the number of horses would be so much reduced that the expense of £5,000,000 ($25.000,000) would be annually saved to the public. . . . . In short, the public and private advantages resulting from the improvement of our highways would be incalculable." .

The roads of New England and the Middle States are far from being satisfactory as to their location, direction and construction. They pass through places that offer the greatest resistance to economic traffic. . . . .

SUGGESTIONS AND CRITICISMS.

2. The money raised for making roads must be used for that purpose, and the majority of it should not go into the pockets of surveyors, lawyers, inspectors and contractors. Enough money is collected to put the roads in good order, but in many places the effect of the work is not visible, and in others it were better if they had been left to nature.

The highways should be in charge of a committee, and there should be no more plowing up of the, sides and making of cultivated patches. The mud should be removed from the ditches, and a good coating of gravel should be spread over the roadbed. We need good gravel, common-sense and government aid.

3. The National Government should issue bonds for the construction of roads, and the supervisors should be elected as at present.

4. The model road would consist of two flat tramways of iron eighteen inches broad by one-quarter of an inch thick.

5. The principal cities should be connected by macadamized roads thirty-six feet wide, built and maintained by the State. The counties should build similar roads twenty-four feet wide; the townships, eighteen feet wide, half of the width being met-

aled. These roads should be laid out and supervised by competent State and county officers, and be constructed of the best and cheapest material on hand, and by contract.

———

6. Let the county commissioners or the court appoint a road commissioner, and, with a tax laid on every citlzen of the county, let him build a good durable road, and have power to abandon such as are difficult to keep up or are not necessary for the accommodation of the public. The law should state explicitly the material, width, wages per diem, and make it a penal offence for any political influence or intrigue to enter into any appointment. There should be sub-commissioners appointed in each township, whose work should be approved by the commissioners.

———

7. It would be sheer folly to attempt to enforce the construction of macadamized roads, because the great portion of the country is *entirely* destitute of limestone (the only stone that would make a good macadam road).

Have the election of supervisors by vote of the people *entirely* abolished, and let the appointing power be placed in our courts, making it *imperative* with the judges to appoint none but men of known reputation and ability, having some practical knowledge of their work. There should be one or two supervisors to each township, who should be allowed a liberal *per diem* and be required to furnish and select their own implements and employés, to fix wages, to assess and collect the road tax, and inflict a penalty for extra heavy hauling while the ground is soft and full of water. Bonds should be required.

———

8. Do not put logs in a new road; nor cover a sluice with small stones; remove all roots and stumps; apply the stones in thick layers and let them be well broken; do not allow the road to be ruined by a rain or flood when an hour's work will turn the water.

9. The present way of working out taxes is entirely wrong, and should be abolished. A road supervisor should be appointed for each county with power to employ assistants for each district.

---

10. A law should be passed requiring all road tax to be paid in money collected as other taxes. The State should pay one-half of all road tax. One or more road masters should be appointed in each township by the judge of the court, by petition from the citizens, to serve for three years ; to give bond and be returnable for neglect of duty.

10. All main roads should be forty feet wide, thirty-two between gutters ; all other roads thirty-three feet wide, twenty-five feet between gutters and four feet foot-walks on either side.

---

11. Pennsylvania roads are laid out two rods wide, but it is doubtful if one-half of their length exceeds twenty-five feet in width. Property taxable for State purposes is wholly exempt from paying road taxes. This seems inequitable. Real estate is taxed for county, school and road purposes to an extent in each case equal to the State tax on personal property. This should be more equitably distributed.

The State and National Government might with propriety be asked to aid in building roads as well as improving rivers or assisting the railroads.

The township officers should be authorized to issue bonds clear of taxes, if desired, to build roads and provide the necessary machinery. There should be two supervisors to each township. No civil engineer will be necessary.

---

12. Old, obstructive road laws should be repealed and new ones enacted that would enable our supervisors to enforce the authority necessary for the fulfillment of their many duties. They should be elected for a longer term than one year, and not be in fear of being defeated by the votes of near-sighted tax payers

who will not see that the annual cost of maintaining poor
roads is more expensive than improved ones. Give them full
power to select their employés.   .   .   .   Let them organize
themselves as a board, holding monthly meetings, with the town
clerk as secretary.

The proposition to grant State aid is attended with many
difficulties, because of the Constitutional prohibition to special
legislation, which would prevent enterprising townships that
would be willing to guarantee a just expenditure of such aid
from so doing because of the non-concurrence of others.   This
may be overcome by the board of supervisors making a certified
statement before a judge of the court that they have expended
10 per cent. or more of the road tax in permanently improving
certain roads in their district, and thus entitling them to draw a
like amount from the State treasury to be expended in a similar
manner.   It may be well to have a State superintendent of
roads, whose duty shall be to advise and recommend necessary
regulations and adjust disputes between contiguous districts.

———

17. The interest of every good citizen and every corpora-
tion are identical in having good roads, consequently the
expenses entailed in their construction and maintenance should
be fairly apportioned.   .   .   .   .   Without the aid of a practical civil engineer any efforts for permanently improving public
roads will be worse than useless.   .   .   .   .   All the present
road laws should be repealed, and new laws enacted dividing the
State into districts; a practical engineer should be appointed
by the Governor after examination, with a competent salary.
He should appoint his own assistants in charge of townships.

The tax should be paid in money, hauling or material, for
which vouchers should be given by the engineer.   .   .   .   .   It
would be useless to pass a law specifying any particular system
of road making for the entire State, but it should regulate the
width and grade.   .   .   .   .   Heavy teams should be made to
use wide tires.

No one should think of referring this matter (road construction) to the legislature. What does the average member know or care about the roads of the Commonwealth? The Act of June 2d, 1887, authorized the condemnation and vacation of turnpikes, and relegated them to the care of the borough, to be kept "up as other public roads or streets." That means to cover them with dirt and revert them back to what these roads were before, and even much worse. In one case the supervisor attempted to keep up the turnpike by hauling a few loads of stone thereon, and was in consequence defeated at the next election. The citizens, it seems, are unwilling to be taxed for any kind of road making. Thus because some single turnpike had to be condemned the entire commonwealth was burdened with this foolish law.

But there is need of improvement, and the people should be educated through the schools, where the children should be shown the defects of our existing roads, and be taught how to remedy them. There are arbor days, why not have road days? . . . Turnpike roads are enterprises undertaken by chartered companies. As a question of economy the State ought not to build or authorize townships or counties to construct them. Under the best private management but comparatively few make more than a common profit of from 4 to 6 per cent. The cost of maintenance is far greater than is generally supposed—$200 per mile per annum is about the average, while the original cost of construction is about $5000. . . .

Between the Telford and macadam systems, the Telford is the better. The only difference is that Telford starts the foundation with large stones while macadam breaks them small. The large stones form a barrier against heavy teams cutting through, especially in wet seasons or when the frost comes out of the earth. All the old turnpikes from Philadelphia were constructed in this way, and they have a solid bottom and maintain their integrity much better than the modern ones built on the macadam plan, and they cost less for repairs.

18. There are no roads in Pennsylvania which either Mr. MacAdam or Mr. Telford would be willing to accept as representing their modes. MacAdam formulated the proposition that the wear of roads is proportioned to the weight and velocity of the carriage running upon a given breadth of the tire of the wheels. From which his practical deduction was, that a road to be good should have a smooth solid surface, so flat that a carriage might stand upright; the stones should not exceed one inch in any of their dimensions.

Philadelphia has lost enormously by looking too much at the mere hardness of the material, and too little at its small size. The House of Correction stone if broken to the true MacAdam size would make a very suitable material.

20. It would not be advisable to macadamize our country roads under existing conditions. The cost is generally placed at too low a figure. If the main roads are to be metaled the State should take the matter in hand. . . For many years to come our main dependence must be dirt roads, which must be properly improved by being graded, drained, harrowed, rolled and honed at the right time and in the proper manner. . . It is quite certain that our road laws must be radically changed before *any* improvement can take place. . . Roads must be placed in the hands of engineers—men educated for the business. Europe has good roads because they are built and maintained by engineers.

21. Most decidedly the farmers ought not to build stone roads without State aid. . . Should there be a commission appointed, engineers, or superintendent of public highways, so as to have uniformity in the roads? Emphatically, No. The farmers are already burdened enough without having to pay for a lot of useless officers. It does seem paradoxical that what road laws any farmer of any brains could make in five minutes, and what any railroad paddy, who could pound stone, could

execute, were not made long ago. What do we elect men to the legislature for, if they are not competent to give us a road law ?

Our roads are not better because there is no law compelling the commissioners to make them so. They should be required to levy a tax to be paid in money, but be authorized to give the farmer a rebate on taxes for all stone delivered along the roadside during the year at a price per perch, and if they wished to work they should be paid for the work done, and not for the time put in. Then, as each mile is completed, the State should pay its part.

23. In the country sheet asphalt will rot in about ten years. Proper legislation will require a State board composed of a member from each county. The county should also be divided into districts, with a supervisor in charge of each to look after the contractors. The roads should be built and maintained by a State tax.

24. To make a good road only requires honest work with pick and shovel, hammer and drill, supplemented with horse and cart and scraper, as may be required.   .   .

The road law of 1836, with some local changes, is the law of to-day. It is exceedingly comprehensive, and is suited even better for the present times than for the period in which it was enacted. The trouble is not with the law, but with the people who do not avail themselves of its advantages. They prefer to ascend hills of ten degrees slope rather than help to pay to cut them down to five degrees, as the law requires ; to drive in the mud and stick in ruts rather than gutter and drain the road ; to make the width eighteen or twenty feet rather than forty or fifty to save land. Such roads are just narrow enough to prevent them from being effectually made. The fault is not with the law, but with the people, and they have what they want and do not complain.

17

26. The system of working out the road tax should be abolished, as not many men go on the road to work but to put in time and get credit for taxes. It is said of a certain township that it pays $2000 to $2500 per year, and the roads are never in decent condition, whereas $1000 applied in the proper manner would produce much better results. . . . The legislature should appropriate all the money the State can spare for roads. If one-half the losses caused by bad roads were applied to their improvement, it would not be long before they were better.

27. Efforts have been made from time to time to induce the officers to stone portions of the roads, with some success, but when the tax was increased to do more than the absolutely necessary repairing, dissatisfaction has resulted in defeating the re-election of the officers.

28. State aid would be desirable with laws to make it available if the State furnishes the money and would construct and entirely keep in repair leading roads in each township or county; but not so if the townships were required to furnish the money for the State to spend. . . . A law is needed requiring all taxes to be paid in money, so that the road officers can secure the best labor in the market. . . . *All property*, real and personal, should be taxed for *all purposes for which* the owner receives a benefit. Land in our township is now taxed from ten to twelve mills per dollar on its full value. Thus the farmer pays $120 while the stockholder pays but $30. With taxation equalized, a law requiring not less than 2 per cent. of the mileage in each district improved by stoning or graveling each year would seem to be just.

29. In defraying the cost of roads, the simplest and best method is to assess the whole cost on the county, taking care to improve all the main roads at the same time.

30. One of the first steps in the improvement of the roads

will be to remove the management entirely from political control. Some favor State aid, but those who remember the $40,000,000 State debt and the circumstances under which it was created, will not favor this plan. In any case the property owner must pay the debt. There is no doubt that more miles of road would be built by local effort than by State assistance. The State money would become political plunder. Local jealousies would spring up and matters would be made worse instead of better. . . .

The change proposed is that a competent person should be appointed by the judges of the Supreme Court to be chief engineer or road commissioner. He should appoint the county engineer of roads for a term of five years. These should give bonds for faithful performance of duties, and have entire control of county roads under the county commissioners, who should raise from $25,000 to 50,000 in a county every year to be expended on roads. The townships may levy a tax of from two to five mills on the dollar to be spent on township roads under the engineer.

31. I would build the roads all over the State with the money of the State, which will in a short time be completely out of debt. For four years I would appropriate $2,000,000 annually, and after that a much larger sum to be divided among the counties according to population.

There should be three county commissioners, one of whom should be a civil engineer, and they should be elected by a convention. The work should be done by contract.

32. In wet seasons our roads are nearly impassable, because there is no system of drainage and no outlets for water, and usually the centre of the road is the lowest part of it. The only thing they are good for is a ditch for all the surrounding fields to drain into. . . . . The legislative feature is the keynote for good roads. The present supervisor should be buried and forgotten. He has been one of the most indepen-

dent and powerful of county officers. No action of his could
be questioned; his books could not be seen without a criminal
proceeding in court. He has been, in most instances, a farmer,
with his farm to look after. His election depended on his
money and popularity, not on his ability. His term is one
year. His salary is not fixed; he has a commission on the road
tax he is able to collect, and gets, besides, $2.00 per day when
on the road, and $1.50 for his horse. His first year he makes
the taxes so low as to ensure his re-election, but in his second
and last year he increases them 100 per cent. His salary from
this source varies from $500 to $1000. The hired laborers are
his political friends, old and inefficient, or they are land owners
working out their taxes. He will not work on the roads when
his farm needs his services, consequently the work is done at
the worst time and in the most ineffective manner, or not at all.
With such supervision and wholesale robbery, is it to be won-
dered at that our roads are in their present state?

The system of working out the road tax is all wrong, and
should be abolished.

The State should build the roads, levy a sufficient tax on
property and a poll tax of from three to five dollars on all not
property owners.

Turnpike companies should be bought out by the State, as
the principle of private corporations taxing public travel is all
wrong, or else they should be compelled to maintain a certain
standard of excellence. The Governor should appoint engineers
in each county to supervise all State roads, subject to a State
board of overseers.

———

33. To maintain our earth roads in a passable condition we
should have a State law that will be practical, and not as many
different laws as there are townships in each county.

The great trouble with our present system is not that the
work costs too much, but that it is impossible to have it done
when it should be, because we have too many contractors and

too many incompetent supervisors. The courts should appoint them and require surety for the faithful performance of duties, giving them a competent salary. The man who will work for nothing is dear at his board. . . Make all road taxes payable in money, and employ road laborers continuously. . . The county should prepare—that is, grade and drain the roadbed, which may cost from $500 to $1500, after which the State should put on the macadam, as it can be done cheaper in large contracts by employing machinery. . . The National Government should release the tax on whiskey and tobacco, and if necessary the State could collect and devote it to roads. Manufactured articles should be taxed as well as real estate and live stock. After the roads are built the counties should keep them in repair.

---

36. The present method of raising a specified sum of money for roads and allowing an inexperienced and incompetent person to expend the same is erroneous. The highway supervisor is elected without the first thought as to his fitness for the position. Often the care of the roads is given to the lowest bidder, and the money is expended before half the year has expired ; again, a large part of the money is spent where it will benefit the backers of the man in charge. When an overseer has learned something of his duties another takes his place and begins his experience at the expense of the roads. There is as great need of civil service reform in these matters as in those of national politics. The right man should be retained.

Not less than three road commissioners should be appointed in each town, the latter being divided into districts. Every three districts should have one commissioner, who should examine the roads and report to the town meeting. The repairs should be let out by contract, in sections of not more than five miles each. There should be no day's labor employed, and no tax-payer should be permitted to work out his taxes on the road. The tax should be paid in money. The indolent will then be obliged to contribute his share, and the burden will not fall

upon the few.   The old system is wrong; and good roads, convenience, comfort and economy, with increased happiness of
country life, demand a change.

---

38. The present system of working roads always was bad,
and the longer it exists the worse it becomes, so that it should
be abandoned.   Education is necessary, and it is possible that in
the next generation we may have better roads. . .   A super-
vising engineer should be appointed for each district.

39–41. Our roads should be divided into two, if not three,
classes.   1st. The main roads, which should be maintained
equally by the State and counties through which they pass. 2d.
County roads. 3d. Lateral or township roads.   The county
roads should be built and maintained by the county through
which they pass, while the township roads should be similarly
sustained by the township's officers.   A map of all roads should
be filed in the county clerk's office, and the board of overseers
should be authorized to levy a tax not to exceed one-fourth of
one per cent. of the assessed value of the taxables in the
county, or if preferred, to issue bonds at a low rate and provide
a sinking fund.   The debt should not exceed 3 per cent. of the
assessed valuation.

The country road law of New Jersey puts one-third of the
cost on the city, town or borough through which the road passes,
and two-thirds on the county at large.   Convicts and tramps
should be employed in breaking stone at a per diem and under
proper supervision.   As to supervisors, poor pay and penurious
treatment will weed out good men, if they happen to get in, and
leave the roads in unskilled hands.   They should be nominated
by the town officials, and after examination, be balloted for by
the people.   The examination should consist of 100 questions
on local features, road laws, road making, best materials, location, cost, trees, bookkeeping and mensuration.

40. Important points to be observed in the maintenance of roads : 1. All mud and dirt should be removed as frequently as possible ; 2. The entire drainage system should be carefully maintained ; 3. Constant repairs wherever ruts or depressions begin to show ; 4. Careful sprinkling three or four times a day in dry weather ; 5. The frequent use of the two-and-a-half-ton roller.

Legislation. 1. Abolish the present system of working out taxes and have them paid in cash ; 2. Each county should have a superintendent of roads, either appointed or elected for a term of years, well paid for his services. Each township a supervisor subject to the county superintendent ; 3. The road taxes for each township should be expended by the supervisor subject to the township board. He should be under bonds ; 4. There should be a standard set of specifications for all the roads of the State.

----

43. A country road should have attention when the weather is favorable. The scraper and roller should be freely used to destroy ruts.

CONSTRUCTION.

The roadbed may be of any material, exclusive of clay and quicksand. After the construction of the bed, curbstones, fourteen to sixteen inches high, and four to six thick, should be placed on either side, and the space between them set with stones nine to twelve inches high, and be keyed-together. Upon this rough pavement should be laid a four inch layer of two and a-half inch stones, rolled under a pressure of from ten to twelve tons, until completely settled. A second layer five to six inches thick of two inch stones should then be added and compacted by rolling. Finally, a layer one inch thick, of fine stuff, is spread upon the top, moistened thoroughly and rolled down smooth. The total depth of this metaled surface is about two feet. No estimate of the cost is submitted.

8. A cheap road for heavy traffic may be made by preparing a foundation seven feet wide and twenty inches deep of broken stones, and covering it with ten inches of coal ashes or creek gravel. The remaining thirteen feet of the width should be carefully freed from stones.

For small bridges of ten feet span, use old railroad T rails and cover them with flagstones under two feet of earth and gravel.

———

9. The cheapest and best way of making a good road is: 1st. To deposit a layer of coal ashes ten inches deep; 2d. A layer of broken stone eight inches thick; 3d. Succeeded by another stratum of coal ashes eight inches thick. The result will be a dry, clean and durable road, costing nothing for material and but little for labor.

———

10. Where macadam is used the stone should be placed only on one side of the road, and the earth which is removed should be used to raise the other side and to fill in low places, as thorough drainage is the main feature in road making.

———

11. Earth roads may be much improved by crowning the road with a good scraper, handled by a team and two men. To construct a good stone surface the stones should be broken by a crusher, to pass through a one-inch ring. It should be placed on a portion of the surface, say twelve feet wide and six inches deep on dry soil, with greater depth when required. It should not be screened, but deposited as it leaves the crusher, coarse and fine together, to form a compact mass, and thoroughly rolled. Hard stone is preferred when procurable. One mile will require about 2000 perches at, say seventy-five cents per perch for breaking or hauling on road.

———

12. The old process of throwing the sods into the middle of the road and the stones under the fences must be reversed if we would have good roads.

14. There are six kinds of metal which make very good hard roads, viz.; (*a*) stone of all kinds; (*b*) gravel; (*c*) sand; (*d*) brush; (*e*) straw; (*f*) cornstalks; each of which has been successfully used under heavy traffic. . . . The roads should be 22 feet wide having grades of 8 inches to the rod ($=\frac{1}{22}$), should be properly drained and made hard. After draining and ditching the roadbed, plow up the bottom 4 inches deep, harrow fine, put on a layer of 3½ or 4-inch stone closely placed but not crowded; roll with a 500-pound iron roller until bedded. Add a layer of 1¼-inch broken stone, 6 inches thick; roll down even; add a layer of coarse sand or stone dust 2 inches thick.

Where quicksand exists, common straw may be used to make a roadbed when nothing else will do. Dig out the bed to a depth of 4 feet; twist the straw into a rope of say 3 inches as iron moulders do; double and twist again until the rope is about 1 foot thick; lay the ropes across the bed; cover with dry clay or sand 3 inches thick; then another layer of straw rope followed by sand, etc., until the trench is filled to within 6 inches of the top; finish with clay or other material at hand.

17. In some sections a peculiar sand is found from disintegrated limestone, sometimes micaceous and siliceous, but it makes a good road throughout the year.

Each township should be provided with a portable stone-crusher, horse and cart, and a regular force of laborers, under a competent foreman. All work should be done by contract. . . On good sustaining ground from 8 to 12 inches of metaling will be required, broken in sizes varying from 2½ inches at the bottom to screenings on top. They should be rolled down on a well-drained, correctly-shaped surface. When a good bed cannot be found, then Telford, beginning with 14-inch stone at the centre, diminishing to 8 inches at the gutter for a 16-foot wide road. Then ram, cover with sand and a top dressing of 2½ inches of ballast, then a layer of 1½-inch metal and 1½ inches of screenings, each to be rolled separately with a heavy roller. On the average country road macadam will be found the cheapest and just as durable, and it need not be over 8 feet wide.

---

18. Stone, broken small, as a true macadam requires, arched over the natural earth with proper supports at the sides, would be as compact and strong as if made up piece by piece with brick and stone, and save immensely in the cost of the expensive foundation thought to be essential in all self-sustaining pavements. But always provided the natural surface is dry.

---

21. First-class roads should be 10 feet wide and 1 foot deep, filled with finely-broken stone. Second-class roads should only be 8 feet wide. Never allow any water to stand on the road. For third-class roads, round them up, don't make them too wide; keep out the stones and you have very good roads when the weather is fine. Macadamizing, from the fact that stone is most abundant of all materials, recommends itself as being the only plan whereby we may have good roads at all times.

---

22. The turnpike should not be less than 35 to 40 feet between fences, thus permitting room for a drain and Summer road.

---

23. A good road should be about 36 feet wide. There is economy in making the roadbed 27 feet wide or even less. The earth should be 1 foot deep. There should be paved gutters 2 feet wide on each side. Ballast composed of loose or broken stone 8 or 10 inches in depth, should be placed over the entire bed between the gutters, and the remaining depth of 2 to 4 inches is to be filled with small broken stone or clean, screened, coarse gravel, rolled and covered with sharp sand. . . . The farmers have more stones picked off their fields than would be needed, and of such sizes as would make a good ballast of 2 to 3 inches cube, with smaller stones to fill in the middle layers, and crushed stone or screenings for the top course.

24. The base of a Telford road ought to be graded about 6 inches higher in the middle of a 20-feet wide roadbed, the larger of large stones, 8 inches thick, set on edge, and closely compacted, then 8 inches more of broken stone at the centre, sloping to 4 inches at the side. To make a complete finish, gravel or very fine broken stone should be put on top of the broken stone, and the whole surface rolled with a 15-ton road-roller until perfectly level and solid. . . .

A common road should never be less than 30 feet wide, of which 26 feet should be graded, leaving 2 feet of gutters on either side. Ruts should be filled up as soon as may be practicable, by using an improved road scraper.

26. To make a good road, make the cross section of the roadbed concave, with a slope toward the centre of 1 inch in 3 feet. Then make a drain 4 inches deep along the centre of the concavity, and lay 3-inch tile carefully end to end with a grade of 1 inch to a rod. It should run out every 300 feet to the side drain. Then fill up the roadbed with stone till it becomes convex, cover this with 3 inches of broken stone and just enough soil to make it smooth. The road and ditches need constant attention. This road will cost from $1000 to $2000 per mile.

27. Concerning plowing and filling up the public roads as customary, from 1 to 10 inches high all over, I consider it the greatest nuisance that can happen to it.

29. For a main road from 25 to 40 feet is sufficient, and for cross-country roads 16 feet will answer.

32. For a main thoroughfare I would recommend a width of 30 feet from out-to-out of side ditches, and for a cross road 22 to 24 feet will be ample.

There are two well-known systems of stone roads. The Telford requires greater skill and more care in making; consequently, is the most expensive without being more durable or satisfactory. The macadam, all things considered, is the best suited to our purpose, and is everything that can be desired.

A lot of broken stone of all sizes spread three or four inches deep and left to travel to pack, will never be satisfactory, yet this is what is known as macadamizing. In his latest practice MacAdam did not allow any stone larger than a cube of one-and-a-half inches or two inches on edge to be used; he caused splinters and thin slices and spalls to be excluded, and laid great stress on uniformity of size and freedom from dust, sand or earthy matter. It has been proved to be a mistake to exclude the smaller fragments and detritus, as the road cannot be compacted into a smooth hard surface by rolling or by traffic. If the forms are angular and of all sizes below the maximun prescribed, the fragments will unite more firmly and very little if any binding material will be necessary.

For very hard stone a two-inch ring gauge is sufficient, but for softer varieties a two-and-a-half inch gauge may be used. MacAdam considered ten inches of well-compacted materials enough for very heavy traffic. In this country of severe frosts the standard minimum thickness should not be less than ten inches. . . . . Except in large towns a width of sixteen feet for metaling will suffice, applied in the centre of the road, and good gravel may be spread over the wings. . . . . Cross roads may be made excellent if covered with ten inches of gravel applied on the centre of the road for a width of ten feet. It should be coarse but not to exceed one-and-a-half inches, and contain enough clayey loam to bind it together firmly. Boiler ashes may be used, but are not so good nor durable.

----

33. We want first, firm beds of stone, which can only be obtained by hand placing, whether we use the macadam or pike, and a good finish of hard stone firmly broken, that the roads may be alike proof to the action of wheels and water. Very few sections of road have stone hard enough for top dressing, and if of

medium grade they will soon wear into ruts. Single track may be made seven feet wide, but for double track, always to be recommended, they should be sixteen feet wide.

---

36. For purposes of draining, the road should have a grade of at least 1 foot in 130, and the greatest slope should not exceed 1 in 35. No road should be wider than is necessary for the travel over it. For two vehicles to pass, the width should be at least 16½ feet, but it is far better to increase this to 20 feet. The surface should be raised above the general level of the surrounding land, and good ditches be placed on either side. Thorough drainage is one of the first requisites of a good road.

For gravel roads the material should be dug from pits and screened so as to separate all sizes over one-and-a-half inches and under one-half inch in diameter. It should be applied in three coats, each of three inches thickness, and rolled

Charcoal Roads.—In some of the Western States, where wood is plenty, roads have been made through swampy forests as follows : Logs from six inches to two feet in diameter and from twelve to twenty-four feet long are cut and piled lengthwise along the road about six feet high, being nine feet on the bottom and two on top, and then covered with straw and earth, or simply with sods, and burned in the manner of coal-pits. The covering is taken from the sides of the road, and the ditches thus formed afford good drainage. After the timber is converted into charcoal, the earth is removed to the sides of the ditch and the coal drawn each way having a gentle slope from the centre to the sides. Such a road, though expensive, is very durable, and always presents a smooth, hard surface.

Plank roads should be made of twelve by twenty-four inch sleepers sixteen feet long and bedded on the flat side three or four feet apart, filled in between with earth beaten or rolled down so as to leave no air spaces underneath the planks. These should be eight feet long and four inches thick, preferably of oak, and from six to twelve inches wide, laid square across the

stringers.   They should then be covered with a coating of coal
tar and an inch of coarse sand or fine gravel.

Stone Roads.—If the bottom consists largely of clay it is
better to apply a coating of several inches of sand or gravel
before applying the road metal.   Sometimes a close floor of
boards will serve as well.   After the excavation is made and
drained, broken stone is laid upon the prepared bed in two or
three layers three inches thick and rolled successively, and then
a coating of one inch of sand is spread over the top and rolled
into it with plenty of water.   Such is the method in England.
Some consider it better to dispense with the coating of sand.
From six to ten inches of road metal is a proper maximum depth.

No large stones should be used.   The proper size is a one-
and-a-half inch cube, or two inches on the longest diagonal,
broken by hand or in a crusher.

The best materials are the basaltic and trap rocks, syenite,
granite and some limestone, but flint or quartz rocks, gneiss,
mica—slate and sandstone should never be used.

Earth roads are full of defects.   They contain many ruts,
especially in clay soil.   On sandy soil six inches of clay will be
an improvement.   In filling ruts coarse sand or gravel should be
used free from vegetable mould.   Stones should never be used
unbroken.   The plow and scraper should never be used to
repair a road.

The full width should not be less than forty nor more than
sixty feet, but the paved portion need only be from eighteen to
twenty-four feet, eighteen feet being ample for the majority of
country roads.

The lateral slope of the surface should not be less than
one-half nor more than three-quarters of an inch to the
foot.

For the top dressing of Telford pavements granite or trap
rock will be found to give entire satisfaction.   Although costing
more at first, it is much cheaper in the end than some of the
softer stones.   This has been proven beyond a doubt by prac-

tical experience. A very light coat of clay upon this covering will be found advantageous in binding it together.

For the macadam road, place first a layer of broken stone of two-and-one-half to three inches in size for a depth of six inches; cover this with another six-inch layer of stones broken to one-and-one-half to two-inch size, thoroughly rolled; then a light coat of clay, followed by stone screenings, sprinkled and thoroughly rolled. There is much difference of opinion as to which of these two methods is the best for a general road pavement, but there should not be to anyone who has watched the results of heavy travel upon Telford and macadam when laid on similar soil and under similar conditions. It will be found that ruts form sooner in the macadam than in the Telford pavement, especially in the Spring of the year. The macadam is excellent for light travel, but is not equal to the Telford for general traffic. A much cheaper road than either can be made by using the Telford foundation, and covering it with about four inches of gravel containing sufficient clay to make it pack well. This makes a hard, smooth surface, is easily kept in repair, and is an excellent road for light travel.

---

43. The grade should not exceed six feet per hundred, nor be less than one. Where the subsoil is strong loam or clay, it should receive a layer of iron moulder's sand or coal ashes to a depth of about two inches. Good gravel six inches deep will greatly improve the road. All loose stones should be picked off and used for macadamizing the worst portions.

RELATIVE COST OF MACADAM VS. TELFORD.

Other things being equal, the cheapest road will be the best, but it is often a difficult problem to determine how much more may be expended on the first cost of a road that its ultimate expense for maintenance may be a minimum. Upon this point there is great difference of opinion, and the tendency of popular opinion is to lean toward the lesser first cost, even if

the road does require a larger outlay to maintain it in passable
order. While this policy is not always the best nor most economical, it is often necessary to secure any improvement whatever.

For the more ready comparison of the cost of these systems, the prices as given by the several contributors are arranged in parallel columns :

MACADAM.	TELFORD.
15. One mile, 30 feet wide, and 14 inches deep in centre, from $7000 to $9000, according to material and distance. With a good old foundation, it would cost $3500 to $4000.	One mile, 20″ deep, in layers, with good rolling, can be made for $5000 to $7000, according to material and distance. On an old foundation it would cost from $3000 to $3500.

A macadam road is the best road, and, being the best, it is
the cheapest.

Estimate for roads thirty feet wide, fourteen inches deep
at centre, with one yard of borders in grass and two sidewalks
six feet wide :

MacAdam would cost, ... $9,236	Telford, ... $8,236
If on old foundation, ... 6,686	" old foundation, . . . 5,686
" " but with-	Telford, sans accessories, . . 3,000
out walks, border, etc., . 3,350	

Resurfacing every sixth year, $900 per mile.

---

17. One mile, single track, 8 feet wide, ... {$ 800 / 1,200 | One mile, single track, . . {$2,500 / 6,000

COST OF OTHER ROADS.

15. A good road, with a surface of gravel laid on ten
inches of stone, with two side drains, can be built for $2500 to
$3000 per mile.

With one side drain and eight inches of broken rock, the
road would cost from $1500 to $2500 per mile.

---

17. One mile of plank road, good for eight years, $1000 to
$3400.

18. In the vicinity of Philadelphia, and near stone quarries and crushers, the cost of making the ordinary stone road is about $1.00 per square yard. As such roads are constructed near the city, having Belgian block gutters for drainage and flag crossing-stones every two or three hundred feet, the first cost of these pseudo-macadam roads is nearly $2.00, and then brick, as a mere question of first cost, can successfully compete with it. A dollar a square yard is, however, probably all the generality of property could stand under a general road law. But the enormous cost of repairs to these roads must not be lost sight of. . . . . The brick used in Philadelphia has to be brought by rail 300 to 400 miles. If it costs a dollar a square yard for broken stone, that requires an annual attention that doubles its cost in ten years, while if the brick road will last twenty-five years without showing any material wear, at $1.50, $1.75 or even $2.00 a square yard, it requires no demonstration to determine which is the better.

21. I am confident that a stone road such as is described (ten feet wide by one deep), in counties where stone is abundant, would not cost over $1.50 per lineal rod.

22. The cost of building a turnpike, including grading, culverts, bridges, toll-houses, etc., varies from $1500 to $2000 per mile, taking all things into consideration, together with the difficulty of obtaining stone at all points.

23. The cost of a stone road with paved gutters would be eighty cents per square yard, one foot deep exclusive of arches and bridges, the masonry of which would cost about eight cents per cubic foot, complete. Repairs would cost about $25 per mile.

28. In a township containing about 100 miles of public roads the average cost of annual repairs for ten years past was

18

$3500, and the rate of taxation on the full value of the land 3½ mills. There is an excellent turnpike crossing the township, about five miles, which cost $3000 per mile forty years ago, and which requires an average expense of $80 per mile, exclusive of salaries, to keep in repair.

---

29. A good macadam road fourteen inches deep can be built for $7000 per mile. The interest of that amount at 5 per cent. is $350, while the cost of maintenance, including material, watering and labor, would not exceed $400 per annum—a total of $750 per mile. This amount would be very light indeed, and in the enhancement of land values would be returned ten-fold.

---

30. The expense will run from $1000 to $10,000 to thoroughly build and macadamize one mile of road.

---

32. As to cost, it is impossible to give any correct figures. It can only be said that it is always more economic in the long run to use the best material and follow the best plan.

---

40. The cost of earth excavation will vary from sixteen to thirty cents per cubic yard; rock excavation from fifty to seventy-five cents. Stones suitable for a Telford foundation can be quarried and delivered for $1.00 per cubic yard, or for an eight-inch foundation, about twenty-two cents per square yard. Four good pavers can readily place 300 lineal feet, eighteen feet wide, per day (150 square yards per man). This will give two and one-third cents per square yard for laying the foundation.

Broken stone can be delivered for $1.25 per cubic yard, or about fourteen cents per square yard, four inches deep. Allowing seven cents for screenings, sprinkling and rolling, the total cost of a square yard of Telford pavement will be forty-six cents under the most favorable conditions. The limit may run up to ninety-five cents. This does not include grading, draining, bridging, etc. There is comparatively little difference between the cost of a Telford and macadam road of the same depth. A good gravel road on a Telford foundation will cost about thirty-five cents per square yard, exclusive of grading. For reconstructing old turnpikes the cost will be from thirty to forty-five cents per square yard.

FOREIGN ROADS.

French roads are divided into national, departmental, military and country cross-roads. The national roads are maintained at the expense of the Empire. The second-class roads are provided by the departments ; the country roads by the communes.

In 1873 there were 223 national roads, aggregating 23,180 miles in length. They are fifty-two-and-a-half feet wide, of which the roadway is 19.68 feet ; sidewalks 19.68, and ditches and embankments 13.12 feet.

The department roads are thirty-eight feet wide and embraced 29,167 miles. Of cross-roads there were 338,273 miles. France covers 204,091 square miles, or 4.436 times the area of Pennsylvania.

36. The maximum grade allowed on the French roads is one in twenty, or 5 per cent. On the great Holyhead road in Wales it is limited to one in thirty ; but there are two places where it was necessary to make .it one in twenty-two and one in seventeen. On the roads crossing the Alps, at the Simplon, Splugin and St. Gothard Passes, the steepest grades are one in thirteen. These roads are from twenty-five to thirty feet wide. In Great Britain the width as fixed by law varies from twenty to sixty feet.

BENEFICIAL RESULTS OF IMPROVED ROADS.

In those portions of Ohio which have taken advantage of the statute, an increase of 50 per cent. in value is not uncommon, and 25 per cent. is the least estimate resulting from the improvements. Moreover, the people of those sections would not be deprived of their good roads at any price. Nor would they consent to go back to the old system of mud roads. They pay their 'road tax cheerfully, and without any longing for the annual picnic, commonly called "working the roads," which they formerly regarded as an inestimable right. "We find it pays to macadamize the roads, and our people would not like to be restricted to a tax of seven mills, because we sometimes want to spend a great deal more than that. We have learned that it pays to make good roads, no matter what they cost. Everybody says, 'if you will make the roads good, we do not care for the tax.' It is when you have nothing to show for the money expended that they complain, which is the objection to this working-out system."

Any enterprise which reduces the cost of transportation 40 per cent. and increases the value of land from 25 to 50 per cent. should commend itself to the self-interest of every farmer in the State. It would be difficult to devise any scheme that would contribute so. largely to the general prosperity as a large and immediate outlay, judiciously expended in the construction of first-class roads.

---

26. The good roads benefit all classes, for when they are in good condition there is a rush, and when they are poor there is a scarcity. This state of affairs has a bad effect on the business of the traders as well as on the pockets of both producers and consumers. Many farmers having a choice of two markets will go to that one having the best roads, for it is an important question to them whether they go once or twice to carry a given load.

---

36. The opening of the great military road by Marshall Wade through the Scottish highlands has done more for the civilization of that region than the preceding efforts of British monarchs. Estates have greatly increased in value and annual returns; former wastes are now producing large crops of wheat;

neat farmhouses and herds of cattle are seen where was once a desert, and the habits and morals of the people are greatly improved. . . By the opening of a road to the people of Steinthal, in Alsace, by Oberlin, a wonderfully moral and intellectual development ensued. The Japanese government recommends good roads to promote agriculture and civilization, and the Persian Shah is pursuing a similar policy.

CONTRIBUTIONS SUBMITTED BY KNOWN
CORRESPONDENTS.

A number of papers were also submitted by persons interested in the subject over their own signatures, with the hope that their suggestions might be of some service to the public.

Thus, a gentleman from Utica, N. Y., writes, laying great stress upon the injurious effects of water on earth roads, and urging thorough drainage and a plan for compacting the surface so as to render it waterproof by what he calls " the principle of compression." That is, he would first " moisten the earth to the proper consistency " and then pass over it low, long furnaces or troughs, having fires in them, to parbake the earth, which should have been previously thoroughly rolled by fifteen to twenty-ton rollers. The estimated cost per mile is only $800.

A writer living at Glen Olden, Delaware County, Pa., recommends the Telford road as being the best, attributing the failure of many old pikes to imperfect foundations. He believes that " nothing would increase both the valuation and population in Delaware, Montgomery, Chester and Bucks Counties so much as good roads," which could be built by county bonds.

Westmoreland County furnishes a typical illustration of how not to do it, from which the more prominent features are extracted. The writer says : " We certainly need a change in the road laws, and a new system of making roads. The reasons are : The supervisors are elected for their politics, regardless of other qualifications; they are made to do as their constituents wish ; they are not allowed to levy a tax sufficient to make the roads good. For example, a supervisor is elected, has the tax levied, and is ready to work. He notifies as many citizens as

(278)

the case demands. They meet at the place appointed, some with tools, some without; instructions are given, and for an hour or two all goes well; then work slackens, and they begin to show that they consider their service as an accommodation to the supervisor, who cannot discharge them. The result is that but little is accomplished in proportion to their wages. Again, they all want to be boss, each doing what he desires; they dump large stones into a rut, and pronounce it a good job; or the property owner objects to opening drains into his field, so the water is made to course along the road and settle in the depressions, because the law says where the road is thirty feet wide the water must be confined to it. Many instances of slovenly work are cited till the day wears away and evening comes, when the supervisor settles up and finds that children, laggards and delinquents are expected to be counted as full-grown, able-bodied men for a full day's labor. The whole thing is a swindle, sanctioned by law, and the roads are always in poor condition."

Road making should be applied as a science. The supervisor should be elected for each county, who should examine township officers, and, if qualified, hire them; buy tools, furnish teams and laborers, and whatever may be required for making or maintaining good roads. He should have power to change the location of a road when necessary, to open new roads, and vacate those which are unnecessary; to adopt plans and methods, build bridges, culverts, etc.; to audit accounts, and make reports to county officers monthly. All tax should be paid in money. Stones to be broken to pass through a two-inch ring, and the metaled part of the road to be not less than eight feet wide.

Lycoming County divides roads into two classes, and recommends separate treatment for those in level country from those over hills. It lays stress upon thorough drainage, and advises the reversal of the usual method by "flooding the fields instead of draining them," with other points already stated elsewhere relating to construction.

Lehigh County voices its views to the effect that there is but one alternative, that is " to pike the roads with limestone, gravel or cinder," but if the legislature passes an act it will ruin two-thirds of the land owners, who can now scarcely make both ends meet.   The road commissioner is no good in a county. The old law should be repealed.   People should not work out their taxes, as it makes poor roads.   Our supervisors do the work, and begin at any hour and call it a day.   No *side gutters* are opened, no cross drains made, and the road machines are of no use.   But how shall we raise the money?

Berks County suggests that the State should purchase a stone crusher for each county, and that the privilege of working out the tax should not be repealed ; that there is no need of an engineer or supervisor, but that suitable men can be found in each township to do the work if only some uniform rules were prepared for their guidance.   The taxes should not be increased.

A Bucks County farmer says main roads should be 50 feet wide, and cross roads 33.   They should have a shallow ditch on either side, with frequent openings.   The earth from the ditches should be thrown into the middle of the road and rounded up, so it will be 8 inches higher than the sides.   Then cover this surface with 6 inches of broken stone about the size of a guinea's egg.   The bed of the road should be 20 feet wide.   The stones should not be too hard.   A road built in this way costs a good deal, but it is cheapest in the long run.   To keep it in repair, let it to the farmers in one-half mile lengths.

A Philadelphian recommends a clause regulating the breadth of wheel tires, and that roads be built of layers of stone and cinder, alternately, but no dimensions are stated nor any estimates given.

Snyder County is represented by an experienced " foreman," farmer and supervisor for the third term, who says roads should be made in the Summer, from May to September, of hard stone, broken for the bottom, to be covered with gravel and rounded up. As the farmers cannot work on roads at this time of year, they don't get the work they should have. At least one good man should be appointed by the judge of the court, in each township, and he should be endorsed by at least twelve good citizens. The supervisor should not be elected, for if he don't let the farmers work when it suits them, he will stand a poor chance for re-election, and a goodly number are not used to doing an honest day's work. Under the engineer system the foreman will hire his laborers, and get a good day's work out of them. Farming land is taxed entirely too high to raise grain. The taxes in Union Township run from 25 to 28 mills on the dollar, and this is more than poor land will stand. The State ought at least to pay the supervisors and keep the old stage roads in good repair.

———

Another farmer from Berks believes that three-fourths of all the road tax is, wasted, and if properly spent at least three miles of good roads could be built each year, and in from five to seven years every township in the State would have good roads without increasing the taxation.

NOTES BY THE SECRETARY.

Judging from the general tenor of the papers the feeling prevails among farmers that their taxes are already greatly in excess of those of other citizens, and that the cost of transforming mud roads into macadam is so great as to be impracticable.

The success of any important measure is assured only after those most interested in it become convinced that it will result greatly to their benefit. To this end the estimates and results of experience, as to the benefits conferred by improved roads, are presented, that the farmers may look upon the other side of the picture and come to realize the enormous gain to themselves and others from improved highways. The statement that $4,000,000 are wasted in Pennsylvania alone in consequence of her poor and often impassable roads, is a moderate one. Even the saving of 25 per cent. of the horse-power required for traffic in Great Britain is estimated at $100,000,000. Again, it is stated that the road tax for Pennsylvania is about $4,000,000, and there is nothing to show for it, because of the useless attempts to build a permanent structure out of incoherent, perishable material over improper locations, and because of unskilled labor and imperfect supervision. Thus another direct waste is added to the indirect one, causing a loss of $8,000,000, which, under proper legislation, should be converted into a permanent benefit. It is also a fact that the cost of maintenance decreases as the surface of the roads is improved, so that it will be far more economical to maintain them after the work is done than before. If the money now annually wasted were gradually applied to permanent works there need be no increase in taxation, while before many years the reconstruction would be an accomplished fact.

The cost of keeping one horse is placed at $125 per annum,

and it is clearly shown that the improvement of the roads will enable three horses to do the work of four, and in many places one may easily haul the loads now requiring two, yet the law that would tax the farmer to this extent each year would be regarded as oppressive, merely because the economy of a good road is not appreciated. It is none the less a fact which will only come to be realized after it has been tried.

The difficulties to be overcome in this *move for better roads* are ignorance and distrust. Ignorance as to the great benefits to result from improved highways, both directly and indirectly, and which it is, in part, the object of these papers to remove; distrust as to the integrity of those who may be selected or appointed to conduct the work and handle the means. This can be met by employing a class of men of well-known probity and ability, whose reputation for skill and honesty is worth more to them than money, and such a class will be found in the civil engineers and surveyors resident in the great Commonwealth of Pennsylvania, who are deeply interested as citizens in promoting this long-needed reformation.

Again, the injustice of placing the burden of taxation for roads upon real estate is one which calls forth vehement protest/ from the farmer, and the possibility of increasing this burder. begets general opposition, so that no legislator would be safe i.1 his seat who would advocate so radical a measure.

Practically, therefore, it becomes a question of Ways and Means, which must be provided by enactments in such a manner as not to increase the rate, but to equalize and distribute it more generally over the entire community which will be benefited; and to secure far greater efficiency from the expenditures than now obtains under the "working out" system with supervisors.

When it comes to be realized that good roads are a benefit to all classes of citizens, whether farmer or manufacturer, consumer or producer, banker or merchant, corporations or individuals, the injustice of so unequal a distribution of the road tax will be better appreciated and be more equitably distributed.

It should be remembered that the cost of any article, whether of luxury or necessity, is made up of two items, viz.: that of production and that of transportation and storage, and that the resistance encountered on roads and streets forms the larger percentage of the cost of movement. If this be diminished the profit to the producer must be greater or the cost to the consumer less.

Roads are but parts of an interdependent system of transportation, and form the most important feeders to the railroads. There are many reasons why the trunk lines as well as the branches should use every effort to improve these important auxiliaries to their traffic and keep their rolling stock more uniformly employed at all seasons. There are no organizations that would be so greatly benefited as the transportation companies by the improvement of our highways, and it is therefore eminently proper that their taxes should be applied to this purpose.

WAYS AND MEANS.

Various suggestions are made as to the proper method of providing the funds for improving the roads ; among them it is proposed, (1), that counties or townships shall be authorized to issue bonds at a low rate of interest up to a stipulated amount, and to levy sufficient tax to pay the interest and provide a sinking fund ; or (2), that a poll tax for roads be laid on every male citizen or alien, whether property holder or not ; or (3), that joint stock companies be permitted to build or improve pikes and collect tolls. (4) Some writers think the State should build free turnpikes between principal cities, leaving it for the lesser divisions to extend the system by branches ; or (5), that the State should loan the counties a *pro rata* depending on mileage, population or subscription to its own road fund ; (6), others again go so far as to endorse a movement by the National Government in loaning its credit to the States for the improvement of its roads as postal routes as it does for rivers and harbors or for railroads

As outlined above, it is the writer's opinion that an equitable readjustment of the taxes with proper restrictions as to the intelligent supervision and distribution will be amply sufficient to incorporate the movement.

There are serious objections also to the stock company proposition, as it prevents uniformity of action and equitable taxation. Some roads will cost less and be taxed more than others, and it is always difficult to enforce a standard as to the condition of the highways or to compel companies to maintain it. Witness the streets of Philadelphia.

The plan which commends itself to the writer as being the simplest, most direct and least objectionable is that of State aid under proper restrictions. For example, let the amount that can be spared be appropriated for the construction, not maintenance, *of permanent roads*, to become available after a certain limited date, by which time the various counties should notify the State Treasurer what amount of money they were willing to subscribe and appropriate for the same purpose for the current year, when the State appropriation should be allotted *pro rata* among the counties subscribing to the road fund, and the county treasurer be authorized to draw on the State Treasurer by instalment as the work progressed and was accepted by the board of engineers and inspectors. The location, inspection and approval of the roads should be under a board consisting of the resident, county and State engineers, or their deputies, and four reputable citizens of the county appointed by the judge of the court, or elected by the citizens.

No public work of this character should be undertaken until a competent civil engineer is appointed to represent the interests of the State, who should carefully revise the character and location of every road before the work of metaling the surface is authorized. The economy of such an office will be very great in effecting far more in preventing useless expenditure than the cost of the office. The best is the cheapest in this case, and it is well said that " the man who works for nothing is not worth his board." While other States find it to the interest of economy to maintain an engineer, Pennsylvania has been content to entrust the supervision of her public works to the rotation of a political office and suffer accordingly from indifference and neglect. It is said that $200,000,000 will not cover the waste due to imperfect roads alone.

Upon the question of working out the tax or paying it in money there is but one opinion, and that is to the effect that the former system should be abolished, and also that the length of the term of the supervisor should be increased to at least three years, and that he should not be elected but appointed by the courts or by county or township officers during good behavior, and should be required to give bonds, be regularly employed, and be authorized to let work by contract or to employ laborers as he might consider most effective.

Since it is proposed to invite a prize competition for the best draft of a legislative bill, the writer does not feel justified in further elaborating upon the special features which should be included in such a measure.

CONSTRUCTION.

Many opinions are presented on this head, showing great diversity as to dimensions, material, and mode of construction, notwithstanding the general impression that "we know all about road building that is worth knowing." This knowledge, according to some, may be condensed into the brief requirements of thorough drainage and an impervious, smooth and hard surface. But the methods and materials for accomplishing the end are so various and so local as to show the necessity for great latitude in this direction to meet the resources of the ever-varying geological features of the State. The same individuality is found to exist as to the dimensions, grades, forms of sections, etc., as well as to the units employed in estimating quantities. In framing a law it is very important that the terms be general yet free from ambiguity, so that there may be no misconstruction. Thus the ton and perch, which have a variety of values, should be excluded as units of quantity. Moreover, the specific gravity varies so greatly even in materials of the same species that a ton conveys no definite idea as to the space it may occupy.

Linear measurements should be made by the foot, yard or mile, superficial measurements by the square yard or acre, and cubic measurements by the cubic yard. All of these have the same basis, viz., the foot. In regulating the widths of roads the ratio of length to area as of the mile to the acre should be made the unit of widths, and some multiple of this should be made the width of the road ; thus the acre (43,560 square feet) divided by the mile (5280 feet) gives 8¼ as the ratio. Let this be called the road unit or *demirod*. Or, in other words, a road one mile long and 8¼ feet wide will contain one acre ; a road four times this width (33 feet) will require four acres to the mile. This width between fences would be ample for cross-country roads. The *unit* is also a good width for the wagon track, with sufficient allowance for hubs and clearance. For double track, 16½ feet, or 1 rod of metaled surface would be ample, = 2 acres per mile. On this basis a single trackway, if 1 foot deep, would contain 1613⅓ cubic yards. A double trackway, if six inches deep, the same. At one dollar per cubic yard the cost would be $1613.33 per mile for metal. In one acre, or unit of area, (1 mile long by 8¼ feet wide) there are 4840 square yards. Cost by the square yard of one foot depth, 33⅓ cents.

Roads of six units in width, or 3 rods (49½ feet) 6 acres per mile, would give either three or four trackways with sufficient room for sidewalks and drains—furnishing a good width for main lines ; while for boulevards, they may be 8, 10 or 12 units (66, 82.5 or 99 feet) according to circumstances.

The importance of limiting the grades is mentioned by a number of writers, who restrict it to the angle of repose, which varies for different surfaces. For ordinary cases 5 per cent. should not be exceeded, yet there may be exceptions when the engineer would not be warranted in observing the limitation, so 'nat discretion should be given him to be exercised where the traffic would not justify so great an outlay.

The privilege should be secured of making outlets into any natural drainage channel. The width of tire should be such that the load should not exceed 400 pounds per lineal inch, and it would be a great improvement and effect a large saving in maintenance if the axles of all wagons employed in heavy hauling were made with one axle shorter than the other by an amount equal to double the width of the tire. The effect would be to distribute the pressure over double the usual surface of the road and prevent ruts, reducing the force of traction, and causing the wagons to act as road rollers.

As to the relative merits of the Telford and Macadam systems, it will be seen that there are experienced supervisors who advocate either, and that some claim that Telford costs less than Macadam, others the reverse, according to their experience. In fact, it is found that there is very little difference under similar conditions for equal depths and widths. On good subsoil, well-drained, the foundation course of Telford may be omitted, in which case it becomes a light Macadam. From the figures submitted, it will be seen that a 9-inch metaling may be built for from $2500 to $3000 per mile or less, according to the accessibility of material, and the cost of maintenance varies from one per cent to ten, according to the efficiency of the administration and material of which the road is built.

In these notes no allusion is made to the several prize papers, as they are submitted in full for the information of those interested.

The Secretary desires to submit, in this connection, a few notes on the adaption of soils to road construction, the literature of which appears to be meagre.

SOILS AND THEIR ADAPTATION TO ROADS.

It is the province of the engineer to adapt his materials to the work which they are intended to perform in the most judicious manner, yet there would seem to be no branch of engineering in which this desideratum is more generally neglected than in that of road making. Here, it is true, many other more important considerations have made this element subservient, and in many cases it is almost entirely ignored. The road is frequently located where land is cheapest and poorest, without reference to its sustaining power, composition, condition or porosity, yet there are many cases where a little attention to these requirements and a readjustment of the alignment would convert a road, at times impassable, into a permanently good highway, capable of being maintained at small expense.

Although much has been written and said upon the application of stone to the surfacing of roads, there is comparatively little information to be found in modern literature relative to the utility of the various soils for road making purposes; yet it is a matter of every day observation that there are some formations where country roads are found to be in uniformly good condition. It is important that the natural conditions existing at such localities should be studied and extended as far as practicable, and that the effects of the elements upon the sustaining power of soils should be better known.

That road will be found to be most durable whose bed is least affected by rain, frost, sun and wind; that is to say, *that material which retains most nearly a constant volume when subjected to great ranges of temperature, moisture or pressure, will make the best roadbed.* This result is usually sought to be attained by "thorough drainage," but this is an expensive remedy, requiring constant supervision, and is not, therefore, so effective as a location upon soil which does not require so much attention to maintain its immobility. In a general way, it is well known that sand will contract when wet, while clay will expand under the same conditions. Loam and gravely earth expand largely from frost and contract from heat, thus breaking up the surface in a short time. Shaly and porous rocks *in situ* are not materially changed in volume by these natural forces, and usually present a good wearing surface; but when exposed on steep

19

slopes, the detritus is rapidly abraded, leaving exposed the ragged edges of other and harder rocks with which they may be interstratified.

With a view to determine the relative sensibility of various earths, a series of experiments was conducted by Messrs. Hulme and Fisher,[1] to determine the absorption, expansion, angle of slope, etc., of crude materials. They began with dry clay, and, by adding water, by weight, found the average absorption to be 27½ per cent. The time required to reach the limit, for the quantity of clay tested, was about five hours. The experiments on expansion gave average results as high as 12 per cent., or one-eighth of an inch for every lineal inch of clay. When mixed with 16 per cent., by weight, of water, it was found that the clay was unable to sustain a pressure of thirty pounds per square inch, or two tons per square foot.

Unfortunately, time was lacking for the completion of this series of experiments with other materials, but this loss may be in part supplied by the following data, compiled from experiments by Mr. Schübler, as to the shrinkage, absorption and saturation of the various soils :

Character.	Specific Gravity.	Wt. per Cub. Ft.	Saturation in lbs per Cub. Ft.	Per cent. of Saturation.	Absorption. 1000 grains of earth on a surface of 50 square inches absorbed in			
					12 hours.	24 hours.	48 hours.	72 hours.
Siliceous sand,	2.653	166	27.3	16.5	0 grains.	0	0	0
Sandy clay, . .	2.601	163	38.8	23.8	21	26	28	28
Loamy clay, .	2.581	161	41.4	25.6	25	30	34	32
Brick clay, . .	2.560	160	45.4	28.4	30	36	40	41
Pure gray clay,	2.533	158	43.3	27.4	37	42	48	49
Pipe clay, . .	2.440	152½	47.4	31.0	—	—	—	—
Arable soil, . .	2.401	150	40.8	27.2	16	22	23	23
Garden mold, .	2.332	146	48.4	33.2	35	45	50	52
Humus, . . .	1.370	91	50.1	55.0	80	97	110	120

From the table, it appears that siliceous sand does not absorb water, and that the practical limit with the clay compounds is reached at the end of the forty-eighth hour, or possibly earlier. For arable soil, the percentage is but 2.3, while for pure gray clay it is double this, or 4.8 per cent.

⁻niversity of Pennsylvania, 1890, for their Post-Senior Thesis.

On the other hand, with reference to the effects of heat, the same authority states that in 100 parts the same soils shrink in the following proportions :

Siliceous sand, . . .	No change
Sandy clay, ...	6 parts.
Loamy "	8.9 "
Brick, "	11.4 "
Pure gray clay, . .	18.3 "
Arable soil, ...	12.0 "
Garden mold, . . .	14 9 "
Humus, ...	20 0 "

Peat, strong clay and humus will shrink one-fifth of their bulk in dry weather and expand correspondingly in wet. They are, therefore, the worst kinds of material for a substratum.

These data show that the pure sands are those which are least liable to change of volume from the action of natural agencies, and they are, therefore, those best adapted to the purpose of foundations for the wearing surface, provided only that the tendency to lateral movement be neutralized by suitable curbing, to prevent the sand from being washed out.

In making a selection from the siliceous sands, the coarser varieties will be found best, as the quantity of water absorbed is much less than in the fine grades. The ability to retain moisture varies greatly with different soils, as well as with their depth. Thus the "containing power of water of the earths as determined from the amount of water evaporated in four days" was found by Schüber to be,

For calcareous sand, ... 29 per cent.
  " light garden mold, ... 89 "
  " very light turf soil, ... 366 "
  " arable, ... 60 "
  " black turf, not so light, ... 179 "
  " white fine clay, ... 70 "
  " gray " . . . . 87 "

"The fine gray clays, after fourteen days, exhibited still a damp surface, while the turf soils were perfectly dry many days earlier."

These experiments all demonstrate the unsuitable character

of clay or its compounds for the purpose of a substratum for roads, and indicate the care which the engineer should exercise to avoid argillaceous formations when possible, or else to provide a suitable substitute which is not readily affected by frost or heat, moisture or dryness.

With due attention to the character of the soils, the expense of maintenance and the resistance to traffic may be greatly reduced, while the character of the road will be much improved.[1]

[1] Reference is made to the 41st and 42d Reports of the State Board of Agriculture on Roads, edited by Thomas J. Edge, Secretary, Harrisburg, Penna., 1890, for much valuable information.

RESURFACING.

Past experience has shown that in resurfacing old or worn-out roads success was mainly due to the attention paid to the size and form of the stones which were carefully broken by hand on the roadside. They were so small that the passage of a wheel did not produce the rocking movement inherent to larger stones, hence it was very easy to keep the roads in good condition until the entire surface had worn down uniformly to the lower stratum when it was resurfaced. So far as possible, the toughest stones were reserved for this purpose. It is manifest, therefore, that *size, form* and *quality* were the elements relied upon to secure durability in the roads repaired by the earlier road masters.

The same care in the selection and application of the materials should produce equally good results to-day under similar conditions of climate and traffic, but, unfortunately, the experience of the last century is not often utilized in practice. Stones very much too large for the purpose are freely used, the quality is inferior, and to facilitate their binding together, clay, the most injurious of materials, is frequently added. Carefully drafted specifications are often rendered nugatory by a too liberal construction on the part of incompetent supervisors appointed to enforce them, resulting in failure and extravagance.

Of all materials available for metaling, that variety of stone is the best which possesses greatest resistance to crushing and wear, greatest toughness and density, and which breaks most nearly into cubical or angular forms.

Such material is comparatively rare, it is true, but where it exists it is economical to transport it considerable distances for use in remetaling, as its greater durability will save the cost of the more frequent transportation and labor when softer varieties are used.   Thus if a trap rock has twice the strength of a granite at the quarry, it would be worth more than double the price on the road, since the expense of one hauling and laying would be saved.

For resurfacing in Philadelphia County the present specifications conform very nearly to the requirements insisted upon by MacAdam, and should result in good and durable roads where they are enforced.   They provide "That repair to macadam surfaces shall be made with hard, durable stone, broken to sizes such that the greatest length of the largest pieces will not exceed two inches put on in quantities sufficient to completely fill all depressions, then be rolled or rammed and covered with stone screenings."   Where these specifications are strictly enforced, the result should be a good and durable wearing surface, which may be readily maintained in the same good condition by that constant supervision which every macadamized road should receive.

As a road wears down by travel, it is only possible to maintain it in such good condition by constant vigilance on the part of the roadkeeper, who should go over it daily and make the repairs immediately wherever there may be any indications of weakness.   The surface of a road should never be allowed to wear into ruts and holes before resurfacing, but the instant a break of any kind, however small, occurs, it should be at once repaired.   The maintenance of a common road should receive the same skill, care and attention as that of a railroad.   B.

The following rules, published by The Road Improvement Association, of No. 57 Basinghall Street, London, E. C., will be found useful to roadmen, and are therefore submitted *in extenso*:

1. Never allow a hollow, a rut or a puddle to remain on a road, but fill it up at once with *chips* from the stone heap.

2. Always use *chips* for patching, and for all repairs during the summer months.

3. Never put fresh stones on the road if by cross-picking and a thorough use of the rake the surface can be made smooth and kept at the proper strength and section.

4. Remember that the rake is the most useful tool in your collection, and that it should be kept close at hand the whole year round.

5. Do not spread large patches of stone over the whole width of the road, but coat the middle, or horse track, first, and, when this has worn in, coat each of the sides in turn.

6. Always arrange that the bulk of the stones may be laid down before Christmas.

7. In moderately dry weather, and on hard roads, always pick up the old surface into ridges six inches apart, and remove all large and projecting stones before applying a new coating.

8. Never spread stones more than one stone deep, but add a second layer when the first has worn in, if one coat be not enough.

9. Use a steel-pronged fork to load the barrows at the stone heap, so that the siftings may be available for "binding" and for summer repairs.

10. Never shoot stones on to the road, and crack them where they lie, or a smooth surface will be out of the question.

11.   Go over the whole of the new coating every day or two with the rake, and never leave the stones in ridges.

12.   Remove all large stones, blocks of wood and other obstructions (used for diverting the traffic) at nightfall, or the consequences may be serious.

13.   *Never put a stone upon a road for repairing purposes that will not pass freely in every direction through a two-inch ring*, and remember that still smaller stones should be used for patching and for all slight repairs.

14.   Recollect that hard stone should be broken to a finer gauge than soft, but that the two-inch gauge is the largest that should be employed *under any circumstances* where no steam roller is employed.

15.   Never be without your ring-gauge. It should be to the roadsman what the compass is to the mariner.

16.   If you have no ring-gauge, remember MacAdam's advice, that any stone you cannot put easily into your mouth should be broken smaller.

17.   Use *chips*, if possible, for binding newly-laid stones together, and remember that road sweepings, horse droppings sods of grass and other rubbish, when used for this purpose, will ruin the best road in creation.

18.   Remember that water-worn or rounded stones should never be used upon steep gradients, or they will fail to bind together.

19.   Never allow dust or mud to lie on the surface of the road, for either of these will double the cost of maintenance.

20.   Recollect dust becomes mud at the first shower, and that mud forms a wet blanket which will keep a road in a filthy condition for weeks at a time, instead of allowing it to dry in a few hours.

21.   See that all sweepings and scrapings are put into heaps, and carted away immediately.

22.   Remember that the middle of the road should always

be a little higher than the sides, so that the rain may run into the side gutters at once.

23. Never allow the water tables, gutters and ditches to clog up, but keep them clear the whole year through.

24. Always be upon your road in wet weather, and at once fill up with "chips" any hollows or ruts where the rain may lie.

25. When the main coatings of stone have worn in, go over the whole road, and, gathering together all the loose stones, return them to the stone heap for use in the winter to follow; for loose stones are a source of danger and annoyance, and should never be allowed to lie on any road.

CONTRIBUTORS.

ADDIS, T. B. M.

ALCORN WM., W. & CO.

ALLEN, ROWLAND D.

ALTEMUS, JOSEPH B.

ASSOCIATED CYCLING CLUBS OF PHILADELPHIA

ATKINSON BROTHERS

AUSTIN, RICHARD L.

BAILY, JOEL J.

BAILY, JOSHUA L.

BAIRD, HENRY CAREY

BAIRD, JOHN

BAIRD, JOHN & SONS

BARKER, WHARTON

BARNES, WILLIAM H.

BARTOL, H. W.

BARTON, HENRY H.

BEATTIE & HAY

BELFIELD, T. BROOM

BENSON, EDWIN N.

BERGNER & ENGEL BREWING COMPANY

BERWIND, CHARLES F.

BLAKELY, JOHN

BLANKENBURG, RUDOLPH

BORIE, BEAUVEAU

BROCKIE, WILLIAM

BROOKE, F. M. & H.

BROWN, T. WISTAR

BRYANT, WALTER H.

BULLITT, JOHN C.

BURGESS, HUGH

BURNHAM, GEORGE

BUSCH, HENRY E.

BUTTON, CONYERS

CASSATT, ALEXANDER J.

CHANDLER, THEOPHILUS P., JR.

CHENEY BROTHERS

CHESNUT, JOHN H.

CHILDS, GEORGE W.

CLARK, CLARENCE H.

CLARK, EDWARD W.

CLYDE, B. FRANK

CONVERSE, JOHN H.

COOKE, JAY

CRESSON, GEORGE V.

CROWE, WILLIAM J.

DICKSON, SAMUEL

DINGEE, JOHN H.

DISSEL, CHARLES

DISSTON, HAMILTON

DOBBINS, EDWARD T.

DOUGHERTY, JOHN A.

DREER, FERDINAND J.

DWIGHT, E. P.

EDELHEIM, CARL

ELKINTON, JOS. S. & THOS.

ERBEN, SEARCH & CO.

EVANS, S. W. & SON

FARR, THOMAS H.

FARRELLY, STEPHEN

FELL, JOHN R.

FELS & Co.
FELTON, SAMUEL K.
FISHER, JAMES LOGAN
FRANKS, HENRY L.
GARRETT, C. S. & SON
GAW, H. L., JR.
GERHARD, WILLIAM
GIBBS, WILLIAM W.
GILBERT, SAMUEL H.
GILLINGHAM, JOSEPH E.
GODFREY, LINCOLN
GOODWIN, WILLIAM W.
GRAVES, N. Z. & Co.
GREGG, WILLIAM H.
GRIFFIN, NICHOLAS J.
GRISCOM, CLEMENT A.
HACKER, WILLIAM
HAINES, HENRY
HANCE BROTHERS & WHITE
HARPER, SMITH
HARRAH, C. J.
HARRIS, GEORGE S. & SONS
HARRISON, CHARLES C.
HART CYCLE COMPANY
HARTSHORNE, CHARLES
HAUPT, LEWIS M.
HENSZEY, W. C., (Agent for
    Carpenter Estate).
HENSZEY, WILLIAM P.
HINCHMAN, CHARLES S.
HINCHMAN, HOWARD & SON
HIPPLE, FRANK K.
HIRSH & BROTHER
HOUSTON, HENRY H.
HOWELL, ZOPHAR C.

IRVINE, WILLIAM B.
IRWIN, HENRY
JAMISON, B. K.
JAYNE, EBEN C.
JENKS, JOHN STORY
JUSTICE, WILLIAM W.
KEIM, GEORGE DE B.
KEMBLE, WILLIAM H.
KENNEDY, FRANCIS W.
KIMBALL, F. S.
KNIGHT, EDWARD C.
LAMBERT, JOHN
LANE'S, D. M. SONS
LEA, ARTHUR H.
LEA, HENRY C.
LEE, JESSE & SONS
LESER, FREDERICK
LEWIS, SAUNDERS
LIPPINCOTT, CHARLES, & Co.
LIPPINCOTT, CRAIGE
LONGSTRETH, EDWARD
MACBETH, REV. HENRY
MASON, HENRY T.
MATHEWS, EDWARD J.
McCARGO, DAVID
MILLBOURNE MILLS COMPANY
MITCHELL, JAMES E.
MUNDELL, JOHN & Co.
NEWMAN, M. M.
NIMLET, DAVID C.
OGDEN, EDWARD H.
ORNE, JOHN F.
PARTRIDGE & RICHARDSON
PHILADELPHIA BICYCLE CLUB
PHILADELPHIA TRUSS Co.

POLEY, WARREN H.

POPE, ALBERT A.

PORTER, CHARLES

PULASKI, M. H.

RAMBO, WILLIAM B.

REDNER, LEWIS H.

REEVES, PARVIN & CO.

REYNOLDS, J. & SON

RHAWN, WILLIAM H.

RICHARDSON, CHARLES

ROBERTS, GEORGE B.

ROGERS, WM. D., SON & CO.

ROWLAND, BENJAMIN

RYERSS, ROBERT W.

SCHMIDT, JOHN G.

SCOTT, GEORGE W.

SCOTT, WILLIAM H.

SELLERS, JOHN, JR.

SELLERS, WILLIAM

SHARPLESS, HENRY W.

SHARPLESS, JOHN & CO.

SHARPLESS, SAMUEL J.

SHELMERDINE, WILLIAM H.

SHINN, JAMES T.

SHORTRIDGE, N. PARKER

SIMES, WILLIAM F.

SIMONS, JOHN F.

SMITH, WILLIAM P., JR.

STEPHENS, HORATIO S.

STRAWBRIDGE, JUSTUS C.

TAYLOR, J. HARRY

THOMAS, GEORGE C.

TOBIN, PATRICK

TOWNSEND, EDWARD Y.

TOWNSEND, HENRY C.

WARREN, E. BURGESS

WEBSTER, EDMUND

WEIGHTMAN, WILLIAM

WELSH, JOHN LOWBER

WHARTON, CHARLES W.

WHARTON, JOSEPH

WHEELER, ANDREW

WHITNEY & KEMMERER

WILSON, J. SIMS

WINSOR, J. D.

WINSOR, W. D.

WOOD, REV. CHARLES

WOOD, WALTER

WRIGHT, JAMES A.

WRIGHT, PETER, & SONS

WRIGHT, TYNDALE & VAN RODEN

YARNALL, FRANCIS C.

YATES, DAVID G. & CO.

YOUNG & SONS.

INDEX.

CONTRIBUTIONS TO SCIENCE.

The frequent calls for the publications of the undersigned having nearly exhausted the supply, the writer has determined to reprint some of the more important pamphlets for sale, and will be pleased to fill any orders which may be addressed to him, enclosing the price. These papers are, in general, illustrated with cuts and maps.

LEWIS M. HAUPT, C.E.,

Professor of Civil Engineering, University of Pennsylvania.

107 N. 35th St., Philadelphia, Pa·

MUNICIPAL ENGINEERING.

MARITIME ENGINEERING.

RIVERS AND HARBORS.

TRANSPORTATION.

MISCELLANEOUS BOOKS.

Reprints by Permission from the following societies, Journals or Proceedings: *a*. Lecture delivered before the Manufacturers' Club of Philadelphia; *b*. Report of Pennsylvania State Board of Agriculture, 1890; *c*. American Association for the Advancement of Science; *d*. American Society of Civil Engineers; *e*. Proceedings of Engineers' Club, of Philadelphia; *f*. Journal of Franklin Institute; *ps*. Proceedings American Philosophical Society; *s*. American Economic Association.

www.ingramcontent.com/pod-product-compliance
Lightning Source LLC
Chambersburg PA
CBHW021120270326
41929CB00009B/979